Following the
SANTA FE
TRAIL

A Guide for Modern Travelers

Following the
SANTA FE
TRAIL

Marc Simmons and Hal Jackson

Third Edition/Revised and Expanded

Ancient City Press
Santa Fe, New Mexico

International Standard Book Number paperback : 1-58096-011-1

Third Edition

Cover illustration by Ron Kil
Cover design by Janice St. Marie
Book design by Kathleen Sparkes, White Hart Design
Line drawings by Roger Balm

Library of Congress Cataloging-in-Publication Data

Simmons, Marc.
Following the Santa Fe trail : a guide for modern travelers / by Marc
Simmons and Hal Jackson. — 3rd ed.
_____ p. _____ cm.
Includes bibliographical references (p.) and index.
ISBN 1-58096-011-1(pbk.: alk. paper)
    1. Santa Fe National Historic Trail — Guidebooks.   2. Automobile
travel — Santa Fe National Historic Trail — Guidebooks. I. Jackson, Hal
(Hal E.) II. Title.

E786.S56   2001
917.8 — dc21   98-6968

10   9   8   7   6   5   4   3   2   1

FOR BEVERLY

CONTENTS

LIST OF MAPS

PREFACE

The aim of this book is to assist contemporary travelers in finding their way over the Santa Fe Trail. Modern paved highways parallel much of the old wagon route, but in some places graded county roads must be followed for short stretches. With the directions we have provided, anyone should be able to retrace large sections of the trail with comparative ease, although we have not tried to describe the route precisely mile by mile.

Today, trail travel, whether by automobile, foot, horseback, covered wagon, or bicycle (and we have met persons who have used all these means), affords numerous opportunities for adventure. This is because traveling with a purpose offers a deep and fulfilling experience, which is seldom the case in random sightseeing. Another attraction is the magic and beauty that persists in much of the landscape through which the Santa Fe Trail passes.

Background reading is essential preparation for any historical trip, and in the Introduction we give the titles of useful and interesting books that will provide basic information on the subject. There is also commentary about road conditions and the best times of the year to plan a trail excursion. And we include a discussion of the types of markers and historical monuments that will be encountered.

With only a few exceptions, we have not attempted to make recommendations regarding lodging and meals. That information is easily obtained from standard guides and tourist brochures. Requests for this type of material can be addressed to the Chamber of Commerce in larger places such as Independence, Kansas City, Fort Leavenworth, Council Grove, Dodge City, Trinidad, Raton, Las Vegas, and Santa Fe. Most tourist destinations also have web sites on the World Wide Web. Travelers should keep in mind that smaller towns may offer very limited accommodations. For example, Council Grove, a focal point on the trail, has only two motels, although it does have a splendid restaurant, the historic Hays House, dating from covered wagon days.

The main text briefly describes the chief points of interest along the Santa Fe Trail and furnishes precise directions for finding them while using standard road maps. We have tried to provide sufficient detail so that those venturing out upon the Santa Fe Trail for the first time can avoid wild goose chases and have more time to spend at sites worth a prolonged visit. No attempt has been made, however, to recount the full histories of individual trail sites, a task requiring a book many times larger than this guide. Rather, we give a few summary details to place the point of interest in proper perspective, leaving the traveler to learn more through additional reading. In some places, though, we have added unusual bits of information not available in standard sources.

Historic pioneer trails serve as some of the most fascinating links to our nation's past. Retracing them can be an exhilarating and educational experience. An added pleasure, we have discovered, comes from meeting people along the way who are dedicated history buffs and know many obscure details of the trail story in their localities. We have found such individuals, including most private owners of trail sites, unfailingly friendly and eager to share information. They enjoy talking with persons who are retracing the old wagon road, and if you are open and courteous, you will have a splendid chance of becoming acquainted with America at its grassroots.

Numerous changes have occurred since Ancient City Press published the first edition of Marc Simmons's *Following the Santa Fe Trail* in 1984 and a second edition two years later. For one thing, public interest in the trail has mushroomed. Also, President Reagan signed a congressional bill in May 1987 designating the Santa Fe Trail a National Historic Trail, thus bringing it under the jurisdiction of the National Park Service for purposes of interpretation and commemoration.

Another landmark event was the 1986 founding of the Santa Fe Trail Association (SFTA), with headquarters in Larned, Kansas. Through its historical and promotional programs, supported by twelve local chapters, the SFTA is engaged in mapping and marking the trail, sponsoring publications, and holding regular conferences. The public interest growing out of its work has attracted the attention of scholars and writers, and created a new awareness by state tourism bureaus of the value of actively promoting the Santa Fe Trail. The Association's fine quarterly journal, *Wagon Tracks*, contains recent trail scholarship, news, and a calendar of current events.

The growing enthusiasm for exploring and learning about this distinctive trail has made updating this guide imperative. Because Marc Simmons was occupied with other projects, in 1999 Hal Jackson, formerly a geography professor at California's Humboldt State University and now a resident of Placitas, New Mexico, offered to retrace the trail and make the needed corrections and additions for this revised edition. During ensuing months, he made numerous trips along the Santa Fe Trail and became familiar with the landscape of the entire route.

Subsequently, Jackson rewrote those sections of the original guide that needed updating, and then he and Simmons reviewed the manuscript to ensure accuracy and clarity. In addition, new maps were drawn and new illustrations selected. It is hoped that this latest edition will be received with the same enthusiasm as earlier editions.

In compiling this guide we have incurred many debts. First, our thanks go to all the people who assisted Simmons in the first and second editions of *Following the Santa Fe Trail*. Their contributions carry over into the present work, and their names are noted in the original prefaces.

With regard to the current edition, we would first like to thank two Missourians at the eastern end of the trail, both trail "blue bloods" since their families were in that area when the wagon caravans rolled. Denny Davis spent many hours with us around Franklin pointing out locations of historical importance. He also provided us with a copy of the original Franklin plat. Roger Slusher of Lexington, whose ancestors were among the first to settle on Tabo Creek east of town, was of great help in explaining the complexities of the Santa Fe Trail in his county, and he increased our knowledge substantially.

The most challenging part of the trail for today's travelers is that section running from Independence, Missouri, to Lenexa, Kansas, which includes the Kansas City metropolitan area. More new information has come to light and trail reinterpretation has taken place here more than anywhere else. Craig Crease, who has studied the trail in western Missouri and eastern Kansas and published his findings in *Wagon Tracks*, the SFTA quarterly, spent many days informing us of his research. Ross Marshall, who also knows the Kansas City area, deserves our thanks for accompanying us from Independence to Lenexa.

Ed Harmison of Overland, Kansas, showed us his part of the trail, and we thank him for his time and effort. The SFTA is very fortunate to have dedicated members such as Don Kress of its Flint Hills Chapter, an expert on the trail around Council Grove who helped us in many ways, especially with the old route east of there. The chapter can provide information about an annual summer wagon caravan he leads from Burlingame to Lost Spring.

No chapter of the SFTA has been more active in researching its part of the trail than the Wet/Dry Chapter in Larned, Kansas. Dr. David Clapsaddle, the trail master between Pawnee Rock and Dodge City, spent many hours showing us where the various branch trails were located in this section. He was also the leader of a group of three marking George W. Sibley's campsite in Larned. The Wet/Dry Chapter merits special praise for its placement of a series of handsome trail markers.

Paul Bentrup, an official Trail Ambassador for the SFTA, has devoted years to protecting and promoting the trail. He has long maintained Charlie's Ruts west of Deerfield, Kansas, where he has kept a mailbox filled with printed information about the entire trail. He accompanied us to every important location in his area to make sure we understood its importance.

Bentrup referred us to Lawrence McMillan in Granada, Colorado, and thanks to the information he provided us, we were able to add a section on Old Granada. In La Junta are two individuals deserving of our gratitude. Phil Peterson, a longtime active member of the SFTA, gave us considerable help. Bob Jones, who has worked tirelessly on the trail, bought the land on which Hole-in-the-Rock site is located and donated it to the Archaeological Conservancy to ensure its future protection. He escorted us from La Junta up

Timpas Creek as far as Hole-in-the-Rock and gave us facts about the site that we have included in this guide.

In northern New Mexico, Nancy Robertson of Raton gets our thanks for sharing information about her section of the trail. Richard Louden of Branson, Colorado (east of Raton), led us to Tollgate Canyon on a branch of the trail that is new to this edition. He is also an expert on trail traveler Marion Russell, having known her daughter-in-law, who wrote down Russell's memoirs in the early 1930s.

In the area around Clayton, New Mexico, we were fortunate to have Billy Mock and Jimmy Hall for guides. On Mock's land is famed McNees Crossing, to which he allows public access. (Shut the highway gate behind you to keep in the livestock.) Hall, our other guide, works for the Kiowa National Grasslands in Clayton and is familiar with every trace of the trail in northeastern New Mexico. Our thanks to both of them.

Rancher Faye Gaines is owner of Point of Rocks, one of the trail's highlights in New Mexico. We are delighted that she has made her site available to the public. A side trip off the highway to this beautiful area is a must. Brian King of the Doolittle Ranch (the trail-era Watrous House and adjacent land) took us to the location of Barclay's Fort, and we appreciate his time and interest.

Harry Myers, the superintendent at Fort Union National Monument, is one of the most knowledgeable historians around. Michael Olsen, a historian at New Mexico Highlands University in Las Vegas, and Myers shared with us their extensive knowledge of the trail in San Miguel County. In addition, through research the two of them did an excellent job of unraveling the story of Becknell's 1821 meeting with Mexican troops at Kearny Gap.

Over several years, Michael Macklin mapped the old wagon road between Watrous and San José, New Mexico, sharing his findings with us. We believe he determined the accurate location of the trail here and thank him for helping us on this section.

Tom Steel of the End of the Trail Chapter of the SFTA clarified some points for us within the limits of Santa Fe. He is one of the lucky people with wagon ruts running through his property.

Two other people helped considerably in completing this edition. To Roger Balm goes our thanks for drawing the historical sketches included throughout the guide. Also we wish to express our gratitude to Pat Macklin for reading early drafts of the revisions and making many helpful suggestions for improvement.

Finally, the Kansas City Public Library generously provided us with the photo of the Gillis House Hotel included in the Kansas City section. And Greg Franzwa has let us use his photo of the Durham trail ruts, included in the Introduction.

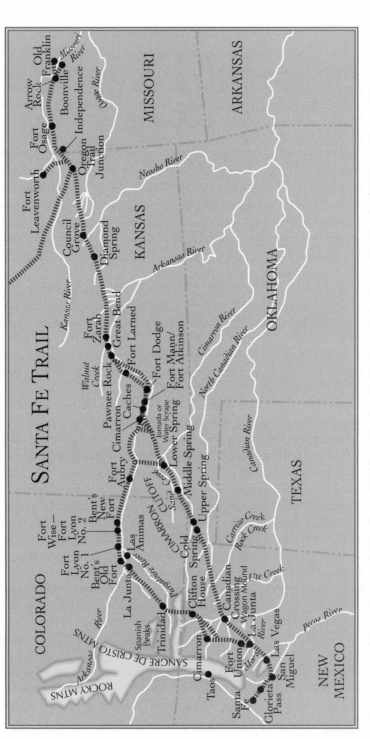

Map recreated from Larry M. Beachum, William Becknell: Father of the Santa Fe Trade (El Paso: Texas Western Press, 1982). Used with permission.

INTRODUCTION

The Santa Fe Trail was the first and most exotic of America's great trans-Mississippi pathways to the West. Its opening in 1821 preceded by two decades the birth of the Oregon and California Trails. Unlike them, the Santa Fe Trail began in the United States and ended in a foreign country, Mexico, at least for the first quarter-century of its existence. The strange customs, unfamiliar language, and breathtaking scenery found at the foot of the trail exerted a strong appeal and filled overlanders bound for New Mexico with special excitement.

The trail to Santa Fe was first and last a highway of commerce. In that, it differed markedly from trails farther north whose traffic consisted mainly of pioneer settlers, ranchers, farmers, and miners pushing toward the Pacific Ocean in quest of new homes and opportunities to be won from the land. The Santa Fe Trail was opened by a merchant, William Becknell, who foresaw profits to be made in transporting American goods across the southern prairies to eager Hispanic customers in the Republic of Mexico's far north. The merchants who followed him with mighty caravans of freight wagons merely enlarged upon a commercial opportunity that Becknell first brought to public attention. Within a short time the Santa Fe trade ballooned into a million-dollar-a-year business, pouring Mexican silver coin and raw products into the state of Missouri and precipitating a minor economic boom in what heretofore had been a depressed area on the American frontier.

The twenty-five years in which Mexico controlled the western end of the trade are generally regarded as the heyday of the Santa Fe Trail. In that period occurred many of the most dramatic events associated with trail history, including noted Indian fights, weather disasters that befell several caravans, the survey of the route in 1825, the first experimentation with military patrols, and the travels of Josiah Gregg, whose book on the subject, *Commerce of the Prairies*, first publicized this chapter in America's far western adventure.

After Gen. Stephen Watts Kearny led a conquering army over the Mountain Route of the Santa Fe Trail in 1846, the first year of the Mexican War, and brought the Southwest under United States rule, the character of overland commerce changed. With both ends of the trail in American hands, the traffic was no longer of international scope. Forts were added along the route to guard against Indian attack, and the freighting of military supplies became a new business. Stagecoach and mail services were inaugurated. More varied types of travelers put in an appearance. Where once the trail had been frequented only by merchants, their wagon masters, and ox drovers, by the late 1840s one could begin to meet, besides U.S. Army soldiers, newly appointed government officials, gold seekers bound for California, Catholic priests and nuns, a sprinkling of Protestant missionaries, and even a few emigrant families.

The last phase of the trail story unfolded during the 1870s as railroads pushed across Kansas and into the Southwest, creating a new railhead with each advance and progressively shortening the Santa Fe Trail. When the train reached Las Vegas in summer 1879, only 65 miles remained of the original wagon route to Santa Fe. In February 1880, with that last gap closed by rails, newspapers in New Mexico's capital proclaimed in bold headlines: "The Santa Fe Trail Passes into Oblivion."

The subsections that follow are aimed at assisting modern travelers in enlarging their understanding of the trail and increasing the enjoyment that comes with retracing the wagon tracks of the pioneer merchant men from Missouri. Recommended background reading, maps, and travel tips are discussed. Markers, monuments, and trail ruts are also described.

RECOMMENDED READING

The literature on the Santa Fe Trail is vast, almost overwhelming for the beginner. Basic for anyone doing serious research on the subject is Jack D. Rittenhouse's *The Santa Fe Trail: A Historical Bibliography*. Published in 1971 to commemorate the 150th anniversary of the opening of the trail by Becknell, it contains an annotated listing of 718 titles. Since its publication, of course, new works have appeared, so the number of books and articles relating to the trail must now be around 1,000.

The titles recommended here comprise a basic reading list that should be consulted by all those planning a trip over the trail. Everyone should read at least one general Santa Fe Trail history chosen from among the several suggested. Failure to do so will seriously diminish the value and pleasure of a tour. Also read as many of the firsthand accounts as time permits. Primary journals or diaries and recollections of trail life by individual participants impart a taste and feel for the past like nothing else and give a sense of what caravan travel was like.

When exploring the trail, it is wise to carry a small library of one's own books in the backseat of the car. Then, at each historic stop you can consult an appropriate volume and read the words of a traveler who preceded you to that place by 150 years. How remarkable, for example, to stand in Independence Square and read Matt Field's lively description of a noisy and colorful wagon caravan preparing to depart for Santa Fe; or to climb Pawnee Rock with Susan Magoffin's diary in hand and to consult the entry for July 4, 1846, recounting her experiences and emotions there; or to reach the eastern limits of Santa Fe and turn to Josiah Gregg's vivid recital of the arrival of an ox train at the trail's end. With such books we are able to look backward as through a prism and make the entire, grand Santa Fe Trail adventure part of our own experience.

For background reading before the trip, ask your bookseller to order what you need from the publisher. If you are unable to do this, bookstores located on or near the trail often have many of the following titles in stock. Although they will not be available for background reading before starting, many items can be purchased along the way. In addition, a number of specialized books and pamphlets will be found only at the historic sites they describe. At places like Arrow Rock, Council Grove, and Santa Fe, for example, keep a lookout for small historical publications that are of value to trail buffs.

National sites or monuments such as Fort Union, Fort Larned, Bent's Fort, and Pecos sell pertinent books in their visitors' centers. So, too, does the National Frontier Trails Center, Independence; the Santa Fe Trail Center at Larned; the Taos Book Shop across the street from Kit Carson's house; and the Museum Shop at the Palace of the Governors, Santa Fe.

You might also send a legal-sized SASE to the Last Chance Store, P. O. Box 31, Woodston, KS 67675 for a list of current trail books, including activity books for children. The store is sponsored by and benefits the Santa Fe Trail Association. Many of the volumes we recommend can be obtained from this source in paperback editions. All the following books are available at the time of writing.

GENERAL HISTORIES

Robert L. Duffus, *The Santa Fe Trail* (University of New Mexico Press, 1999). First published in 1930, and thus somewhat outdated, this is still the best survey of the trail for the general reader.

Stanley Vestal, *The Old Santa Fe Trail* (University of Nebraska Press, 1996). This is a highly readable account of the main events in trail history.

Max L. Moorhead, *New Mexico's Royal Road: Trade and Travel on the Chihuahua Trail* (University of Oklahoma Press, 1995). In spite of its title, this book is mainly about the commercial aspects of the Santa Fe Trail prior to 1848.

Josiah Gregg, *Commerce of the Prairies* (University of Oklahoma Press, 1990). This classic account of the Santa Fe trade, 1831–1844, is a book you should carry with you.

James A. Crutchfield, *The Santa Fe Trail* (Wordware Publishing, 1996). This episodic history serves as a useful introduction to the subject.

William Y. Chalfant, *Dangerous Passage: The Santa Fe Trail and the Mexican War* (University of Oklahoma Press, 1994). This is a valuable account of the crucial middle years of trail history.

Marc Simmons, *The Old Trail to Santa Fe* (University of New Mexico Press, 1996). The first chapters of this book provide an overview, followed by sketches of unusual interest.

Gene and Mary Martin, *Trail Dust: A Quick Picture History of the Santa Fe Trail* (Martin Associates, 1991). A handy little survey that makes a useful companion to Duffus's *The Santa Fe Trail*.

Mark L. Gardner, *Santa Fe Trail: National Historic Trail* (Southwest Parks and Monuments Association, 1993). An excellent introduction, beautifully illustrated.

TRAIL GUIDES

There are few accessible guides for the Santa Fe Trail. With luck, copies of out-of-print books such as Hobart Stocking's *The Road to Santa Fe*, or Gregory M. Franzwa's *The Santa Fe Trail Revisited* or his *Maps of the Santa Fe Trail* (both Patrice Press) can occasionally be found. Otherwise, the following resources may prove useful.

Gregory M. Franzwa, *The Oregon Trail Revisited, Silver Anniversary Edition* (Patrice Press, 1997). This book is especially valuable in following the Santa Fe Trail through Independence and metropolitan Kansas City.

Kathleen Ann Cordes, *America's National Historic Trails* (University of Oklahoma Press, 1999). This book includes a historical summary of the Santa Fe Trail and lists points of interest.

William E. Hill, *The Santa Fe Trail, Yesterday and Today* (Caxton Press, 1992). A helpful handbook containing a lengthy section of historical photos.

Elaine Pinkerton, *The Santa Fe Trail by Bicycle* (Red Crane Books, 1993). This book will appeal to individuals interested in the several annual organized bicycle treks along the Santa Fe Trail. It also has information of interest to the general traveler.

William W. White, *The Santa Fe Trail by Air* (Western Airtrails, 1996). Although this publication contains primarily specialized information for pilots, trail hounds will want the book for its aerial photos.

MEMOIRS, JOURNALS, AND BIOGRAPHIES

Books by and about individuals who traveled the Santa Fe Trail help us capture the spirit and flavor of those thrilling days. The following titles are especially recommended. Check Jack Rittenhouse's bibliography for others.

Mrs. Hal Russell, ed., *Land of Enchantment: Memoirs of Marian Russell Along the Santa Fe Trail* (University of New Mexico Press, 1993). This is a favorite. If you fail to read it beforehand and do not carry a copy on the trail, your trip will suffer.

Magoffin, Susan Shelby, *Down the Santa Fe Trail and into Mexico, 1846–1847: The Diary of Susan Shelby Magoffin*, edited by Stella M. Drumm (Lincoln: University of Nebraska Press, 1982). Regarded as a classic of trail literature, this book should be read entry by entry as you move west on your tour.

Kit Carson, *Autobiography* (University of Nebraska Press, 1966). Carson crossed the trail many times on his way west to further adventures.

Lewis H. Garrard, *Wah-to-yah and the Taos Trail* (University of Oklahoma Press, 1979). An account by an observant seventeen year old, this book is engagingly written. Garrard participated in stirring events along the trail in 1846 and 1847.

W. W. H. Davis, *El Gringo: New Mexico and Her People* (University of Nebraska Press, 1982). The first chapters of this book describe Davis's trip by stagecoach over the trail in 1853. The rest gives a picture of life in territorial New Mexico.

John E. Sunder, ed., *Matt Field on the Santa Fe Trail* (University of Oklahoma Press, 1995). Impressions of a trail trip in 1839 makes this an entertaining and informative book.

James Josiah Webb, *Adventures in the Santa Fe Trade, 1844–1847* (University of Nebraska Press, 1995). A businessman's account of his trail experiences.

Mark L. Gardner and Marc Simmons, eds., *The Mexican War Correspondence of Richard Smith Elliott* (University of Oklahoma Press, 1997). This book consists of letters of a soldier describing his march over the trail with Stephen Watts Kearny's conquering army.

Marian Meyer, *Mary Donoho: New First Lady of the Santa Fe Trail* (Ancient City Press, 1991). This is one of the few books about women on the trail.

Marc Simmons, ed., *On the Santa Fe Trail* (University Press of Kansas, 1986). This book contains short memoirs by some interesting trail travelers.

SPECIAL STUDIES

Scholars have produced authoritative studies on various phases of trail history. Following are some of the best.

Morris F. Taylor, *First Mail West: Stagecoach Lines on the Santa Fe Trail* (University of New Mexico Press, 2000). Taylor's fine volume is the only one on stagecoaching, and more still needs to be written on the subject.

David Lavender, *Bent's Fort* (University of Nebraska Press, 1972). Lavender's book is essential reading for background on the Mountain Route of the trail.

Robert W. Frazer, *Forts of the West* (University of Oklahoma Press, 1977). This compendium includes capsule histories of all the military posts established on the Santa Fe Trail.

Kate L. Gregg, ed., *The Road to Santa Fe: The Journal and Diaries of George Champlin Sibley* (University of New Mexico Press, 1995). This book contains accounts of the trail survey of 1825 and is useful for those dedicated to finding every significant point of interest along the route.

Thomas B. Hall, M.D., *Medicine on the Santa Fe Trail* (Friends of Arrow Rock, 1987). This volume gives details about a neglected but important subject in trail history.

Leo E. Oliva, *Fort Larned* (Kansas State Historical Society, 1997). This handsome and well-written small book gives the military side of Santa Fe Trail history.

MAPS

Following the Santa Fe Trail must be used in conjunction with standard highway maps. American Automobile Association maps are quite good, particularly for the Kansas City/Independence area. Maps of the five individual trail states are issued by the respective Highway Departments or Tourist Bureaus in each state. Usually these maps are offered free at tourist information centers or through the mail. Many states and cities along the trail now have web sites that can provide valuable information about travel on the trail.

In addition, a number of specialized maps are available. Very handy is the National Park Service's Official Map and Guide of the Santa Fe Trail, showing the original route and campsites along with modern roads. The Last Chance Store sells two large illustrated trail maps, plus a reproduction of Josiah Gregg's 1844 Santa Fe Trail map.

The SFTA, through its chapters, has undertaken a long-range project to map the entire trail. The Wet/Dry Routes Chapter was the first to publish the results of its survey in central Kansas: *A Directory of Santa Fe Trail Sites*, compiled by David K. Clapsaddle. The chapter has also printed a *Self-Guided Auto Tour of the Santa Fe Trail* for its area. To obtain these while traveling, check at the Santa Fe Trail Center, Larned, Kansas.

Moreover, the United States Geological Survey (USGS) has a wide variety of maps that best depict the nature of the trail. The western portion of the trail is shown on these maps in most cases. They can be consulted at some large libraries. The maps in this guide were drawn using the USGS 30 x 60 minute quadrangles for the base map. For a list of other maps available, write to: USGS Information Services, Box 25286, Federal Center, Denver, CO 80225. Their toll-free number is 1-800-HELP-MAP. Index maps for each state are free from the USGS and are very helpful as you decide which maps you need. The Santa Fe Trail maps (1:100,000) from east to west are:

Moberly, MO	Ulysses, KS
Jefferson City, MO	Leoti, KS
Marshall, MO	Lamar, CO
Kansas City, MO-KS	Las Animas, CO
Olathe, KS	La Junta, CO
Lawrence, KS	Walsenburg, CO
Council Grove, KS	Trinidad, CO
Salina, KS	Raton, NM
Hutchinson, KS	Springer, NM
Great Bend, KS	Roy, NM
Larned, KS	Santa Fe, NM
Kinsley, KS	Villanueva, NM
Dodge City, KS	

Maps for the Cimarron Cutoff from Lakin are:

Ulysses, KS	Capulin Mountain, NM
Hugoton, KS	Clayton, NM
Springfield, CO-KS-OK	Springer, NM
Boise City, OK-CO-TX-KS	Roy, NM

If you need any topographic maps from the USGS quickly, the following company can get the maps to you in short order: Timley Discount Topos, 9769 West 119th Drive, Suite 9, Broomfield, CO 80021; phone 303-469-5022.

INTERNET RESOURCES

Another source of information that is becoming increasingly important and useful is the World Wide Web. Although no attempt has been made to list every Web address that might provide useful information, one site that is particularly helpful is maintained by the University of Kansas: http: www.ukans .edu/heritage/research/sft/sft-cities.html. This site can also be found by searching under "Santa Fe Trail." Many other web sites have links to this site, and it is revised at regular intervals to assure up-to-date information. It will lead you to travel information as well as trail research.

HISTORIC PRESERVATION

NATIONAL PARK SERVICE
In 1968, Congress passed the National Trails System Act, which recognized historic trails and scenic trails throughout the country. Not until 1987, however, was the Santa Fe Trail added to the system, by special legislation. The National Park Service's Long Distance Trails Group Office at Santa Fe has jurisdiction over the Santa Fe Trail for preservation, interpretive, and marking purposes. It has developed and installed distinctive signs designating the auto tour route that parallels the trail. The official logo shows an ox-drawn freight wagon.

The federal program also works with private landowners who seek voluntary certification of historic sites on their property. To qualify, strict standards must be met.

The National Park Service publishes the *Santa Fe Trail Official Map and Guide*, a spectacular accordion brochure in color with a superb trail map, historical illustrations, and detailed text. It is a must for all travelers and can be found at national monuments and state tourism offices.

SANTA FE TRAIL ASSOCIATION
In 1986, at Trinidad, Colorado, the Santa Fe Trail Council, afterward renamed the Santa Fe Trail Association, was established to promote all aspects of the trail, including preservation, marking, research, publication, and travel. More than a dozen chapters develop programs at the local level. In odd-numbered years the SFTA holds a three-day symposium featuring lectures, tours, and period entertainment. The association's quarterly, *Wagon Tracks*, has become a major source of information on both the historic and contemporary trail. The SFTA coordinates its efforts with the National Park Service. As you drive the trail, you will likely note the distinctive "XING" signs that mark trail crossings. These have been placed by local chapters with the cooperation of the Park Service.

The administrative office and archives of the SFTA are located at the Santa Fe Trail Center, RR 3, Larned, KS 67550. For a membership brochure, send a legal-sized SASE to the SFTA office.

MARKERS AND MONUMENTS

Today, much of the excitement in following the Santa Fe Trail comes from seeing actual physical remains like ruts, old forts, or period artifacts preserved in museums. Natural landmarks like Pawnee Rock, the Cimarron River, and the Wagon Mound, which were there when the merchant caravans passed by, are also fascinating to see.

By contrast, since markers and monuments represent recent additions to the trail, all installed in the twentieth century and some during the past few years, many travelers pay little attention to them. However, this is unfortunate since such markers and monuments provide a sense of continuity, calling attention to the location of the trail on stretches where no original remains can be found. They serve as reminders that modern travelers are on the right course, and those with a text offer valuable historical information. Some, like the monument paid for by Kansas schoolchildren at the Cottonwood Crossing, are one of a kind. Others are part of a series placed by government agencies or private groups. In several instances, interesting stories connected with the programs initiated to raise money for markers constitute part of the history of the modern trail. Some of the marker and monument groups that you will encounter are described below.

DAUGHTERS OF THE AMERICAN REVOLUTION (DAR) MARKERS
The DAR launched the earliest, and to date the most ambitious, effort to commemorate the old Santa Fe Trail. Between 1902 and 1912, DAR chapters in all the trail states except Oklahoma relocated the fading route through research, raised funds from private and government sources, and placed handsome incised red or gray granite markers along the trail. Although the precise number of markers placed by the organization has not been determined, since no record was kept and additions have been made from time to time over the years, research has provided some information. Twenty-nine markers were placed in Missouri. Further, according to Mrs. T. A. Cordry's little book *The Story of the Marking of the Santa Fe Trail* (Crane and Co., 1915), ninety-six markers were installed along the trail in Kansas. But others were added later, including the one at the Little Arkansas Crossing (1979), so the actual figure must be over one hundred. Moreover, special DAR markers with a bronze plaque attached to granite were placed at various points between Kansas City and Santa Fe. Originally there were supposedly ten of these, but only six can be now be located. The Kansas Society Daughters of the American Revolution published the fine book *Ninetieth Anniversary Survey of the Santa Fe Trail DAR Markers in Kansas* in 1998. They located all the markers except one and provided locations and descriptions.

The Colorado chapter of the DAR placed thirty-four markers between

DAR markers in Kansas City, Missouri. Markers in Missouri have the location incised on the base.

1906 and 1909 and an additional one in 1928, most of them on the Mountain Route. However, four were located on the north side of the Cimarron River, where the Cimarron Cutoff angled for a few miles across the southeastern corner of Colorado. A total of nineteen markers were placed in New Mexico. Oklahoma had no markers originally but today has one new marker near the New Mexico State line.

Due to changes in the highway system, some markers in all the trail states have been moved from the original sites. In many cases these markers could be moved back to where the DAR placed them. For example, in New Mexico the Highway Department has relocated three markers to Interstate 25 rest stops so more people can see them, but it would be more educational and interesting for travelers if they could be viewed at their original sites on the trail.

We have made no attempt to locate all the DAR markers along the Santa Fe Trail. Instead, we have tried to call attention to those that are particularly visible, especially ones at major sites. Many others are scattered almost randomly along highways and back roads, often obscured by weeds or bushes. The majority of the markers bear a simple and quite similar text, but a few have special inscriptions, and we have emphasized the locations of these. After a few days on the trail, the DAR markers become familiar friends, and by scanning the roadsides, new ones will be discovered in unexpected places.

PIONEER MOTHER STATUES

As an outgrowth of its success in marking the Santa Fe Trail, the DAR joined with other interested groups to provide monuments for the National Old Trails Road. Established by an act of Congress in 1806 as the first federal road, it began in Cumberland, Maryland, and eventually was extended to St. Louis. From there an extension across central Missouri known as Boone's Lick Road led to a hookup with the Santa Fe Trail, which was considered part of the system after the federal survey of the trail was initiated in 1825. By 1837, with the boom in railroading, the government abandoned upkeep of the National Road.

In 1912, citizens in Kansas City formed the National Old Trails Road

The Pioneer Mother statue in Lexington, Missouri. This monument was dedicated by Harry S. Truman.

Association. Its purpose was not only to research and mark the historic route from coast to coast but also to encourage Congress to develop a national highway system with the advent of automobiles beginning to challenge the supremacy of railroads. The DAR became closely involved with the association's program. Red, white, and blue historical signs were adopted, and the same colors were painted in alternating stripes on telegraph and telephone poles along the National Road. Today, however, no evidence of this work remains.

More enduring was the DAR's project of installing twelve statues of the Pioneer Mother in each of the states on the National Road from Maryland to California. Four of the statues were intended for the Santa Fe Trail: one each at Lexington, Missouri; Council Grove, Kansas; Lamar, Colorado; and Santa Fe, New Mexico. For reasons explained later in this guide, the last was installed at Albuquerque instead of Santa Fe. Standing 10 feet high on a 6-foot base, the statues are made of pink algonite stone. The figure, a mother in sunbonnet with two children, was executed by St. Louis sculptor August Leimbach. The four on the Santa Fe route have special trail inscriptions around their bases.

Unrelated to these statues are two other Pioneer Mother memorials in the Kansas City area. One is a heroic bronze statue in Penn Valley Park, the other a red stone monument at Old Westport. In addition, women are also honored by the special DAR marker atop Pawnee Rock and the Plainswoman statue on the campus of Dodge City Community College.

OFFICIAL STATE HIGHWAY MARKERS
Each Highway Department or Tourist Bureau in the five trail states (Missouri, Kansas, Colorado, Oklahoma, and New Mexico) has placed attractive historical markers at major sites along the route. These contain some of the longest and most authoritative texts of any markers, and their locations have been carefully noted.

Trail travelers see such signs on highways along the SFT. This one is in Springer, New Mexico.

SPECIAL MARKERS AND MONUMENTS

Several groups of associated markers and sites related to a particular individual or event are worth mentioning. In your background reading pay special attention to the stories behind them.

Charles and William Bent were closely identified with the saga of the Santa Fe Trail. Places of interest related to their careers include: William Bent's house, Kansas City; Bent's New Fort (ruins), west of Lamar, Colorado; Bent's Old Fort (reconstruction), near La Junta, Colorado; William Bent's grave, Las Animas, Colorado; Charles Bent's house, Taos, New Mexico; and Charles Bent's grave in the National Cemetery, Santa Fe, New Mexico.

Christopher (Kit) Carson is another famous name firmly linked to the trail's history. As a boy he left from the site of Old Franklin, Missouri, on his first trip to Santa Fe. The State Historical Marker near Pawnee Rock refers to his stop at that renowned site. See the chapel marking the spot where he died in 1868 at Fort Lyon, Colorado, as well as the large equestrian statue in Kit Carson Park at Trinidad, Colorado. A reconstruction of Kit's house is at Rayado, New Mexico, and his principal residence is preserved nearby in Taos, where his grave is located. Santa Fe also has a Kit Carson monument.

William Becknell, Father of the Trail, is commemorated on markers at Franklin, Arrow Rock, Council Grove, Pawnee Rock, Dodge City, Cimarron, and Wagon Mound. Strangely, Josiah Gregg, who made such a large contribution to the trail story, is badly neglected by markers, with his name only mentioned in passing on a few. However, a tall granite Josiah Gregg Memorial Monument is located on the campus of Palo Duro High School in Amarillo, Texas. It commemorates an alternate "Santa Fe Trail" that Gregg helped blaze in 1840 from Fort Smith, Arkansas, across Oklahoma and the Texas Panhandle to New Mexico. Ruts of that trail are said to be visible on the school grounds. There are some fine ruts adjacent to TX 136 north of Amarillo and about 30

Local chapters have placed these signs at locations where the SFT crosses highways.

miles south of the town of Fritch. An official Texas Highway Marker, with reference to Gregg, marks the site.

Spanish explorer Francisco Vásquez de Coronado and his chief friar, Father Juan de Padilla, receive considerable attention along the Santa Fe Trail, although they traveled it some three hundred years before its formal establishment. Markers or monuments honoring them can be visited in Kansas at Council Grove, Herington, Lyons, and Fort Dodge. There is a Coronado mural in Santa Fe's main post office. Moreover, a little-known monument to Father Padilla is at the west end of Ellwood Park in Amarillo, Texas.

Members of the Mormon Battalion, who marched over the trail to Santa Fe and on to California during the first year of the Mexican War (1846), are remembered by five new markers installed in 1983 at Fort Leavenworth, Council Grove, McPherson, and Larned in Kansas, and on the courthouse square at Boise City, Oklahoma. One additional marker is in New Mexico located along Interstate 25 between Santa Fe and Albuquerque.

Modern-day exploration of the Santa Fe Trail will prove most interesting and enjoyable if it is preceded by careful planning. Therefore, it is advisable to study this guide, read background sources, collect and carefully peruse maps, and create an itinerary tailored to your interests and needs. At that point you will be ready to shout, as did the early wagon masters, "Catch up! All's set! Ho, for Santa Fe!"

TRAIL FEATURES

Among the most interesting features of the modern trail are the ruts, or tracks, of the original trace left by the heavy wheels of freight wagons. In recent years,

Rut

the word *ruts* has become the favored generic term for traces left in the earth by wagons and their draft animals. Most people can scarcely believe that such ruts can still be seen after more than a hundred years. Of course, in many places agriculture or urban expansion have destroyed all signs of the trail. Yet, here and there from Missouri to New Mexico, Santa Fe Trail ruts have been preserved. Some are very short lengths, carefully protected in parks or lots. Others, particularly on the western third of the trail, run for miles where the land has remained largely undisturbed.

Ruts accessible to the visitor have been noted throughout this guide. Although a few are well marked, such as those at Fort Leavenworth, Baldwin City, Fort Larned, and Fort Union, most are not. Moreover, their appearance and character vary considerably, and it requires some practice to identify them. What follows is a brief description of rut formation and how to recognize ruts and other features in the field.

Ruts usually appear as wide depressions in the ground, heavily grassed over. What might be called a standard rut has this form in cross-section: The width of the depression is slightly greater than that of a heavy freight wagon. Its sides may be sloping sharply or almost vertical and the bottom or floor comparatively flat, usually without a center mound.

The ruts seen today were produced by the cutting of the sod by wagon wheels and the chewing up of the surface by hooves of mule teams, or by six, eight, or more yokes of oxen followed by the erosive action of rain and wind.

Expectations of how ruts are supposed to look often prevent travelers from recognizing them. Many newcomers to the trail, hearing of ruts, expect to see something resembling tire tracks of a car or pickup truck, sometimes called a "two-track." However, trail ruts are quite different, and the inability to see beyond such expectations accounts for the problem people often have in recognizing ruts, even when they are standing in them.

In addition, Hollywood films showing wagon trains moving west in a single line have conditioned the public to believe that this was the accepted and traditional caravan formation. However, wagons moved in various formations depending on terrain, safety, or comfort. The fact is that upon reaching the open prairie beyond Council Grove and continuing across the southern plains to the foot of the Rockies, Santa Fe wagon masters habitually spread wagons out in four parallel files. By traveling four abreast, the wagons could more readily move into a defensive square in the event of an Indian attack, and such a formation also

Two-track

A SFT rut (left) and a modern two-track (far right) near Kearny Gap, New Mexico.

allowed more drivers to be in front, out of the lung-stinging dust that formed a canopy over the train. In Josiah Gregg's *Commerce of the Prairies*, there is an engraving of a Santa Fe-bound wagon train moving in four columns.

Further, when wagon wheels had churned a deep track through mud or dust, successive caravans, for ease of travel, often moved to the left or right,

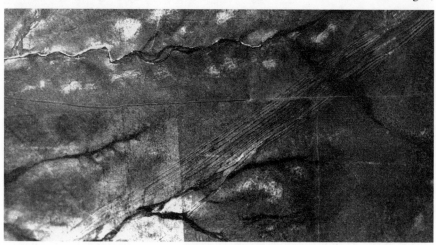

Multiple ruts, southwest of Watous, New Mexico, seen on a 1939 soil conservation aerial photo.

Swale

SFT swales at Black Jack, near Baldwin City, Kansas.

Notch

A swale with notch ascending from the Missouri River at Fort Leavenworth, Kansas.

establishing a new trail on undisturbed ground. Today, the wide band of tracks left from that practice may be partially filled by wind-blown soil and grassed over. Viewed laterally from afar, the low-mounded ridges of the tracks then appear as ripples in the prairie.

Moreover, when ascending a ridge coming out of a stream or river valley, wagons generally formed a single file, so that in time a deep depression was

The SFT with a small check dam across it at Tecolote, New Mexico.

worn up the hill. Often heavy wagons would have a second team hitched up to assist in the climb, further deepening the path. Frequently, the sides of such depressions eroded into gentle slopes, producing a feature now described as a swale. A good example can be seen at William Minor Park west of the Blue River in Kansas City. The distinction between swale and rut is that a swale has gently sloping sides in contrast to the distinct "break," or steep side, of a rut.

Sometimes associated with a swale is a cut in the crest of the ridge, resembling an open gunsight, which we call a notch. Good examples of this feature can be found at Fort Leavenworth and the "Bugle Notch" at Rayado, New Mexico.

Two other trail features, both produced by erosion so excessive that little semblance of the original trail trace remains, are washouts and blowouts. A washout is caused by heavy water erosion widening and deepening a rut until it resembles a dry streambed (called an arroyo in New Mexico and a gully elsewhere). To identify this feature, it is helpful to locate undisturbed trail remains either above or below the washout. Also, a washout is often quite straight, a likely indicator that it was once part of the trail. Sometimes the Soil Conservation Service or landowner has placed a low earthen dam across a washout to prevent further erosion.

A blowout occurs when wind gouges a relatively deep depression well beyond the limits of the original rut. The trail may have been through soft, sandy soil and oriented in such a way that the prevailing wind scoured it. True blowouts are uncommon, but a fine example has been photographed on private land southwest of Durham, Kansas.

This wind-scoured blowout is on the trail near Durham, Kansas. Photo courtesy Gregory Franzwa.

Finally, on open flats travelers will occasionally see a mere imprint of the trail, the original ruts having long since been filled in by surface or windblown sand. In such cases, although no depressions remain visible, discolorations in the earth and differences in or absence of vegetation may faintly or even clearly mark the original wagon route.

PLANNING YOUR TRIP

Josiah Gregg tells us that traders waited until the first green grass appeared in late April or May before setting out on the trail since they wanted to be sure of adequate feed for their animals, and the greening signaled the end of the blizzard season. No man wanted to be caught on the open plains in a snowstorm. Stories of a few improvident individuals who dared a winter crossing and suffered fearfully or even perished in the attempt were known to all.

The warning implicit in those early stories is also best heeded today. In his guide *The Road to Santa Fe*, Hobart Stocking speaks of a blinding snowstorm he encountered while following the Cimarron Cutoff through the Oklahoma Panhandle. His car stalled on an icy highway, and he had to be rescued. Consequently, except for short trips when there is a near-term promise of good weather, travel on the Santa Fe Trail should be avoided in winter. The best times of the year to travel the trail are late spring, early summer, and early fall. The extreme heat of midsummer, especially in Missouri and Kansas, discourages many people from sightseeing, although cool Santa Fe (at an elevation of 7,000 feet) offers an escape from the East in July and August.

In addition, a rainy spell can set in at any time during the warm season, after which unpaved roads quickly turn to quagmires, making travel impossible. If in doubt about weather, check locally on conditions before leaving the paved highway.

Since the original starting point of the Santa Fe Trail was the river town of Franklin, Missouri, in the central part of the state, that place is the logical beginning for this guide and for your tour. Following the trail to its fork in western Kansas, you can there take the Cimarron Cutoff to Santa Fe and then return by way of the Mountain Route (or vice versa) so as not to miss any of the sites. Individuals living near the western end of the Santa Fe Trail will also want to drive east on one of these routes and return via the other, but on the journey out they will have to follow the guide in reverse. For those unable to devote the several weeks required to cover all the trail at once, brief excursions of a few days can be made along convenient sections of the route.

SITE ACCESSIBILITY AND ALTERATION

The majority of historic trail sites described in *Following the Santa Fe Trail* are open and accessible to the public. Although a number are on private property, many of these can be easily viewed from a nearby public road. Those wishing to enter must get permission from the owner, as for example at Diamond Spring. In a few noted instances, such as at McNees Crossing, the owner freely admits visitors without advanced permission. Remember to close gates behind you upon entering and leaving. Of course, visitors should respect all sites, and observation of unauthorized digging or vandalism should be reported to local authorities.

Every guide of this kind is to some degree already out of date by the time it leaves the printer. Roads change, markers are added or removed, historical sites are altered and even destroyed by vandals. In our collections are photographs and slides of landmarks and monuments that disappeared soon after we shot them. Some of these include the Nebraska House Hotel on Independence Square, demolished to make way for a parking lot; the small but significant Point of Rocks a few miles west of Dodge City, destroyed when the highway was widened; Uncle Dick Wootton's two-story adobe house in Raton Pass, torn down by its owner. And even after extensive efforts at education and raising awareness about the importance of the trail, the destruction continues. In 1997, a church near 85th and Manchester in the Kansas City area destroyed many yards of Santa Fe Trail ruts for a soccer field. A few years later, despite the public outcry over the first destruction, it leveled the remaining ruts to enlarge the soccer field. The list of stolen or vandalized markers would run to several pages. As one example, a beautiful one placed and dedicated at the Wayne City Landing on the Missouri River was vandalized within two weeks but fortunately was later restored.

As a result of such threats to trail sites, we have deliberately excluded several places on the trail because they are particularly vulnerable to damage, mainly from treasure hunters. In addition, references to two other places were deleted because they are on private property and the owners prefer not to have visitors.

We believe we have found all major and most minor sites on the trail. However, we admit that during every new trip we find something of interest previously overlooked. By keeping a sharp watch, readers will make their own discoveries and thus add to the fun of trail travel.

ABBREVIATIONS COMMONLY USED IN THE TEXT

DAR = Daughters of the American Revolution

SFT = Santa Fe Trail

SFTA = Santa Fe Trail Association

State highways in the trail states are abbreviated by state (KS, MO, CO, OK, NM) and number; for example, Kansas 7 = KS 7.

Federal highways are abbreviated by US and number, for example US 56.

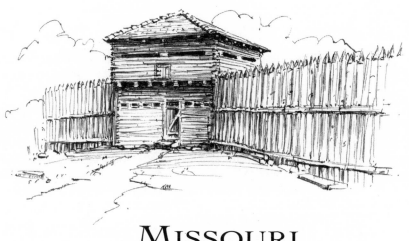

MISSOURI

FRANKLIN, FORT OSAGE, AND LEXINGTON

FRANKLIN

The original starting point of the Santa Fe Trail (SFT) was Franklin, Missouri. Platted in 1816 on a low floodplain on the north bank of the Missouri River, it was named in honor of Benjamin Franklin. The town was the center of what was called the Boonslick Country, which stretched over several counties along the Missouri River. The name Boonslick (originally Boone's Lick) referred to a salt lick probably discovered by Daniel Boone about 1800. Around 1807, the lick was developed commercially for salt production by his sons Nathan and Daniel Morgan Boone. After 1815, the Boonslick Country's population expanded rapidly for two reasons. First, the War of 1812 ended, diminishing threats of Indian hostilities. Second, in 1811 there had been a major earthquake in New Madrid, Missouri, where settlers lost their farms. They were given certificates for land in other parts of the state, and while some of these people came to the Boonslick Country, the majority of certificates were sold to others who then settled in this area. Many of the irregularly shaped landholdings here are a result of claims based on these certificates.

The first steamboat, the *Independence*, made it up the Missouri River to Franklin in 1819. The citizens greeted the event enthusiastically and were certain that this voyage would make Franklin even more important. Unfortunately, other than military supply craft, Franklin was not to have another steamboat visit until 1826.

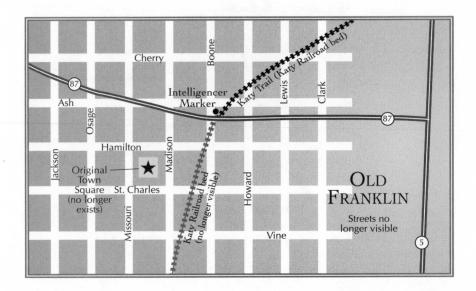

The first flood to threaten Franklin also occurred in 1826, and an even larger one in 1828. The principal commercial district of Franklin was closest to the river and hardest hit. Consequently, in the latter year, businesses and many residents began moving to higher ground 2 miles away in what was to become New Franklin. Not all business left Old Franklin, but certainly its importance was in decline by 1828.

It was in 1821, the year that Missouri became a state, that Franklin became linked with the SFT. In that year William Becknell, the Father of the Santa Fe Trail, departed for New Mexico. Franklin was also the home of the teenage Kit Carson, who in 1826 ran away from his job as a saddler's apprentice to join a wagon train headed for Santa Fe. Kit's father, Lindsay, is listed as one of the men at Fort Hempstead (a log fort near Franklin) during the War of 1812, so undoubtedly young Kit was also there at this time. As the first outfitting center for the infant Santa Fe trade, Franklin was also the residence of numerous other men closely identified with the trail, among them Meredith Miles Marmaduke, the Coopers, and David Workman, the saddler who employed Carson and later went to Santa Fe himself.

Access to Old Franklin is from Interstate 70, the main St. Louis to Kansas City highway. Exit at Boonville (Exits 121, 104, or 101), drive north through the center of town, and cross the Missouri River on a new concrete bridge. You are on US 40. Just north of the bridge, MO 87 intersects from the left (west). Before taking MO 87, turn sharply right (back onto the old highway). The Old Franklin DAR marker is located on the east side of the old highway, although it may be moved to the mini-park on MO 87 in the future.

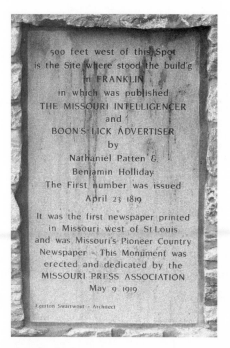

500 feet west of this Spot
is the Site where stood the build'g
in FRANKLIN
in which was published
THE MISSOURI INTELLIGENCER
and
BOON'S LICK ADVERTISER
by
Nathaniel Patten &
Benjamin Holliday
The First number was issued
April 23 1819
It was the first newspaper printed
in Missouri west of St Louis
and was Missouri's Pioneer Country
Newspaper - This Monument was
erected and dedicated by the
MISSOURI PRESS ASSOCIATION
May 9 1919

Egerton Swartwout - Architect

The restored Missouri Intelligencer *marker at the site of Old Franklin, Missouri.*

Here go west .25 mile on MO 87, and on the right, near a row of trees, is a small park. This park is on the site of the Old Franklin terminal for the Missouri-Kansas-Texas Railroad, known popularly as the "Katy." Here the Katy Trail enters from the north, a walking and biking trail from St. Charles, Missouri, that follows the old bed of the railroad. Of SFT interest is a marker with an inscription commemorating two newspapers, one of them the *Missouri Intelligencer*. This marker replaces one lost in the flood of 1993. The *Missouri Intelligencer* was the first weekly newspaper established (1819) west of St. Louis, and today the back files of this paper are a prime source for information about the history of the SFT. Its pages carried the first announcement of Becknell's initial trip to Santa Fe and, on October 12, 1826, a notice that the boy Christopher Carson had fled his apprenticeship. Soon after, the *Missouri Intelligencer* moved its offices 15 miles north to Fayette, the new county seat. The marker notes that the original newspaper office was "500 feet west of this spot," which would be the center of Old Franklin. You are standing very near the corner of what was Boone and Ash Streets in Old Franklin.

The center of Old Franklin was located two blocks southwest of the marker. In 1973, a flood uncovered traces of the town in the fields on both sides of MO 87. Old Franklin was 1.5 by 1.5 miles, so it is no wonder it extended across this road. (Modern maps show a Franklin west of New Franklin, but this is not the original town.)

Heading west on MO 87, you will be following the SFT after about 1 mile. (There is a faded Franklin sign just west of a turnout.) The trail left the square in Old Franklin and headed west toward the ferry that crossed to Arrow Rock Spring. Note that the highway you are on is only slightly higher than the floodplain (called a bottom here in Howard County) to the left. Traders stayed at the edge of the floodplain next to the adjacent hills. At just under 2.5 miles from the Katy Trail, MO 87 curves right and climbs a hill. Paved Route Z continues straight ahead. Follow it and at .8 mile from the junction is the historic home

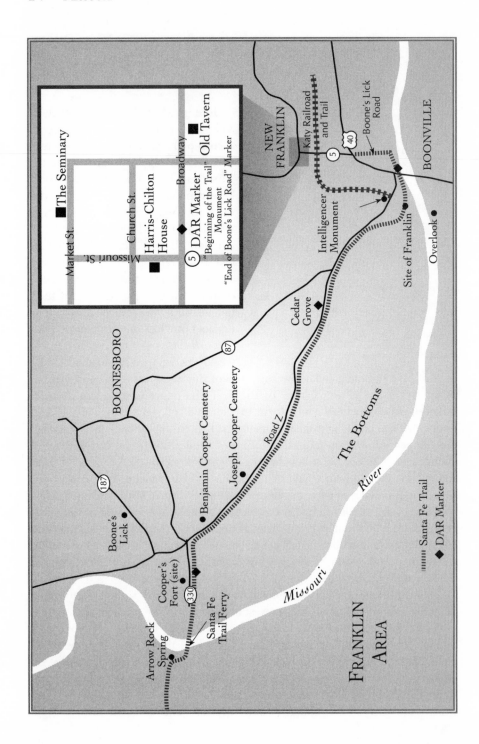

Cedar Grove, on the right. It is on high ground behind a low stone wall with a DAR marker in front. The two-story Greek Revival house has green shutters and a white porch across the front. The builder of the main section, which dates from 1856, was a physician named Dr. Horace Kingsbury. Attached to the left end of the main structure is a small brick Federal-style house dating to 1824. Built by pioneer farmer Nicholas Amick, it is one of the oldest area residences still standing. It is now a private residence. During its earliest years of occupation, Santa Fe-bound caravans passed in front.

Continue ahead on Route Z to a small cemetery on your right, about 4.6 miles from Cedar Grove. This cemetery contains the grave of Joseph Cooper. There is a small sign and a stile for easy entrance. It is a short but steep walk to the cemetery. About 1.6 miles past the first cemetery you come to a second, which contains the graves of Benjamin Cooper and his brother Sarshall, who was the commander at Cooper's Fort during the War of 1812. One grave marker here says "Sarshel Cooper" with a death date of 1815, but a marker at that fort spells his name differently and gives a different death year. There is a small sign, stile, and steep walk here as well.

Continuing on Route Z another .3 mile, you come to the hamlet of Petersburg, where there is only a marker for a post-trail building. There is, however, a gravel road that comes in from the left (County Road 330). Follow this road (weather permitting) for .8 mile, where there is another DAR marker on the left by a telephone pole. The marker is inscribed at the base "Cooper's Fort" but is difficult to read because of silt deposited by the flood. Cooper's Fort was silted over by a flood in 1844, but another flood in 1903 revealed its location. Just beyond, on the right, is a commemorative sign telling about Cooper's Fort.

Brothers Benjamin and Sarshall Cooper built the fort near here for protection of local settlers during the War of 1812, one of five in this part of Boonslick Country. Settlers in the area elected Sarshall Cooper captain of their military company, leading to his command of Cooper's Fort. There were sixty-four men at the fort during this period. In addition to the twelve defenders named Cooper, there was Harmon Gregg. His son Josiah, the future author of *Commerce of the Prairies*, was only six in 1812 when the family lived at the fort. The determination of the Coopers and other defenders is clear from the commemorative sign at the site telling of the following defiant statement, a response made by the fort commander to the U.S. government's order for withdrawal at the outbreak of the war: "We have maid our Hoams here and all we hav is here and it Wud ruen us to Leave now. We are all good Americans, not a Tory or one of his Pups among us and we hav 2 hundred Men and Boys that will Fight to the last and we have 100 Wimen and Girls whut wil tak there places wh. makes a good force. So we can Defend this Settlement wh. Gods help we will do. So if we had a fiew barls of Powder and 2 hundred Lead is all we ask."

Benjamin Cooper led a party with pack mules to Santa Fe in 1822 at the same time William Becknell took the first wagon train over the SFT, Becknell's second trip to Santa Fe. Cooper returned to New Mexico the following year with traders headed by his nephew Steven.

The road beyond Cooper's Fort formerly continued over the bottoms to the Missouri River, where traders utilized a ferry to cross to Arrow Rock Spring. The ferry figured prominently in the early history of the SFT. Becknell may have operated it both before and after his Santa Fe ventures. Turn around here because the road is poor and on private land.

Return on County Road 330 to the pavement at Petersburg. Here turn left on Route J towards Boonesboro (Route Z becomes J because it changes direction). At Boonesboro turn left on MO 87 and go 1.3 miles to the junction with MO 187, which enters from the left. Take MO 187 and drive 2.5 miles to Boone's Lick. Here are important interpretive signs, a DAR marker, and a path leading down to the salt springs.

There is some dispute over who discovered this lick, but a good case can be made that it was Daniel Boone himself. He moved to Missouri in 1799 and is known to have traveled to this area in 1800. To Boone, a professional hunter, the lick was important as it attracted deer to the site. It is clear that the commercial exploitation of the springs was a result of the efforts of his two sons, Nathan and Daniel Morgan Boone. By 1807, they and their crew were making salt by boiling the saline water in large kettles. Salt was a necessity in the early nineteenth century for preserving food. Consequently, this site quickly became known as Boone's Lick and the area around it for hundreds of miles as the Boone's Lick Country (shortened to Boonslick in today's usage).

By 1811, James and Jesse Morrison had bought the lick from the Boones. Before his overland excursion to Santa Fe, Becknell worked for the Morrisons, perhaps as foreman of the large salt-making crew. He was living at the site in 1817, while owning property in nearby Franklin. Joseph L. Morrison, the sixteen-year-old son of James, fell into a kettle of boiling salt water and was scalded to death in 1833. Some years ago, a broken monument marking his grave was reported to be near the top of the curving hillside near the spring.

As there is no bridge or ferry across the Missouri River in this area today, you must return to Old Franklin via MO 87. Where MO 87 intersects US 40, a gravel road goes east. Cross US 40 and take the gravel road about .2 mile to a large mansion on the left. This is Rivercene, which is on the National Register of Historic Places. Now a bed and breakfast, a sign on one of the two stone pillars at the gate reads: "Steamboat Captain's House." It was built in 1869 by a Captain Kinney, who at various times owned nine steamboats on the Missouri River.

The gravel road in front of the mansion is part of a road even older than the SFT. There was an early trail (or trace as it is called here in Missouri) from St. Charles (northwest of St. Louis and on the north bank of the Missouri River) to the Boonslick Country. This trace evolved into Boone's Lick Road. The western end of this road was at the square in Old Franklin. The street on the south side of the square was St. Charles Street, a common way of saying that it was the road to St. Charles.

Return to the intersection of MO 87 and US 40 and turn right (north) toward New Franklin. Turn left on MO 5, and just before New Franklin is a WPA-built bridge over what were the Missouri-Kansas-Texas Railroad tracks (now the Katy Trail). Just beyond the bridge there is a slight rise to the town, the limit of the 1993 flood, which was the largest in recorded history on the Missouri. The one main business street in town, Broadway, intersects the highway, which becomes Missouri Street. Turn right on Broadway one-half block from the Missouri Street-East Broadway intersection, and in the center of the avenue you will find a large red boulder and plaque surmounted by a three-bulb antique streetlight. This is the Beginning of the Trail Monument, placed with much ceremony by the DAR in 1909.

For modern travelers intending to drive (or walk, or bicycle, or ride horseback) all the way to Santa Fe, here is one of the trail's high points. From this spot to the End of the Trail Monument on the Santa Fe Plaza, lie almost 1,000 miles, all studded with history. At the New Franklin monument, your adventure into the past officially commences.

The heading on the bronze plaque reads "Franklin, Cradle of the Santa Fe Trail, 1821." At the top, William Becknell's first packhorse train to Santa Fe appears in sculptured relief. (Other Becknell trains in bronze relief can be seen along the trail at Pawnee Rock and the Wagon Mound.) The full inscription, which we leave to your discovery, will stir all trail buffs who respond to the drama and romance of history. Behind the DAR marker note a separate stone designating the "End of Boone's Lick Road," the road connecting St. Charles with Franklin and the start of the SFT. Actually, these markers properly belong on the square in Old Franklin, but since that site is inaccessible this location will have to do.

Continue east on Broadway to the two-story house at 207, which may be one of the old taverns originally in Old Franklin. We know a tavern was put on logs and moved to New Franklin, and possibly it was this building since locals claim that the upstairs rooms in this house had numbers over the doors before remodeling took place. If it is the old tavern, then it may be the house where the famed Missouri portrait painter George Caleb Bingham, as a boy, watched Chester Harding finish a painting of Daniel Boone. Harding had stopped by Boone's house a year before Boone's death and had him propped up for a portrait. Bingham, himself, went on to become one of Missouri's most famous painters.

The large monument (left) is the "Beginning of the Trail Monument" in New Franklin. On it is a bronze plaque (top right) showing a packhorse train and inscription. The "End of Boone's Lick Road" marker (bottom right) is behind the large stone.

Returning to Missouri Avenue, turn right. In the middle of the first block on the left, at 108 N. Missouri, is the two-story, Federal-style Harris-Chilton House built in 1832. Continue another one and a half blocks to Market Street and turn right. In mid-block on the left, at 110 Market, is a two-story white house with a sign next to a wagon wheel, reading, "Seminary, 1832." This old brick building was the first school, or academy as it was called, in New Franklin.

An interesting side trip can be made north to Fayette at this point. Continue on MO 5 9 miles to Fayette. The town was established in 1823, soon after becoming the Howard County seat. There are many attractive houses here, but the one of interest to trail buffs is that of Joseph Davis, an assistant surveyor on the 1825 Sibley survey and a signer of the treaty made with the Osages at Council Grove, Kansas. Located at 208 South Main Street, the north half (to the right) is older and was likely built about 1826. Davis's great-grandson, Denny Davis, is the owner of the local newspapers and is a valuable source of information on local history. For more information about Franklin, see Davis's article in *Wagon Tracks* (Davis 1993).

Kit Carson sent his half-Indian daughter Adaline to Rock Springs School here in Fayette. Later Adaline attended Howard Female Seminary (afterward Central Methodist College), which still exists in Fayette. Then, in the 1850s, Carson took her back to Taos, New Mexico.

Return to Old Franklin and cross over the Missouri River again to Boonville.

BOONVILLE

Old Franklin, built on the bottoms of the Missouri River on the north bank, had the advantage of being on Boone's Lick Road. Opposite Franklin on the south side steep limestone cliffs rose almost from the water's edge. In 1817, Boonville, named for Daniel Boone, was established atop these cliffs.

Boonville is occasionally mentioned as a starting point for some Santa Fe caravans in the earliest years of the traffic, but its role in the trade was never a major one. Like Franklin and other towns founded later up the Missouri, Boonville had a landing where cargo could be off-loaded from St. Louis steamboats and placed in freight wagons. A steeply sloped cobblestone street led upward from the landing to brick and frame warehouses.

Several early Boonville buildings, while having no direct association with the SFT, must have been familiar to New Mexican traders. Christ Episcopal Church (northeast corner of Vine and Fourth Streets) dates from 1846 and is said to be the oldest Episcopal church west of St. Louis. Thespian Hall, at the corner of Main and Vine Streets, was begun in 1855 and is the oldest theater west of the Alleghenies. And Kemper Military School (Center and Third Streets) was established in 1844. Famed Santa Fe trader Franz Huning of Albuquerque placed his nine-year-old son Arno in this school about 1878.

Today, Boonville is a thriving community with a great deal of interest in its past. Many buildings have been renovated, and it is certainly worth the traveler's time to pause here. Of special interest is Harley Park Overlook, where one has a fine view across the river to the site of Franklin. To get to this overlook, cross the river from the north and continue to Morgan Street. Turn right on Morgan and drive to Parkway, then turn right. Continue one block on Parkway and turn left on Harley to the overlook. From here you can see the "bottoms" across the river, the location of the once-thriving town of Franklin, and a long view up the valley, the route of the SFT to Arrow Rock.

SIDE TRIP TO COLUMBIA, ST. CHARLES, AND ST. LOUIS

Before continuing to Arrow Rock, it is possible to make two side trips of interest to SFT buffs. The first is 27 miles eastward to Columbia, and the second another 120 miles to St. Charles and St. Louis, all on Interstate 70.

COLUMBIA

In Columbia, the State Historical Society of Missouri is located at 1020 Lowry Street on the campus of the University of Missouri. Serious SFT researchers will find excellent facilities here, including:

(a) a library with rare Missouri and western Americana materials;

(b) a newspaper library containing both original papers and microfilm of many early periodicals, among them the *Missouri Intelligencer*; and

(c) the Western Historical Manuscripts Collection, which contains an assortment of primary materials relating to the SFT.

Each of these facilities is located in a separate room in the building, has good indices, and provides photocopying services. In addition, the society maintains an excellent web site (www.system.missouri.edu/shs) with information about parking, hours of operation, available material, and research photos.

ST. CHARLES

Founded in the 1760s by the fur trader Louis Blanchette, St. Charles was the first settlement on the Missouri River. St. Charles is a very interesting small city with numerous buildings from the early nineteenth century. Meriwether Lewis and William Clark visited the town in 1804 on their way up the Missouri on their famous voyage of discovery. Maj. Steven Long also stopped here on his 1819 expedition. George C. Sibley, the leader of the 1825 government survey of the Santa Fe Trail, moved here sometime after completing the survey. He and his wife, Mary Easton Sibley, were instrumental in founding Lindenwood College (now University) in St. Charles. They are both buried on the campus in a small cemetery near the football stadium, in the Easton family plot.

When Independence and Westport became the principal starting points for the SFT, there were still many travelers and emigrants using the Boone's Lick Road from St. Charles to Franklin and then west from Franklin on the trail. The starting point for Boonslick Road is at the intersection of South Main and Boonslick Road (today's spelling) in St. Charles. Also, in a building at 515 South Main was located Eckert's Tavern, where Sibley wrote the final report on his 1825 survey of the SFT. The original building has been replaced with the modern Eckert's Tavern, but there is a marker on the building.

Also of interest is the Katy Trail, which can be accessed just behind Main Street near the river (see Franklin).

ST. LOUIS

Located 15 miles below the confluence of the Mississippi and Missouri Rivers, St. Louis was the nerve center for western exploration and the fur trade in the nineteenth century. Its role in the history of the West is today symbolized by the Gateway Arch at the Jefferson National Expansion Memorial, which has exhibits relating to the SFT. (Access to the arch and museum is from Interstate 70.)

Four St. Louis points of interest associated with the SFT are the following:

A. St. Charles Rock Road and Boone's Lick Road Marker

The marker, located in Kiener Plaza, opposite the old courthouse in downtown St. Louis, designates the beginning of the trunk road that connected St. Louis with the head of the SFT at Franklin. The Boone's Lick Road actually started in St. Charles.

B. Statue of Missouri Senator Thomas Hart Benton

This heroic statue is located in Lafayette Park, bounded by Mississippi, Missouri, Park, and Lafayette Avenues. The splendid statue of Benton, cast in bronze in Munich and erected in 1868, is a gem. It was unveiled by Benton's daughter, Mrs. Jessie Benton Fremont, wife of John Charles Fremont, the Pathfinder. The statue faces west, and at its feet are inscribed the words: "There lies the west; there lies India."

Thomas Hart Benton, elected senator when Missouri achieved statehood in 1821, became the chief spokesman in Washington for Santa Fe traders. He introduced the bill that led to the survey and marking of the trail in 1825 and pressured the secretary of war to provide military protection from the Indians for wagon trains. Surrounding the park are once-beautiful homes, now being restored. It is a rough neighborhood, so visit only in midday.

C. Bellefontaine Cemetery

Bellefontaine Cemetery (pronounced "Bellefountain" locally) is located between Florissant and Broadway, adjacent to Interstate 70, with the main entrance and office at 4947 W. Florissant. The cemetery gates are open seven days a week, but the office has more limited hours.

Since this is a huge cemetery with a maze of lanes, visitors need a map showing notable graves; available free from the office. Several well-known people associated with the SFT and exploration of the West are buried here. Of primary interest to trail buffs is the Magoffin family plot. Brothers James W. (d. 1868) and Samuel Magoffin (d. 1888) were prominent traders well known in Santa Fe, El Paso, and Chihuahua City. Samuel's young Kentucky-born wife Susan Shelby Magoffin (d. 1855) kept an extraordinary diary of her SFT trip in 1846. The plot (in blocks 79–80, lot 1002, behind the elks' statue) has markers for Samuel and Susan. Although a diagram of the casket locations (photocopy available in the cemetery office) shows James located to the right of Susan, in reality, he is buried in San Antonio, Texas, where he died.

A short distance away, under a 15-foot column, rests Gen. Stephen Watts Kearny, who led his army over the SFT in 1846. Before departing New Mexico for California, he entertained Samuel and Susan in the old Spanish Palace of the Governors on the Santa Fe Plaza. Further, Sterling Price, his successor, is buried under another tall column nearby. Early in 1847 Price put down the revolt in Taos, which had resulted in the death of Governor Charles Bent and others. In addition, you will also want to see the impressive monument marking the grave of Senator Thomas Hart Benton, as well as the graves of Manuel Lisa, a founder of the fur trade, and Gen. William Clark of the Lewis and Clark Expedition.

D. Missouri Historical Society, Jefferson Memorial Building

The Missouri Historical Society is located in Forest Park, at Lindell Boulevard and DeBaliviere. The History Museum and Research Center is at 225 South Slinker Boulevard, facing Forest Park. The society maintains a web site (www.mohistory.org), which has a map showing how to get to the museum, hours of operation, and other important information. The collections include excellent materials related to the SFT and fur trade.

ARROW ROCK

From Boonville, go west on Interstate 70 to the Arrow Rock/MO 41 Exit. Turn north on MO 41 and proceed 12 miles to Arrow Rock. As you approach Arrow Rock, the first road to the right leads to a campground that is part of the Arrow Rock State Historic Site. Continue to the second road, which leads you to the visitors' center. This new center has extensive information about the SFT and the Arrow Rock area, as well as three of George Caleb Bingham's paintings. From the center it is an easy walk to the village of Arrow Rock. As you enter the village from the visitors' center, you will be heading for Main Street. The Friends of Arrow Rock have a small shop on Main Street and offer guided tours several times daily to all the important sites in town.

The Arrow Rock site was well known by the time Lewis and Clark traveled by in 1804. They noted it in their journals. When William Becknell passed through here in 1821, he used the ferry from near Cooper's Fort to the landing at the foot of the Arrow Rock bluff. From the landing, traders climbed the bluff and stopped at the spring at the summit. The village itself was not laid out until 1829 by Meredith Miles Marmaduke. By this time the jumping-off point for the SFT had moved west to Independence, so Arrow Rock did not play a major role in the trade. Still, people heading for New Mexico continued to pass through, and Arrow Rock, initially called New Philadelphia, remained associated with the trail for the next several decades.

Although there are a number of early homes of historical and architectural importance, only sites related to the SFT follow:

A. Old Arrow Rock Tavern
A two-story white structure built about 1834 by Joseph Huston, the Old Arrow Rock Tavern is the town's most familiar landmark and a major point of interest related to the SFT. Noted SFT travelers are known to have stopped here. Portraits and relics are on display in the tavern, and a bronze plaque is on the front wall. Historical brochures are available, and fine meals are served.

Stone curb gutters of the kind cut and laid by slaves are in front of the tavern and all along Main Street. According to legend, upon returning from his second trip to Santa Fe, William Becknell cut open leather bags, and Mexican silver coins rolled into these gutters. However, historical evidence suggests that this actually happened in Old Franklin, which had similar gutters. Arrow Rock, after all, was not laid out until 1829, seven years after Becknell returned from Santa Fe the second time.

B. Arrow Rock Official Missouri Historical Marker
The marker is just past the tavern toward the river (north). The sign contains a brief history of the town and references to the SFT.

C. Santa Fe Spring, also called Big Spring and Arrow Rock Spring
To reach the spring, continue two blocks east from the tavern along Main Street (toward the river), then take the second right toward the Scout area. The spring is enclosed in stone and concrete and covered by an open, four-post shelter. There is a white sign with a SFT marker on top identifying the spring as a watering stop for caravans. The river landing was about .25 mile away.

D. Overlook
To find the overlook, continue toward the river. This spot commands a good view of the river landing and, across the Missouri, the Cooper's Fort area.

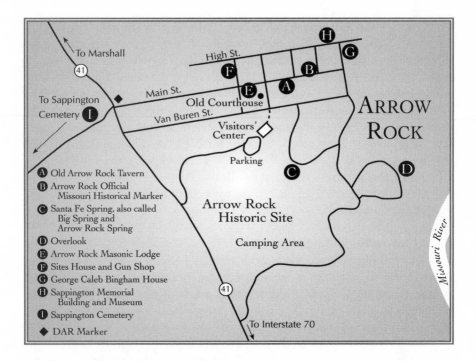

E. Arrow Rock Masonic Lodge
The lodge, founded in 1842, is located on the north side of Main Street, one-half block west of the tavern. Today, the first floor houses a craft center. It is known that a number of its members traveled the SFT.

F. Sites House and Gun Shop
Both buildings are behind the Masonic Lodge. These restored structures belonged to John Sites, Jr., who learned gunsmithing in his father's Boonville shop, which was established in 1835. In 1841, he moved to Arrow Rock, where he opened his own business. Thereafter, Sites catered to the needs of local citizens and supplied guns to individuals heading west on the Santa Fe and Oregon Trails.

G. George Caleb Bingham House
The house is located on the eastern end of High Street. George Caleb Bingham lived here intermittently from 1837 to 1845. The house has been restored and furnished with items from the period.

H. Sappington Memorial Building and Museum
The building is located near the east end of High Street, next to the Lyceum. For Dr. John Sappington's relation to the SFT, see the next section.

I. Sappington Cemetery

From the parking lot of the visitors' center, return to MO 41, and drive west to Main Street. At the junction of Main Street and MO 41, is the Turley Service Station on the northeast corner. Turleys from this area traveled the SFT and were prominent in New Mexico. Simeon Turley operated a distillery at Arroyo Hondo north of Taos. He and his men were killed in the same January 1847 uprising in which Charles Bent perished.

Drive southwest from this junction on Route TT. At .7 mile pass the Arrow Rock Cemetery on the right. Buried here is Joseph Huston (1784–1865), founder of the Old Arrow Rock Tavern. Continue another 4.3 miles until the road ends in a T. Turn left there, and a short distance beyond (on the left) is a sign and gate for the Sappington Cemetery State Historic Site. A lane leads to the actual cemetery, which is surrounded by a low stone wall topped by an iron fence.

Close to the front on the left as you enter the cemetery is the grave of Meredith Miles Marmaduke (1791–1864); two square columns over the grave are connected by a marble arch. In 1824, Marmaduke, famed SFT trader and later governor of Missouri, was a member of the first large caravan to Santa Fe, consisting of eighty-one men and twenty-five wagons. His famous journal of the trip was published in the *Missouri Historical Review* in 1911 (Marmaduke 1911). He married a daughter of Dr. John Sappington.

Dr. Sappington (1776–1856) and his wife Jane (1783–1852) are buried toward the right rear corner of the cemetery under large trees. The inscriptions on top of their aboveground tombs have almost weathered away. The doctor indirectly played a major role in the development of the SFT. In 1832, he began distributing his famous Sappington's Anti-Fever Pills to western travelers. Intended for the prevention and control of malaria, they contained one grain of quinine compounded with gum myrrh and licorice. Sappington revealed the formula for his pills in his treatise *The Theory and Treatment of Fevers* (1844), the first medical book published west of the Mississippi. The pills were produced by the doctor's twenty-five slaves and distributed by traveling salesmen on horseback, one of whom was William Becknell.

Malaria, called ague, then the most serious disease in western Missouri and eastern Kansas, was the scourge of the SFT. It was especially prevalent at Council Grove and along the Arkansas River, where mosquitoes abounded. (Not until 1895 was it learned that mosquitoes were malaria carriers.) Susan Magoffin and many others using the SFT carried packages of Sappington's pills, and every traveler was familiar with his name.

Sappington's large two-story log house, located .5 mile southwest of the cemetery, burned in 1871. An 1834 portrait of him and another of his wife

Jane, painted by famed Arrow Rock artist George Caleb Bingham, are in the Old Arrow Rock Tavern, along with his medicine case and pill roller.

CHESTNUT HILL

From the cemetery, return 5 miles to the junction with MO 41. Turn left (that is, northwest) on MO 41 toward Marshall. At 1.25 miles from the junction, is the Chestnut Hill DAR marker on a bank above the east (right) side of the highway. Behind the marker 200 feet is Chestnut Hill, the white two-story home of Santa Fe trader Phillip Thompson, built in 1844 (now a private residence). One of the area's first settlers, he purchased 1,400 acres of land just west of Arrow Rock as early as 1826. As a result of repeated trips to Santa Fe, Thompson reportedly spoke Spanish better than English.

NEFF TAVERN

At 4.9 miles from the junction at Arrow Rock, MO 41 crosses a small bridge. At .5 mile past the bridge, turn on to a gravel road (County Road 202) that angles in from the left. Go .5 mile to the Neff Place DAR marker in the yard of a farmhouse on the left. In 1837, Isaac Neff built a log tavern here on the SFT. According to Jean Tyree Hamilton: "The Santa Fe Trail went between the tavern and the barn, which later became a stage station, then went west a quarter of a mile, bending around the Neff family cemetery and on northwestward down the grade" (Hamilton 1972). The tavern was torn down in 1890.

The brick residence behind the DAR marker is said to be on the original site of the tavern. To the left rear of this house and visible from the road, is a two-story stone smokehouse, the only structure remaining of Neff's original complex. It is on the National Register of Historic Places. Continue up the road .2 mile to the little Neff Cemetery on the right, marked by a small sign. It contains the graves of Isaac Neff, his wife, and children. Faint traces of the SFT reportedly exist beyond the cemetery, but the area is covered with heavy grass and brush that make it impossible to locate from the road.

MARSHALL TO LEXINGTON

From Arrow Rock, the SFT headed west via modern Marshall and Lexington to Fort Osage. Before 1821, this route was called the Osage Trace. (Stocking's book shows the Osage Trace on Maps 1 and 2.) Stay on MO 41 as far as

Marshall, where a DAR marker is located on the southwest corner of Court-house Square.

At Marshall pick up US 65 west. On the west side of town, begin checking mileage at the junction of US 65 and MO 240. At 5.5 miles beyond this junction, is the Kiser Spring DAR marker on the left (south) side of the highway. It sits on a bank in front of a house, within sight of a bridge ahead over Salt Fork Creek. Four miles farther, in the town of Malta Bend, is another DAR marker just past the only traffic light, on the left (south) side of the highway.

Between Malta Bend and Grand Pass, the highway is actually on a narrow ridge separating the Missouri River on the north from the waters of the Salt Fork River on the south. The Osage Trace followed this route long before the SFT used it. Surprisingly, Grand Pass is really a pass, traversing the divide separating the two rivers.

At 4.5 miles beyond Malta Bend, is the Grand Pass DAR marker, located slightly below ground level in a landscaped area, framed by wagon wheels, on the northwest corner of US 65 at its junction with County Road T. Across the street from the marker (northeast side), is a small cemetery with some very faint trail ruts.

From this point to Lexington, the SFT is almost directly under US 65. After another 4 miles, enter the town of Waverly. Turn right to the Business District and go two blocks to Kelling Street. A DAR marker is in the middle of the block on the lawn of a house directly across from the post office. At Waverly, US 65 turns north, so leave it here and turn on US 24 toward Lexington. The next town is Dover, and there is a DAR marker in a small park on the left (south) side of the highway in the center of town.

At about 2.5 miles west of Dover, the SFT crossed Tabo Creek. There is a DAR marker on the right just before the old road descends to the creek. This was the first water crossing on the trail since Arrow Rock on the Missouri River, and in 1821 the first ferry was established here. Although today the creek does not appear to be a great challenge for wagons, in fact, it lacks a firm bottom and was much wider than it is now. Therefore, a ferry was almost a necessity.

At 5.2 miles past Tabo Creek, on the right (north) side of the highway, look for an antebellum house, Hicklin Hearthstone, built in the 1830s. From the highway you can see the fence and gate in front of the house, and, to the left, the brick slave quarters and overseer's house. The SFT, undoubtedly, passed directly in front of the gate.

This part of Missouri was strongly proslavery before the Civil War, which can be explained by the labor-intensive crops grown here, including hemp and tobacco. Hemp was used for cordage and for burlap, which was sent down the Missouri and Mississippi Rivers to wrap the bales of cotton raised in the Deep South. It can still be seen growing in the ditches here.

LEXINGTON

This town is seldom mentioned in connection with the SFT but, in fact, was linked with the trail's history in several ways. First, Lexington was the center of the giant mercantile firm of the Aull Brothers—John, James, and Robert. Branch stores in nearby Richmond, Liberty, and Independence made this the largest business enterprise on the Missouri frontier and the first chain store in the state. John Aull built his first store and warehouse here in 1822, and by the 1830s the Aulls were leading outfitters for individuals departing on the SFT. After following the American army to Santa Fe and Chihuahua in 1846, the next year James was killed in a robbery at the store he had opened in Chihuahua City.

Second, Lexington was also headquarters for the renowned freighting firm of Russell, Majors, and Waddell, which hauled both civilian and military freight over the SFT in the 1850s. Between April 1860 and October 1861, this company also operated the Pony Express over the central route to California. Alexander Majors, the only one of the partners with extensive trail experience, made his first journey to Santa Fe in 1848.

Formally established in 1822, Lexington, like Boonville, sits atop a bluff on the south bank of the Missouri River. Its old steamboat landing at the base of the bluff was once a major shipping point. Many fine antebellum houses lend the town more of a southern than a western air.

In 1837, Alphonso Wetmore wrote in the *Gazeteer of the State of Missouri:* "Lexington is one of the towns from which outfits are made in merchandise, mules, oxen, and wagons for the Santa Fe or New Mexican trade. The fur-traders who pass to the mountains by land make this town a place of rendezvous, and frequently going out and coming in with their wagons and packed mules, at the same period of going and coming that is chosen by the Mexican traders. Lexington is therefore occasionally a thoroughfare of traders of great enterprise, and caravans of infinite value" (Wetmore 1837).

For valuable information about the trail in the Lexington area, consult Roger Slusher's article in *Wagon Tracks* (Slusher 1991). In addition, if you stop at the Historical Museum on 13th Street, just west of South Street, you can pick up a detailed guide that Slusher compiled for all the local SFT points of interest.

The following are a few of the sites of interest:

A. Martin Lane
As you enter Lexington from the east on MO 224, you will see Martin Lane coming in from the right. The SFT came directly down this curved street heading for Lexington. Drive a few blocks on it to get the feel of the trail here.

B. Old Courthouse Square

To get to the square, follow Main Street to Dover Road and turn south to South Street. Dover Road was a part of the SFT. The large white house to your left is Greystone Park, built in the 1830s, and almost directly on the SFT. It is occasionally open for tours. There are two markers at the site of Courthouse Square. This was the center of Lexington at least through the 1830s, when the focus shifted to the river. The Aull brothers had two warehouses in this area.

C. Lexington Historical Museum

Drive west on South Street to 13th Street. Along this route are some of Lexington's oldest and finest homes. At 13th turn right and drive two blocks to the museum on the right. Built in the 1840s as the national headquarters of the Cumberland Presbyterian Church, it has excellent exhibits featuring the SFT, the Pony Express, and the Civil War Battle of Lexington.

D. Russell, Majors, and Waddell Monument

Leaving the museum, drive north on 13th Street past Main Street, which will take you directly to the Battle of Lexington Historic Site. The entrance to the battlefield visitors' center is on the left about two blocks past Main. After passing the visitors' center, continue to Wood and 15th Streets, where you will see the Lafayette Regional Health Center. At the corner of the parking lot, is the nice monument to Russell, Majors, and Waddell. This was thought (incorrectly) to be the site of pastures for the firm's livestock, a misconception that explains the bovine nature of the monument. Return to Main Street and go right for two blocks.

E. Lafayette County Courthouse

The Lafayette County Courthouse is located on Main Street between 10th and 11th Streets. Built between 1847 and 1849, this structure was familiar to trail travelers of the 1850s. Holding up the clock tower are four columns, and, in the east column is a cannonball fired during the Civil War Battle of Lexington (September 1861). A sign in front of the courthouse calls attention to the cannonball. On the east side of the courthouse is an official Missouri Historical Marker, "Lexington," with text, while at the northwest corner of the grounds (facing Main Street) is a bronze Pony Express plaque with busts of Russell, Majors, and Waddell.

F. Sites on Main Street

Two minor points of interest lie on Main Street west of the courthouse. At the northeast corner of Main and 10th Streets, is the site (not the building) of the office of Russell, Majors, and Waddell. Two doors west at 926 Main Street,

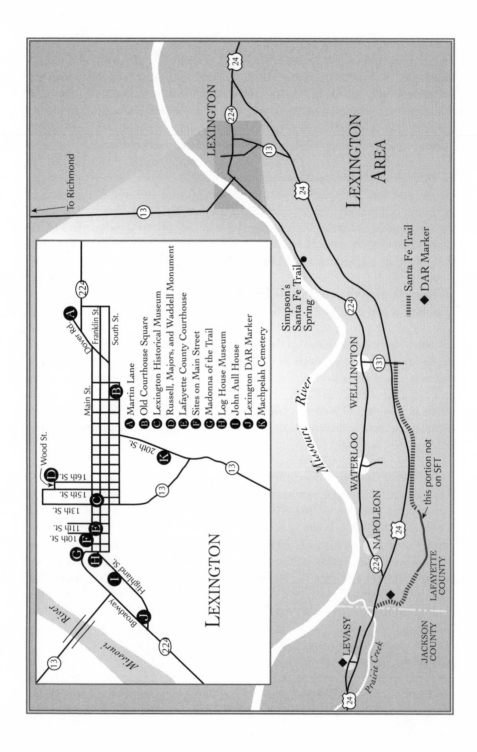

To Richmond

LEXINGTON

LEXINGTON
AREA

Missouri River

Simpson's
Santa Fe Trail
Spring

WELLINGTON

WATERLOO

NAPOLEON

this portion not
on SFT

LEVASY

Prairie Creek

LAFAYETTE
COUNTY

JACKSON
COUNTY

▬▬▬ Santa Fe Trail
◆ DAR Marker

LEXINGTON

Missouri River

Broadway

Highland St.

Wood St.

Dover Rd.

Franklin St.

South St.

Main St.

16th St.

15th St.

13th St.

11th St.

10th St.

20th St.

Ⓐ Martin Lane
Ⓑ Old Courthouse Square
Ⓒ Lexington Historical Museum
Ⓓ Russell, Majors, and Waddell Monument
Ⓔ Lafayette County Courthouse
Ⓕ Sites on Main Street
Ⓖ Madonna of the Trail
Ⓗ Log House Museum
Ⓘ John Aull House
Ⓙ Lexington DAR Marker
Ⓚ Machpelah Cemetery

between 9th and 10th (on the north, or right, side of the street) is a white sign marking a two-story building that was Sterling Price's headquarters during the Battle of Lexington. Price led reinforcements over the SFT in late 1846 and, in 1847, put down the revolt in Taos, New Mexico.

G. Madonna of the Trail
Continue one block on Main Street to Broadway, which angles to the right toward the river. You will be headed toward Richmond on MO 13. At the edge of the bluff above the river, Broadway curves and starts downhill to the left. At this point, on the right, is a small park containing the first of four Madonna of the Trail Monuments located along the SFT. Unveiled in 1928, the statue is of cast stone and stands 18 feet high. The four faces of the base contain historical inscriptions, those on the east and west faces being especially relevant to the SFT. This marker was dedicated by then Jackson County Judge Harry S. Truman.

H. Log House Museum
Almost across the street from the Madonna of the Trail Monument at Broadway and Highland Streets is the Log House Museum. Built in the 1830s, it served as a tavern and private residence. It was originally located one block to the west overlooking the Missouri River, and the river route of the SFT passed directly in front of it.

I. John Aull House
Driving west on Highland Street, you pass by a house at 788 that was used as a temporary bank by Robert Aull in 1845. At 784 Highland you will see the building that was once part of the Elizabeth Aull Seminary. Finally, at 712 Highland is the home of John Aull.

J. Lexington DAR Marker
To get to the Lexington DAR marker, continue on Highland Street, which will descend toward the river. At the bottom of the hill the marker is to the right.

K. Machpelah Cemetery
To reach the Machpelah Cemetery, which is on 20th Street, climb back up the hill, drive east to 20th, and turn right. Drive south on 20th, and as you pass South Street you are about on the "highland route" of the SFT. The cemetery, which is on the right about .5 mile farther, was established in 1849 and contains the graves of many families connected to SFT history, such as the Aulls and Waddells.

SIDE TRIP TO RICHMOND

From the Madonna of the Trail Monument, an excursion can be conveniently made to Richmond 9 miles to the northwest. Follow the highway down to the bottom of the hill and cross the Missouri River on MO 13. In Richmond, find Courthouse Square in the center of town. On the west side of the courthouse, is a magnificent 10-foot bronze statue of Colonel Alexander Doniphan, head of the Missouri Mounted Volunteers, who accompanied Kearny on the SFT to conquer New Mexico in 1846. A plaque on the south base of the statue depicts a sword-waving Doniphan leading his troops at the Battle of Sacramento (north of Chihuahua City) on February 28, 1847. Doniphan died in Richmond on August 8, 1887, but is buried in nearby Liberty.

Go back to Lexington, where you can either return to US 24 and drive west toward Wellington, following the highland route, or you can follow the somewhat more picturesque river route. If you choose the river route, simply turn right (west) after coming across the bridge from Richmond.

WELLINGTON TO FORT OSAGE

The river route, which hugs the narrow ledge just above the floodplain and below the bluffs, was likely used only when the Missouri was not too high. A few miles from Lexington you will come to the Peckerwood Club. (Its real name!) On the right of the tavern is a small marker for "Simpson's Santa Fe Trail Spring."

Continue to Wellington and turn left (south) at MO 131, which will take you back to US 24. Continue beyond this highway to a gravel road marked "Santa Fe Trail." Turn right here and continue west, following the high ground, or ridge line. Where this road veers left and leaves the high ground, you temporarily leave the SFT (see map).

Just before rejoining US 24 turn north and pass a house on the right with a DAR marker in front. At the junction with MO 224, turn west and drive to the small hamlet of Levasy. Turning right into Levasy, there is a DAR marker close to the old highway and the railroad tracks. Return to US 24 and head west toward Fort Osage.

FORT OSAGE

For a brief period in the 1820s, Fort Osage was the westernmost outpost in Missouri and a rendezvous for caravans traveling the SFT. Established in 1808 by William Clark (of the Lewis and Clark Expedition), the palisade walls and log blockhouses sheltered both a military garrison and an Indian trading post run by the government, the latter called a factory. On the summit of a 70-foot bluff overlooking the Missouri River, the fort figured prominently in the fur trade for a time. But it was abandoned in 1825 by the government and the factory system discontinued. In 1827, Fort Leavenworth was established farther up the Missouri for government use.

It was from Fort Osage that a party of U.S. government commissioners set out in 1825 to survey the SFT, actually making Taos and not Santa Fe their final destination. They began recording compass directions and chained distances to New Mexico at a point (the zero milestone) just south of the fort, which was identified by the late Polly Fowler of Independence but is not marked. Because George C. Sibley, the factor, or government trader, at Fort Osage, was the de facto leader of the commissioners, the enterprise is usually referred to as the Sibley survey. (Sibley is buried in St. Charles, Missouri, on the Lindenwood University campus.)

In the community of Buckner, US 24 intersects at the only traffic light with County Road 20-E, which may not be marked. On the southeast corner of this junction in front of a chain-link fence, is the largest DAR marker on the SFT, consisting of three stone panels.

From US 24 proceed north on County Road 20-E 3 miles to Fort Osage, following the small signs. Near the fort, note the Sibley Cemetery on the right, where the paved road turns left in front of the new visitors' center and museum.

The only grave here of major interest is that of famed fur trapper Zenas Leonard. After returning from the Rockies and California, he settled at the site of Fort Osage and became an Indian trader and steamboat operator. His *Narrative of the Adventures of Zenas Leonard* (Quaise 1934) is a well-known account of western adventuring. The modern gray granite headstone, flat and level with the ground, is near the center of the cemetery and behind and to the left of the tall Harrelson Monument. In addition, at the far back corner of the cemetery (that is, on the east side along the Missouri River) is a DAR marker. After touring the cemetery, stop at the visitors' center to see exhibits relating to the history of the fort and the local Indians.

The cemetery served the community of Sibley, founded in 1836 by Archibald Gamble after the dismantling of neighboring Fort Osage. He and George C. Sibley had married sisters, a relationship that no doubt helped him obtain the position of secretary to the commissioners on the 1825 SFT survey. In 1837, overland trader Alphonso Wetmore wrote of the new town of Sibley: "It has already been made a point of landing for Santa Fe goods, and it will probably share largely in the increasing advantages of that trade. The landing and harbor of Sibley are excellent, made so by the eddy-water at the base of the bluff" (Wetmore 1914).

Continue on the paved road 100 feet to the entrance of Fort Osage, where there is an explanatory historical marker at the beginning of the sidewalk that leads to the fort gate. The log fort, reconstructed on its original site in recent years, is today one of the high points at the eastern end of the trail. Blockhouses, soldiers' quarters, and the factory (trading post) can be toured. Shelves in the factory are stocked with trade goods, and the part of the building in which George C. Sibley and his wife lived briefly contains period furnishings. Moreover, a porch at the rear provides a spectacular overlook of the Missouri River.

In 1962, Fort Osage became a Registered National Historic Landmark, and more recently has been certified as a National Park Service Site. Operated by the Jackson County Parks System, a River Days celebration is held here in May.

SIDE TRIP TO LIBERTY

From Fort Osage return to Buckner and go southwest again on US 24 toward Independence. Within a mile you will pass the Independence City Limits sign, about 6.5 miles past this sign on the right (north) side of US 24 is the New Salem Baptist Church. Just beyond it in a small park (also on the right) is the Salem DAR marker.

Continue west to the junction with MO 291, turn right (north), and drive 8 miles to the town of Liberty. Here the one point of SFT interest is the grave of Col. Alexander Doniphan, who led the Missouri Volunteers over the trail in 1846, the first year of the Mexican War. For a brief moment he played a major role in the history of New Mexico. The grave site is in Fairview Cemetery at the south end of Gallatin Street close to the downtown area. Inquire locally for directions. Once in the cemetery the grave can be easily located since it is marked by the tallest monument, a spire about 20 feet high, near the center of the grounds. Although Doniphan was once one of the most renowned men in Missouri, he is now scarcely remembered.

TRAIL BACKGROUND

Before leaving Fort Osage, consider the challenges confronting the earliest traders as they departed this outpost of civilization. In contrast to the danger of the Jornada, or waterless landscape between the Arkansas and Cimarron Rivers, here at the eastern end of the trail the threat was not a shortage of water but a surplus of it.

Along the route of the SFT in western Missouri, there was a sequence of streams, tributaries of the Missouri River, with considerable water. Bordering the stream banks were forests (called "bottom timber" in the diaries). Between the streams on the divides were more or less open prairies. For the most part, traders stayed on high ground, that is, on the prairies. They would move along the divide and whenever possible "head" the streams, crossing them where they were smaller. When they did cross streams, they would seek a gravel or rocky bottom and approaches that were passable with some effort (see maps on this page, and on pages 46 and 47).

EARLIEST PERIOD (1821–1827)

In the earliest period, 1821–1827 (see map on this page), there were two routes used. At this time Independence did not exist, and the last settlement was at Fort Osage. The first route left Fort Osage and forded the Little Blue River 6 miles west. After crossing the Little Blue, travelers headed southwest, following the prairie on the high ground between the Big and Little Blue Rivers. The crossing of the Big Blue was finally made in present-day Swope Park about where 73rd Street would bisect the river. From there the route continued southwest, crossing the present state line 9 miles south of the confluence of the Missouri and Kansas Rivers. The trail then continued into Kansas, and passed Round Grove (later known as Lone Elm Campground), located a few miles south of today's Olathe.

The second early route left the Fort Osage area and went south, following

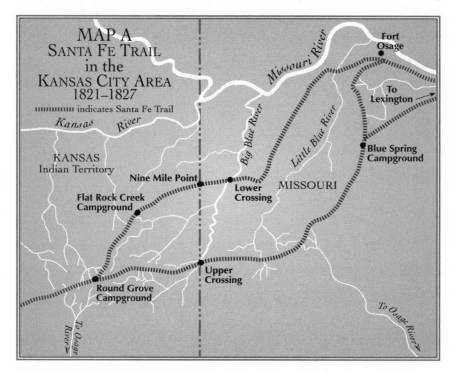

MAP A
SANTA FE TRAIL
in the
KANSAS CITY AREA
1821–1827
||||||||||||| indicates Santa Fe Trail

the road that connected Fort Osage and Harmony Mission farther south. On this route the Blue Spring Campground was an important rendezvous point. Other traders came to the Blue Spring Campground directly from Lexington, and from Cooper, Saline, and Howard Counties. From the campground, the traders continued south and then west, crossing the Little Blue River near its head and the Big Blue River about at 151st Street and State Line Road. From there, the route continued west to Round Grove Campground near where it met the other trail.

Middle Period (1828–1839)

After Independence was founded in 1827, it quickly became the starting point for traders. Transport by water, even on the notorious Missouri River, was easier and cheaper than by land. Consequently, landings were added up the river, and jumping-off points for Santa Fe moved accordingly. As a map of this area shows, the Missouri River, which has been heading west to Independence and upstream, here begins to swing north. However, for travelers going to Santa Fe, the usefulness of the Missouri River ended here. This is the closest they would get to Santa Fe on the Missouri River.

There were two landings for Independence. Blue Mills Landing was first but was quickly superseded by Independence Landing, which is almost due

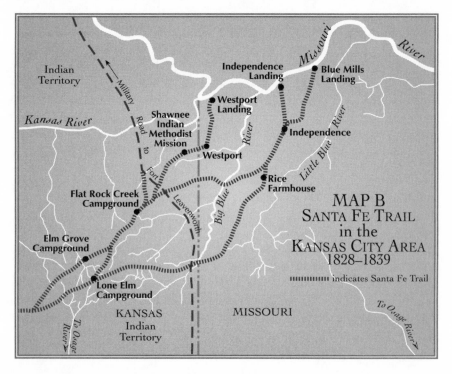

north of Independence Square in Independence and only 3 miles away. From Independence, the trails headed south to connect with the earlier two routes described above (see map on page 46).Thus, the principal entries into Kansas were at the Upper Crossing (near 151st Street and State Line Road) and Nine Mile Point (near 79th and State Line Road). These basic routes were used until about 1839.

Later Period (After 1840)
During the later period (after 1840), a new trailhead was established at Westport, west of Independence. Consequently, from a very modest beginning in the mid-1830s, Westport, 4 miles due south of the Missouri River, became the principal starting point of the trail by the late 1840s. Riverboats used the Westport Landing (also called Kansas Landing) to drop their cargoes bound for Santa Fe. From Westport the trail turned west into Kansas, then angled southwest to join the earlier trails. These routes emerged as the SFT traffic increased because of emigrants bound for Oregon and California using the SFT as far as Gardner, Kansas. At Gardner, the Oregon and California Trails separated from the SFT and headed northwest.

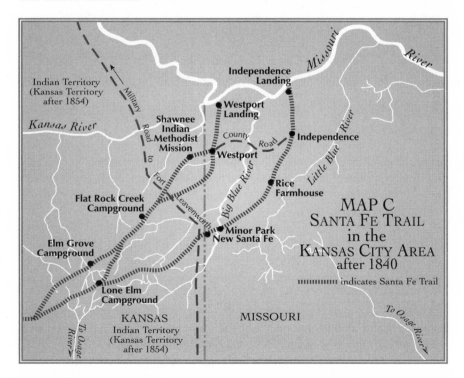

MAP C
SANTA FE TRAIL
in the
KANSAS CITY AREA
after 1840

⁞⁞⁞⁞⁞⁞⁞⁞ indicates Santa Fe Trail

MISSOURI AND KANSAS

INDEPENDENCE, WESTPORT, AND FORT LEAVENWORTH

INDEPENDENCE

From its founding in 1827 until 1850, Independence served as a main outfitting point for the Santa Fe trade. Here goods bought in St. Louis, Philadelphia, New York, and even Europe were transferred from Missouri steamboats to freight wagons bound for Santa Fe. Blacksmiths, wagon and harness makers, sellers of livestock, and local merchants did a lively business in supplying overland travelers, which by the early 1840s included emigrants on the newly opened Oregon Trail.

Before the trailhead shifted westward to Westport and Kansas City in the late 1840s, Independence was a noisy, bustling place frequented by such notables as Kit Carson, Josiah Gregg, Francis Parkman, Samuel and Susan Magoffin, and the long-distance horseback rider Francis X. Aubry. The town is called by the locals the "Queen City of the Trails."

All sites and markers noted here, with one exception, have some association with the SFT. Information about other places of interest can be obtained from the Chamber of Commerce, 210 West Truman Road, P. O. Box 1077, Independence, MO 64051, or from the City of Independence Department of Tourism, 111 East Maple (City Hall), Independence, MO 64050. Visitors interested in following the SFT route through town street by street should use Gregory Franzwa's *The Oregon Trail Revisited, Silver Anniversary Edition.*

A. Harry S. Truman Library and Museum

Entering Independence from the east, stay on US 24, which passes a few blocks north of the downtown area. At the junction with Delaware Street, the library and museum is on the right. At the entrance to the grounds, there is an official Missouri Historical Marker, "Independence," with text referring to the SFT and Josiah Gregg.

Although you may wish to tour the entire facility, the one point of interest for trail buffs is the splendid mural by Thomas H. Benton entitled *Independence and the Opening of the West.* It is located in the main lobby, along with a sales desk that has items of historical interest. The mural depicts scenes typical of the Santa Fe and Oregon Trails. The far right of the mural shows blacksmiths readying wagons for the westward journey. The upper right portrays a caravan heading for Chimney Rock, a famous landmark on the Oregon Trail. The left side is devoted to the SFT. There is a Pawnee warrior with his scalp lock and behind him a Cheyenne chief bartering red fox furs with a trader. At the upper left appears Bent's Fort, best-known stop on the Mountain Route of the trail. Beyond it rise the Spanish Peaks, beacons for all travelers headed toward Santa Fe and Taos. At the bottom, two separate panels show Independence in the late 1840s. The one at the left portrays a steamboat at the Missouri River landing. From it, covered freight wagons are taking on goods for the Santa Fe trade. Finally, the right-hand panel features a caravan forming up on Independence Square with the old 1840 courthouse in the background.

B. Landings

Here we can mention again that there were two landings on the Missouri River north of town. The oldest, founded before 1832, was the Blue Mills Landing located 6 miles northeast of the square. Initially called Owens Landing after Santa Fe trader Samuel C. Owens, Blue Mills was soon overshadowed by Independence Landing, several miles upstream, about 3.5 miles north of Independence Square.

To reach the Independence Landing marker, go north on River Road, which is one block west of the Truman Library. As you follow the River Road, note how it stays on the high ground. This was the principal route of the SFT from the landing. At the "LaFarge" sign, River Road veers left and starts downhill to the cement plant and the original site of the landing. About one block after the turn on the left, is a pullout and Missouri River overlook. At the edge of the overlook is a historical marker, dedicated in August 1983. From this point return south on River Road to Truman Road. Go east on Truman to Osage, then south on Osage to the vicinity of the courthouse.

C. INDEPENDENCE SQUARE

Early writers often described the bustle and color surrounding the courthouse as wagons formed up for the departure to Santa Fe. None of the buildings on the square date from the heyday of the trail. The last, the Nebraska House, built in 1849, located at the northeast corner of present Liberty and Maple, was torn down in 1980 to make way for a parking lot. Even more popular than the Nebraska House as a hostelry was the Merchants Hotel, which was operated by Colonel Smallwood ("Uncle Wood") Noland and soon became known as the Noland House. It was situated on what is now the northwest corner of Main and Maple and also faced the square. The two-story brick building currently there is believed to incorporate some portions of the original structure. The hotel is mentioned by Susan Magoffin, who spent a night under its roof before starting for Santa Fe in 1846.

On the southwest corner of the square (at Liberty and Lexington), the three-story Chrisman-Sawyer Bank Building is on the site of the Aull and Owens Store. (For their role in the Santa Fe trade, see "Lexington" above.)

During the period from 1828 to 1839, the traders left the square and went almost due south to meet the SFT (the SFT as used from 1821 to 1827) near present-day Raytown. Then they continued southwest to cross the Big Blue River in Swope Park. By 1840, they traveled south, crossing the Big Blue River near today's Red Bridge Road. From Red Bridge they then went southwest and crossed into Kansas Territory, where New Santa Fe was located by the early 1850s. From there they passed through Lone Elm Campground. By 1840, the crossing at Red Bridge had gained favor over the Upper Crossing.

The courthouse, inspired by Independence Hall in Philadelphia, is now called the Truman Courthouse since Judge Harry S. Truman had an office there in the 1920s and 1930s. It incorporates the foundations and sections of several earlier Jackson County courthouses dating from trail days. See the restored courtroom on the first floor, which dates to 1852 and was used later by Truman. Offices of the Jackson County Historical Society Archives are also on the first floor. On the west side of the courthouse, is a large equestrian statue of Andrew Jackson, for whom the county is named. Flanking the statue are two monuments, one the DAR marker for the SFT and the other designating the beginning of the Oregon Trail.

D. FIRST LOG COURTHOUSE

The First Log Courthouse, the oldest remaining courthouse west of the Mississippi River, is located at 107 West Kansas Street, one block south of the square. The small structure was built in 1827 to serve as a temporary courthouse until a more permanent one could be constructed.

E. Site of Robert Weston's Blacksmith Shop

The shop was located at the southwest corner of Liberty and Kansas, just west of the First Log Courthouse. This blacksmith shop catered to the needs of Santa Fe traders in the 1840s. The structure was demolished in the 1940s, and the site is now a parking lot. A historical bronze plaque mounted on a red granite monument is on the corner. Robert Weston's father, Samuel, also a noted blacksmith, is honored by a historical marker at his grave site, mentioned in the Woodlawn Cemetery section below.

F. Kritser House

Located at 115 East Walnut, this small residence with a gable roof was built in 1847 by Martin L. Kritser. Reportedly, he traveled the SFT in 1846 and with the profits from his trading venture built this house. A municipal historical marker with text is on the lawn.

G. National Frontier Trails Center

At 524 South Osage, are the buildings associated with the Waggoner-Gates Milling Company. The mill itself was destroyed by an explosion and fire in the 1960s. The headquarters for the Oregon-California Trail Association (OCTA) and the National Frontier Trails Center are now located at this site. OCTA's address is 318 West Pacific. The center has extensive exhibits on the Santa Fe, Oregon, and California Trails, as well as a bookstore with many titles of interest to SFT enthusiasts. The center is a high point of the trail and should not be missed.

In the area north of the remaining mill office (between Osage and Spring Streets), is the Emigrant Spring, whose waters in trail days were said to flow in the volume of "about the size of a man's arm." Here wagons once gathered before departing for Santa Fe.

H. Bingham-Waggoner House

The Bingham-Waggoner House is located at 313 West Pacific. The SFT passed by this residence located just a few blocks south of the square. An early owner of the property was Jacob Hall, a prominent freighter in the Santa Fe and Chihuahua trade and operator of stage lines to New Mexico. His letters and business ledgers are preserved in the Historical Society Archives at the courthouse. A later property owner, John Lewis, built the two-story brick house. He was a saddle maker, also associated with the Santa Fe trade. After changing hands twice more, the estate was purchased by celebrated Missouri artist George Caleb Bingham, who lived there with his wife for six years. In 1879, Peter and William Waggoner bought the house, which was destined to remain in the hands of their descendants for the next ninety-nine years. Today, it is owned by the City of Independence and is open to the public.

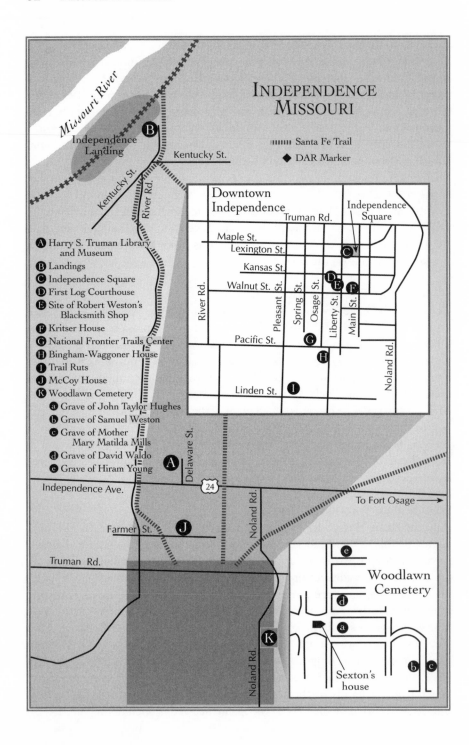

INDEPENDENCE
MISSOURI

Missouri River

Independence
Landing

Kentucky St.

Kentucky St.

River Rd.

⬛⬛⬛⬛ Santa Fe Trail
◆ DAR Marker

Downtown Independence

Independence Square

Truman Rd.

Maple St.

Lexington St.

Kansas St.

Walnut St.

River Rd.

Pleasant St.

Spring St.

Osage St.

Liberty St.

Main St.

Noland Rd.

Pacific St.

Linden St.

Ⓐ Harry S. Truman Library
   and Museum
Ⓑ Landings
Ⓒ Independence Square
Ⓓ First Log Courthouse
Ⓔ Site of Robert Weston's
   Blacksmith Shop
Ⓕ Kritser House
Ⓖ National Frontier Trails Center
Ⓗ Bingham-Waggoner House
Ⓘ Trail Ruts
Ⓙ McCoy House
Ⓚ Woodlawn Cemetery
   ⓐ Grave of John Taylor Hughes
   ⓑ Grave of Samuel Weston
   ⓒ Grave of Mother
      Mary Matilda Mills
   ⓓ Grave of David Waldo
   ⓔ Grave of Hiram Young

Independence Ave.

Delaware St.

24

To Fort Osage ⟶

Farmer St.

Truman Rd.

Noland Rd.

Woodlawn
Cemetery

Sexton's
house

Noland Rd.

I. TRAIL RUTS

Recently a fine set of ruts of interest to trail buffs were discovered in a small area in the southwestern portion of the Bingham-Waggoner estate. To reach the ruts, park your car in the lot immediately west of the Bingham-Waggoner House. From here, look for a paved path at the back of the parking lot leading to the ruts.

J. MCCOY HOUSE

The McCoy House is located at 410 West Farmer. William McCoy arrived in Independence in 1838 and became the town's first mayor in 1849. He was heavily involved in the New Mexico trade, government freighting, and, with Jacob Hall, operating a stagecoach line. The rear wing of this two-story brick residence is thought to have been constructed about 1840 for Samuel C. Owens, famed merchant and outfitter for the Santa Fe trade, while the main section of the house dates from about 1856. A historical marker with text is near the street.

K. WOODLAWN CEMETERY

The cemetery is at 710 South Noland Road. Begun around 1837, reportedly on an Indian burial ground, this cemetery contains the graves of several individuals associated with the SFT, as well as Independence pioneers. Unfortunately, the cemetery attendant cannot help you in finding graves of interest because no records are kept of people buried here before 1900. However, the following descriptions of locations and map will guide you.

(a) **Grave of John Taylor Hughes.** Drive on the right side of the sexton's house and take the first lane leading east, toward the back of the cemetery. Hughes's waist-high stone is on the left next to the lane, with two large cedars just to the north of it. Private Hughes accompanied Col. Alexander Doniphan's First Missouri Mounted Volunteers over the SFT to conquer New Mexico in 1846. Further, he participated in the Navajo expedition to western New Mexico and later was in the Battle of Sacramento north of Chihuahua City. After returning home, he became the official historian for these events when he wrote and published *Doniphan's Expedition* (1997), a book that remains a standard source on the SFT and the Mexican War in the Southwest.

(b) **Grave of Samuel Weston.** From Hughes's gravestone continue straight ahead (east) to the rear of the cemetery, where the lane curves to the right (south). The 6-foot-high Weston marker of red granite is on the right in front of a large tree. Samuel, father of blacksmith Robert Weston (noted above), had a blacksmith shop on Lexington between Osage and Spring Streets. He was also a carpenter and did interior work on two of Independence's early brick courthouses. His headstone is of recent origin and more in the nature of a historical marker with reference to the SFT.

(c) Grave of Mother Mary Matilda Mills. Across the lane from the Samuel Weston grave and a few feet south, Mother Matilda's flat stone, level with the ground, is next to the edge of the pavement. It is in the Stayton family plot. In July 1852, New Mexico's Bishop John B. Lamy was returning to Santa Fe with a party that included a group of Sisters of Loretto. From St. Louis they sailed up the Missouri River on the steamer *Kansas*. Four days out, Mother Matilda, superior of the nuns, died of cholera, and others became gravely ill. Because of his fear of the disease, the captain put Lamy's entire company off the boat 6 miles east of Independence, where they found refuge from the rainy weather in an abandoned warehouse. Mother Matilda lay in a hastily constructed coffin on the riverbank. Lamy finally secured a hearse, but because some of his people still suffered from the dreaded cholera local authorities refused them entrance to the town. Finally, a family named Stayton who learned of the problem offered to let Mother Matilda's coffin be carried to their burial plot in the present Woodlawn Cemetery. There, at night and in secret, Bishop Lamy and Father Donnelly, the local priest, performed the funeral service. Note that in his biography of the bishop, *Lamy of Santa Fe*, Paul Horgan tells of Mother Matilda's death but fails to mention where or how she was buried (Horgan 1975). That information was provided by the late Polly Fowler.

(d) Grave of David Waldo. From the rear of the sexton's house, take the lane leading north and turn right, or east, at the first intersecting lane. The large Confederate monument is immediately on the left, and just past it, on the right side of the lane, is the Waldo monument. David Waldo was a leading Santa Fe merchant, entering the trade as early as 1831. He made numerous trips over the SFT and played a conspicuous role in the conquest of New Mexico in 1846. His younger brother, Lawrence L. Waldo, also a trader, was killed near Mora, New Mexico, early in 1847 during the same disturbances that led to the death of Governor Charles Bent. In the early 1850s, David Waldo was engaged in hauling military freight to New Mexico over the SFT. With Jacob Hall, he also operated the stage line to New Mexico. A brief sketch of his life is included in Ralph E. Twitchell's *The Military Occupation of New Mexico, 1846–1851* (Twitchell 1909).

(e) Grave of Hiram Young. On the next lane north of the Waldo monument is the small Sawyer mausoleum, white with a pitched roof. Across the lane from it, to the northeast, is the chest-high gray granite marker for Hiram Young. In the decade before the Civil War, ex-slave Young gained a reputation as a superb wagon maker. He also carved oxbows by the hundreds for use on the Santa Fe and Oregon Trails. In *Wagons for the Santa Fe Trade: Wheeled Vehicles and Their Makers*, Mark Gardner notes that in 1856 Young had twenty-five large new Santa Fe wagons with 2¹/₂-inch tread, as well as provision boxes and bows, on his lot for sale (Gardner 2000). During the

Civil War, he and his family fled briefly to Fort Leavenworth, and when he returned to Independence he found that his shops (between present Main and Liberty Streets on the south side of US 24) had been destroyed by Union occupation forces. He is pictured, working at his forge, in the lower right corner of the Benton mural at the Truman Library.

Other sites of interest in the Independence area include the following:

JIM BRIDGER'S GRAVE

Drive west on Truman Road to the entrance of the Mount Washington Cemetery. Upon entering, go straight ahead about two blocks, and after crossing a little bridge, Bridger's tall monument is seen immediately on the right, standing alone in a small triangular lot. James Bridger (1804–1881) had nothing to do with the SFT, but as a trapper with Kit Carson in the central and northern Rockies and an associate of Jedediah Smith (both closely identified with the trail) Bridger was a leading figure in the history of the West.

SANTA FE TRAIL PARK

The entrance to Santa Fe Trail Park is off Santa Fe Road, which was formerly McCoy Street, one block north of 31st Street. Caravans from Independence Square passed through the area of the park, headed in a southwesterly direction. Good ruts are visible in the lot just south of the park, and beyond them additional trail ruts can be found in the yards of homes, such as behind 3131 Santa Fe Terrace.

BLUE SPRING CAMPGROUND AND RENDEZVOUS

From Santa Fe Trail Park, drive south on Santa Fe Road to 33rd Street, right on 33rd to Chrysler, and south to Interstate 70. Then go east on Interstate 70 to Woods Chapel Road and turn right. Drive south 1 mile, and when you cross a small stream you are at the site of the Blue Spring Campground and Rendezvous. This was on the Fort Osage to Harmony Mission Road, important in early trail history. The Mission Road actually predates the SFT by a few years. Some traders from Lexington and Franklin came directly to this campground, bypassing Fort Osage. Of this site Alphonso Wetmore wrote in 1828: "Reached the Blue Spring, the rendezvous of the Mexican traders, in season to attend to the election of officers . . ." (Wetmore 1914). Traders would meet here before heading south and then west to Round Grove Campground (later called Lone Elm).

MISSOURI TOWN 1855

Continue south to US 40 and drive east to MO 7. Go south on MO 7 about 3.5 miles and then turn west on Cowherd Road. At the end of Cowherd Road, turn north to the entrance of Missouri Town 1855. This fine living museum, managed by the Jackson County Parks and Recreation Department, consists of residences and businesses built between 1820 and 1860, which have been moved to the site from various locations in western Missouri. Although the place has no direct connection with the SFT, it is so well put together that it helps visitors catch the spirit of trail days. A pair of oxen is corralled on the main street in summer.

Upon completing a tour of trail sites in and around Independence, Missouri Town 1855 is a good point of departure for Raytown. Return north to US 40 and turn left (west). US 40 is also 47th Street here. Continue west on 47th past Noland Road to Blue Ridge Boulevard. Turn left (south) on Blue Ridge, and you will be directly on the SFT route leading into Raytown. Look for the blue SFT signs.

RAYTOWN

The people of Raytown are very conscious of their location on the SFT. Entering the city limits on Blue Ridge Boulevard, note the Santa Fe Trail Professional Building on the left (east) side of the street. Every few blocks are rustic green and white signs designating the route of the SFT, placed by the local Boy Scout troop in the 1970s, as well as more recently placed signs put up by the city. Blue Ridge Boulevard angles diagonally through the center of town. Here the SFT followed the high ground, or ridge, between the Little Blue and the Big Blue Rivers, which was the easiest travel route for wagons. Thus, the name of the road here is Blue Ridge Boulevard.

At 59th Street, turn right (west) and drive three blocks to the intersection of Raytown Road. The City Hall, on the right, is at the site once occupied by the home of George Washington Rhoades. He was the Jackson County surveyor (1840–1844), commissioner of roads, and "an advocate of the Santa Fe Trail." According to *Raytown Remembers*, a book published in 1975 by the Raytown Historical Society, in May 1839 George W. Rhoades "petitioned the County Court to establish a public highway to Santa Fe." The SFT was already well traveled, but owners of adjacent farmlands often put gates across the road to discourage wagons from crossing their properties. Rhoades may have been engaged in trade to the Southwest because his estate inventory included "five Trading Wagons." A cast aluminum plaque referring to the SFT was placed at his homesite in 1975. It is now set in a concrete monument next to the flagpole in front of City Hall.

From this point go south on Raytown Road to the intersection of 63rd Street. Just beyond the southeast corner, facing Raytown Road, is a historical marker with text commemorating the site of William Ray's Blacksmith Shop.

The Archibald Rice farmhouse in Raytown, Missouri.

Ray settled at this spot with his family in the late 1840s, providing wagon repairs for travelers on the SFT. He charged 88¢ to shoe a horse. By 1854, the community that grew up around the shop was known as Raytown, although by that time the smith himself had already migrated westward on the Oregon Trail.

From this intersection drive west on 63rd Street one and a half blocks to the Raytown Museum on the left (at 9705 East 63rd). Some of its exhibits relate to the era of the SFT.

Continue west on 63rd Street .3 mile to Blue Ridge Boulevard, which veers off to the left and after .6 mile intersects with Blue Ridge Extension. Turn left (south) on Blue Ridge Extension, and immediately 66th Street intersects from the left. There on the southeast corner in a large lot, hidden by trees, is the farmhouse of Archibald Rice (8801 East 66th Street). The white frame structure, built in the early 1840s, is little changed except for the later addition of dormer windows in the steep-pitched roof. The SFT passed just north of the house and once beyond it turned left (south) along present Blue Ridge Boulevard. A DAR marker is on the corner facing Blue Ridge Road.

New Orleans journalist Matt Field, who made a trip over the SFT in 1840, wrote: "About half a day's travel [from Independence] brings the Santa Fe bound traders past the flourishing plantation of Farmer Rice, where leisure travelers often linger to enjoy his sweet bacon, fresh eggs, new milk and other nutritious

and unsophisticated luxuries that appease appetite without encumbering diges-
tion" (Field 1995). Field must have stopped at an earlier Rice house since he
came through here before the present house was constructed.

On the west side of the Rice House, facing Blue Ridge Boulevard, is a small
log structure with a stone chimney known as Aunt Sophie's cabin. The restored
cabin is said to have been built in 1837 but in fact was probably built later. This
was one of several cabins Rice provided as quarters for his slaves. All have disappeared except this one, which housed the slave remembered as Aunt Sophie.
Before her death in 1896 at age seventy-seven, she often spoke of the Santa Fe
caravans that had passed by in the early days. She is said to be buried in Independence's Woodlawn Cemetery in the Rice family plot, but we have been unable to locate her grave. Along the street by the cabin is one of the SFT markers
placed by the Boy Scouts. The Rice House is both a Santa Fe Trail and a
California National Historical Trail Certified Site. The National Park
Service markers are in front of the house.

Continue south on Blue Ridge Boulevard about four blocks to the intersection of Gregory. Turn right (west) on Gregory, and almost immediately on
the left (south) is the entrance to the William M. Klein Park. This park is the
creation of a group of dedicated Raytown citizens who formed the Cave
Spring Association to protect and interpret the site. The first portion of a visitors' center, the Art Clark Nature Center, was dedicated in 1982. (Be sure to
note the story of young Art Clark in the center's interpretation.) A map allows
visitors to follow a trail through woodlands to the cave. The SFT did not pass
directly by the cave but some distance to the east.

Return to the intersection of Blue Ridge Boulevard and Gregory, turn right,
and start south on Blue Ridge along the east side of Klein Park. About two
blocks from Gregory is a DAR marker on the right. At this point there are three
choices for the modern trail traveler. A glance at the maps on pages 45, 46, and
47 will indicate that there were two early routes near here and one later route
through New Santa Fe that was used after 1840. Only dedicated travelers will
want to follow all three choices outlined below, but each route has its virtue.

EARLY ROUTE THROUGH SWOPE PARK

The earliest route of the SFT through this area, the one described by George C.
Sibley in the 1825 mapping expedition, left Fort Osage and passed on the east of
the site, which was to become Independence Square (see map on page 45). Then
it continued towards the Big Blue River, crossing at present-day Swope Park.

To get to Swope Park, go west on Gregory. At about the point where
Gregory and Oldham meet, was the crossing point. Perhaps the best early

description of this crossing was by Jacob Fowler, who on July 5, 1822, wrote: "Sot out early and at five miles Crossing a large Crick [the Blue] 50 yards Wide Runs north the Bottoms and Hill Sides are Well Covered With timber- Wr Heare went up a High Steep Hill over some Rocks and Continu over High Roleing ground" (Coues 1965). Fowler wasn't a great speller, but no early chronicler is more enjoyable to read. Although no marker now exists at the crossing, locals are working to get one. It must have been a very difficult descent from the bluff on the east.

The next important location on this route is the place where the early trail crossed into Kansas, Nine Mile Point. To get there, continue west on Gregory to Wornall, turn left (south), and go to 75th Street. Turn right (west) on 75th, then left onto State Line Road, and drive south on State Line. Nine Mile Point is near a Chevron gas station (at this writing) at 79th Street and State Line, although there is no marker. Brown, Sibley's surveyor in 1825, had surveyed the state line earlier (1823) and noted that this point was where the road to Santa Fe passed. His entries at that time read: "South along the west boundary of the State of Missouri. At end of nine miles, raised a mound—Land lies well, and is good clean prairie." Brown went on: "At 9 miles and ten chains [660 feet] to a trace leading from Fort Osage toward Santa Fe . . ." (Brown 1823). This is a very important location, and one hopes that the site will be properly marked in the future.

Turn right at 79th Street and drive west past Mission to Delmar. Turn north and go two blocks to Harmon Park. In this park there are ruts certified by the National Park Service as a SFT site. They were probably on the later route of the trail, connecting Westport and the old trail. In the ruts are some very attractive limestone markers, and at the gazebo is a full-color National Park Service interpretive marker and a bronze trail map.

EARLY ROUTE BY WAY OF THE UPPER CROSSING

To get to the Upper Crossing, start at the Rice farmhouse or Harmon Park. From the Rice House, follow Blue Ridge Boulevard along the divide between the Big Blue and Little Blue Rivers. Continue south to Harry Truman Drive in the city of Grandview. Then turn south to Main Street and right (west) to Arrington Road.

Arrington Road follows a high divide between a branch of the Big Blue River and a very small tributary of the Little Blue River. The SFT followed this prairie along the crest during the second decade of the trail (about 1825–1839). At 139th Street turn right (west) and continue to Holmes, then south on

Holmes to Kenneth Road, and finally west on Kenneth to Big Blue Park. Just before the river is Jackson County Park on the right, and immediately on your left as you enter the park is the Upper Crossing. This was a logical place for traders to cross the Big Blue River, since here the riverbanks are less treacherous, and the water level is lower. From here you can turn right on State Line Road and continue north to New Santa Fe.

To get to the Upper Crossing from Harmon Park, drive south on Mission to 103rd Street, turn left there to State Line Road (State Line becomes Kenneth at 135th Street), and go south to 151st Street. At 151st turn left, cross the Big Blue River back into Missouri, and turn left into Jackson County Park. The Upper Crossing was immediately to the west as you enter the park.

TO NEW SANTA FE

From the Rice farmhouse, continue south on Blue Ridge Boulevard about 2 miles to 83rd Street and turn right. Go to Manchester, turn left, and drive to 85th Street. Here there are nice ruts ascending the hill toward the southwest. These ruts are a certified site on the Santa Fe, Oregon, and California National Historic Trails.

The next stop is Schumacher Park. Drive west on 85th Street to Oldham Road. Turn left (south) on Oldham and continue to 87th Street. At 87th turn left, go a short distance, and turn right on Santa Fe Road. This road is on top of the trail, at least on those portions going southwest. Continue to 93rd Street and turn right (west). Just over the railroad tracks, on the left, is Schumacher Park. The SFT passed through this park, a National Park Service certified site. There is a DAR marker in front of the park.

Continue west on 93rd Street to Hillcrest, then turn left. Drive a short distance and turn right (west) on Bannister. Drive west on Bannister, over Interstate 435, to Elmwood. Turn left at Elmwood, and you will be at Heart Grove, along the creek bottom, now cemented in. It was an important campsite for overland emigrants in the 1840s, with the Donner families, among others, resting here.

Return to Bannister, turn left (west), and continue past another major highway (US 71) to Holmes. Turn left (south) at Holmes and continue about 2 miles to Red Bridge Road. Turn left at Red Bridge and pass by a golf course on the right. As you begin the descent towards the river, Minor Park is on your right. Turn into the parking lot.

At Minor Park there are several National Park service interpretive displays. From here, walk south where you cross several sets of ruts on your left. At about 150 yards, you come to a large red granite DAR marker, located in the deep

Swale with a marker in the notch at Minor Park in Kansas City.

swale of grassed-over SFT ruts that cut through a ridge above the Big Blue River. After the wagons had forded the river, they moved up the slope below the present marker, and their wheels sliced a path in the brow at the top. These are some of the most dramatic trail remains in the Kansas City area.

From the park entrance go west to the intersection of Holmes Road and turn left (south) along the west side of Minor Park. Continue south on Holmes about 1 mile to the intersection of Santa Fe Trail Street. There turn right (crossing Wornall Road) until you come to the Santa Fe Bible Church on the right (north) side of the street. Enter the church parking lot on the west. Adjoining it in the rear is an old cemetery. At the back of the lot is a historical marker, "New Santa Fe," referring to the SFT, but there are many factual errors. A half block west on the northeast corner of Santa Fe Trail Street and State Line Road is a DAR marker.

From Independence, the route of the SFT descended directly from the town (22 miles) in a southwesterly direction via Raytown. By the late 1850s, this route had limited use since the trail became dominated by Westport and Kansas City.

The early history of New Santa Fe is somewhat unclear. A tavern may have been on the site by the mid-1840s, selling whiskey to persons who crossed the state line from the "dry" Indian reservation on the Kansas side. The town site was platted in 1851, and two years later the place boasted two general stores, an inn, a shoe shop, a drugstore, a blacksmith shop, and a post office. New Santa Fe, never much to begin with, withered away after the glory days of the trail.

OLD WESTPORT AND KANSAS CITY

Westport grew up 4 miles south of the Missouri River, the point where the road connecting Independence and the Indian agencies just west in Kansas Territory crossed Mill Creek. In 1833, John Calvin McCoy built a two-story cabin here to serve as a trading post, the beginning of the new community of Westport. About the same time a new landing was cleared on the Missouri River where steamboats could unload their cargoes. First called Westport Landing, the landing went by various names throughout the 1830s and 1840s: Kanzas Landing, Kansas Landing, and finally Town of Kansas. It was about 1.5 miles downstream from the junction of the Kansas (or Kaw) and the Missouri Rivers. The site had a fine ledge of rock jutting out into the water. Goods were first deposited in warehouses, then freighted up the bluff and on to stores in Westport. McCoy was very successful in luring trail outfitters away from Independence.

The small settlement that grew up around the landing afterward was called Kansas City. As the century advanced, Kansas City expanded and, by 1897, eventually engulfed Westport. In the beginning, however, it was Westport, newly booming as a jumping-off point for the Far West, that gave promise of becoming the region's chief population center. By the early 1840s, Independence's monopoly over the Santa Fe trade had been broken, and by the early 1850s Westport virtually controlled the overland traffic. In the decade

Statue of Alexander Majors, John Calvin, McCoy, and Jim Bridger in Westport.

before the Civil War, Westport fairly hummed with activity as Santa Fe traders, mountain men, Indians, and Oregon-bound emigrants mingled in the streets.

Westport remained the main eastern terminus of the SFT as long, or longer, than any of the places that preceded it—Franklin, Lexington, Fort Osage, or even Independence. However, guerrilla warfare prior to the Civil War, and finally the war itself in 1861, brought border disturbances and caused most Santa Fe traders to move their business upriver to Fort Leavenworth, which was more secure. After the war, Westport briefly recovered some of its lost trade, but by 1866 the railroad had pushed into Kansas, and the head of the SFT moved with it.

A large number of sites and markers exist in the Westport-Kansas City area. Those unfamiliar with the region will need to rely on an up-to-date city map. Gregory Franzwa's *The Oregon Trail Revisited, Silver Anniversary Edition*, is also useful for reaching many of the places noted below.

Beginning in Westport, you will see brown and white signs erected by the Kansas City area Historic Trails Association, located at points where the trail crossed section lines, extending from McCoys's trading post in Westport to the western border of Johnson County, Kansas.

KANSAS CITY

The Kansas City metropolitan area takes its role in the history of the SFT very seriously. The phone directory lists forty-one businesses named Santa Fe Trail. There are also six Santa Fe Trail roads, streets, and lanes, and over a dozen schools called Santa Fe Trail, Oregon Trail, or California Trail. Along with this awareness comes an interest in restoring the river front. The original Westport Landing stretched several blocks along the Missouri River from Wyandotte to about Grand. Today's bramble along the old landing will eventually be removed, and foundations of early buildings uncovered as much as possible. This rejuvenation will give us a better idea of the setting along the river.

The city has already developed a park on the Missouri River, which can be reached by driving north on Grand Avenue Viaduct. This will take you to a nice walkway along the river running a mile east of the Town of Kansas site. The landing would have been upstream from the walkway.

The following sites are valuable in gaining an understanding of the SFT from Westport Landing to Westport.

A. Gillis House Site
From Second and Delaware Streets walk north (toward the river) to the foot of the bluff, turn left, and continue one block. On the left is the site of the Gillis

House, built by Benoist Troost in 1849. In 1856, it became known as the American Hotel and was also known as the Union Hotel. Many SFT traders stayed here. Other buildings lined this bluff, continuing eastward several blocks. There are no markers here at the time of writing.

The Gillis House near the waterfront at Westport Landing, post 1860. Photo courtesy Special Collections, Kansas City Public Library, Kansas City, Missouri.

B. CITY MARKET AND STEAMBOAT ARABIA MUSEUM

From the landing return to 3rd Street and turn east to Main Street. The SFT went directly southwest through today's City Market, arriving here by ascending the bluff along what is present-day Grand Avenue Viaduct (see map). The market is full of shops, but most important is the Steamboat Arabia Museum on the east side, which displays a grand collection of goods recovered from the *Arabia*. In 1856, she hit a snag in the Missouri River and sank, which according to museum records was not uncommon. The average life of a steamboat on the treacherous Missouri was three years. The display includes part of the ship and many of the trade items carried in the hold, providing an opportunity to view the kinds of goods that might have been carried on the SFT during this period.

From the museum you can trace the SFT south through Kansas City by using the following directions (see map page 65). If you take this route, you will be following the SFT as far as Penn Valley Park.

1. South from the Arabia to 5th
2. West on 5th to Delaware
3. South on Delaware to 7th
4. West (right) on 7th to Wyandotte (The SFT made this detour because of local topography.)
5. South on Wyandotte to 8th
6. East on 8th to Main
7. South on Main to 12th

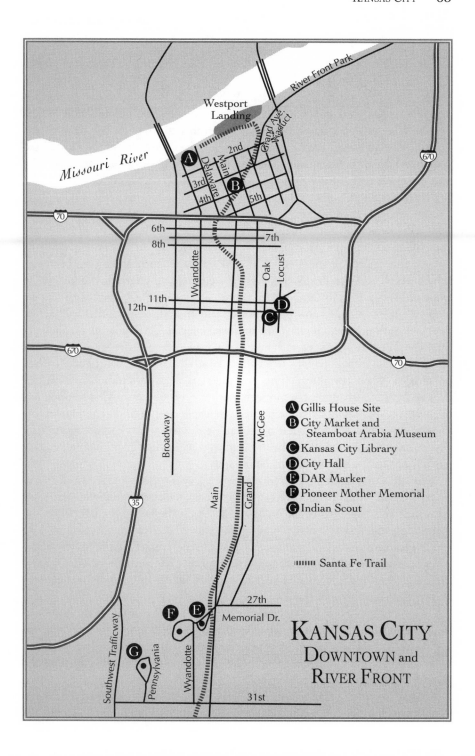

Westport
Landing

River Front Park

Missouri River

Grand Ave. Viaduct

2nd

Main

Delaware

3rd

4th

5th

6th

7th

8th

Wyandotte

Oak

Locust

11th

12th

Broadway

McGee

Main

Grand

Southwest Trafficway

Pennsylvania

Wyandotte

27th

Memorial Dr.

31st

Ⓐ Gillis House Site
Ⓑ City Market and
   Steamboat Arabia Museum
Ⓒ Kansas City Library
Ⓓ City Hall
Ⓔ DAR Marker
Ⓕ Pioneer Mother Memorial
Ⓖ Indian Scout

▓▓▓ Santa Fe Trail

KANSAS CITY
DOWNTOWN and
RIVER FRONT

8. East on 12th to Grand
9. South on Grand to Memorial Drive (The SFT in this stretch is immediately to the west.)

If you followed the trail to Penn Valley Park, you missed two important places. The Kansas City Library (**C** on the map) between 12th and 13th Streets and McGee and Oak has some good research materials on the SFT in the Missouri Valley Room. Further, murals around the ceiling depict the early history of the city, including scenes associated with the trail. Also, just outside the room hangs a copy of the Spalding Map of 1855, which shows the area in the heyday of the SFT.

Another place of interest is City Hall between 11th and 12th Streets and Oak and Locust (**D** on the map). Here major episodes in the city's history are depicted in a frieze of sixteen panels directly above the sixth story.

As you approach the Penn Valley Park area, turn right on Memorial Drive, which takes you into the park. Immediately on your left is a pullout in front of St. Mary's Hospital, where there is a special DAR marker (**E** on the map.) A bronze plaque showing a covered wagon and oxen in relief is attached to a stone monument. Four more of these special DAR bronze plaques are found at points along the eastern end of the trail as far as Lost Spring, Kansas.

Across the road to the west on a small hill is the Pioneer Mother Memorial (**F** on the map). The memorial is a larger-than-life group of bronze figures surrounding a pioneer mother on horseback. This sculpture is unrelated to the series of stone pioneer mothers on the SFT, the first example of which has already been noted at Lexington. To view the sculpture, you must walk up the hill. With the Kansas City skyline rising behind it, this work is beautiful and should not be missed.

Finally, drive south on Wyandotte, which leaves just west of the DAR marker. At 31st Street turn right (west) and go several blocks to Pennsylvania. Turn right here and look for the Indian Scout statue on the hill to the left (**G** on the map), a location that provides another grand view of the Kansas City skyline.

Two more places of interest in the northern part of the city are the Thomas Hart Benton Memorial and the Kansas City Museum of History and Science. They are located in a part of the city where one should use caution and visit in the middle of the day.

The Thomas Hart Benton Memorial is in a traffic circle at the intersection of Gladstone and Benton Boulevards. (Senator Benton's role in developing western trails was mentioned in connection with his statue at St. Louis.) Here a 7-foot granite monument holds two bronze plaques, one of which bears Benton's likeness.

The Kansas City Museum of History and Science is located at 3218 Gladstone Boulevard, two blocks west of the Benton Memorial. Occasional exhibits concerning mountain men, Indians, the Oregon Trail, and the SFT are some of the best anywhere.

From the Indian Scout in Penn Valley Park, return to 31st Street and turn left to Broadway, then follow Broadway south to Westport.

WESTPORT

A. TRAIL MARKERS

A cluster of trail markers is in the vicinity of Broadway and 40th Street, just north of the Broadway and Westport Road intersection and a block northeast of the center of Old Westport. They are in a small triangular park at Broadway and Westport Road.

(1) A DAR marker placed in 1987 is farthest to the north in the park.

(2) A heroic statue of Jim Bridger (mountain man and store owner in Westport), John C. McCoy (founder of Westport), and Alexander Majors (freighter on the SFT).

(3) A large "Three Trails West" terrazzo tile map on the ground showing the Santa Fe, Oregon, and California Trails.

B. HARRIS HOME

The Harris home is at 4000 Baltimore. Built in 1855 by Col. John Harris, who was a participant in the Santa Fe trade, the house was moved to the present site in 1922 from its original location a half-block away at Westport and Main, a spot now marked by a plaque. The beautiful two-story brick house is currently the headquarters of the Westport Historical Society, which has restored several rooms for public view. (Address inquiries to the society at Box 10076, Westport Station, Kansas City, MO 64111.)

C. SITE OF THE HARRIS HOUSE HOTEL

The hotel was located at the northeast corner of Westport and Pennsylvania in the center of Westport. In 1846, Colonel Harris bought the log building at this location when it was known as the McGee Tavern and Hotel, or more popularly the Catfish House, catfish being a specialty of the chef. Owner Allen McGee was selling it to enter the Santa Fe trade. When the building burned, in 1852 Harris rebuilt a three-story brick structure, which was razed in 1922. A plaque now marks the spot. The Independence to Westport road passed by both the Harris home and his hotel. The McCoys Public House Restaurant is now at this site. John McCoy, Westport's founder, had a log trading post here first in 1833.

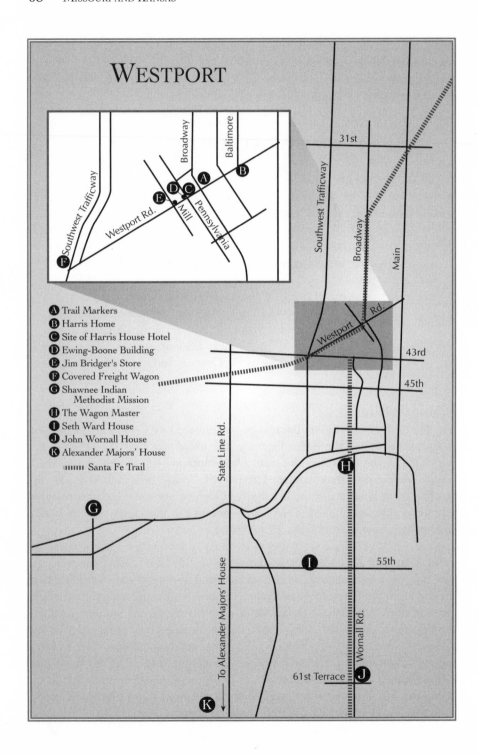

WESTPORT

Broadway
Baltimore
Southwest Trafficway
Westport Rd.
Mill
Pennsylvania

A Trail Markers
B Harris Home
C Site of Harris House Hotel
D Ewing-Boone Building
E Jim Bridger's Store
F Covered Freight Wagon
G Shawnee Indian
      Methodist Mission
H The Wagon Master
I Seth Ward House
J John Wornall House
K Alexander Majors' House
      Santa Fe Trail

31st
Southwest Trafficway
Broadway
Main
Westport   Rd.
43rd
45th
State Line Rd.
55th
To Alexander Majors' House
Wornall Rd.
61st Terrace

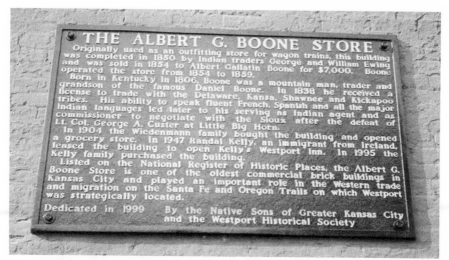

Interpretive sign at the Boone store in Westport, Missouri.

D. THE EWING-BOONE BUILDING

The Ewing-Boone Building is at the northwest corner of Westport and Pennsylvania. Westport's leading historian, the late William Goff, established that this structure was built in 1850–1851. The owners were George and William Ewing, prominent traders with the Shawnees, whose lands lay just across the Kansas line to the west. Albert G. Boone, a grandson of Daniel Boone, bought the building in 1854, the year the Shawnee lands were opened for settlement and the Indian trade declined. It is now Kelly's Bar.

E. JIM BRIDGER'S STORE

Jim Bridger's Store is next to the Ewing-Boone Building on Westport Road. The structure was built in 1850 by Cyprien Chouteau, member of a prominent fur-trading family of St. Louis and Kansas City. Before coming to Westport in that year, he had operated a trading post at Council Grove on the SFT. In 1866, Chouteau sold the two-story store and warehouse to aging Jim Bridger, known in his younger days as "The King of the Mountain Men." Bridger and his son-in-law, Albert Wachsmann, ran a grocery business here for several years. A bronze historical plaque is attached to the outside front wall. The building is presently occupied by a restaurant.

F. COVERED FREIGHT WAGON

The freight wagon is three blocks west of Bridger's Store on Westport Road (which is also 43rd Street) at Southwest Trafficway. This large wagon on the west side of the intersection under the "Old Westport" sign is a replica commemorating trail days. Look for a shopping center behind the freight wagon. There is a "Citizens Commemorative Plaque" in this center listing one hundred prominent early citizens of Westport and Kansas City designated "Old Settlers of Westport and Kansas City."

THE SANTA FE TRAIL FROM WESTPORT

From Old Westport one route of the SFT ran almost due south for a few miles, meandering near and on present-day Wornall Road. From Westport the trail crossed Brush Creek, climbed Brush Creek Hill, and continued on to the "great camping ground." At this well-watered and grassy site, caravans organized for their departure on the SFT. That area now lies between Wornall Road and the state line and is bounded on the north by 67th Street and on the south by 71st Street. At about 66th Street, the south branch of the SFT turned toward the southwest, crossing the state line and meeting the north route at present-day Strang Park in the city of Overland Park.

The other original route leaving Westport went almost due west and then turned southwest. This route led traders by the Shawnee Indian Methodist Mission (**G** on the map on page 68) and near the Shawnee Baptist Mission, as well as the Shawnee Quaker Mission. The Methodist Mission, now a Kansas State Historical Site, is on Mission Road at 53rd Street just across the state line in Kansas. The Shawnee Reservation extended 25 miles south from the Kansas (or Kaw) River through these Indian lands. The Delaware Indians had the lands to the north of the Kaw River. Although the Shawnee Methodist Mission dates from 1829, the location on Mission Road was started in 1839 and was maintained as a manual training school for Shawnee children. Santa Fe Trail travelers and emigrants bound for Oregon often stopped here. Three of the original brick buildings on twelve landscaped acres have been preserved, and a historical marker with text is in front of each.

To reach the Shawnee Mission from the covered freight wagon, drive west on 43rd Street to Mission Road. Turn south on Mission Road to 53rd Street, then right (west) to the mission.

H. THE WAGON MASTER

This bronze, 10-foot-tall equestrian statue of a SFT wagon master is impressive and should not be missed. It is located in front of the Fairmont Hotel on the southern section of Ward Parkway just west of where it intersects with Wornall Road. (Ward Parkway is on both sides of Brush Creek here.) Note the authentic detail of the Santa Fe-style saddle and the long rifle across the pommel. Cast in Italy, the statue was dedicated in 1973.

I. SETH WARD HOUSE

Drive south on Wornall Road to 55th Street. Turn right (west) and go about .5 mile to 1032 West 55th Street. In the yard of this private residence, is a black historical sign with text in gold letters. The two-story white house in front belonged to Seth Ward, who served as post sutler at Fort Laramie on the Oregon Trail. Ward also traveled for a brief period on the SFT, at least part of the time in the employ of famed merchant Ceran St. Vrain. He was a friend of Kit Carson as well. Later, he became a patriarch of Westport, with Ward Parkway named for him. The only sketch of the life of Seth Ward appears in volume 3 of LeRoy R. Hafen's *The Mountain Men and the Fur Trade of the Far West*.

To the rear of the beautiful Ward residence, is a second house that was owned for a time by William Bent, one of the founders of famed Bent's Fort on the Mountain Route of the SFT. Bent commuted between this house, which was the center of a farm, and his fort via the trail. His daughter was married here in 1860. Most of the wording on the historical sign refers to the Civil War Battle of Westport, which took place in the area in October 1864.

J. JOHN WORNALL HOUSE

Return to Wornall and drive south to 61st Terrace. On the northeast corner of this intersection, is the handsome antebellum residence of John Wornall, built in 1858 by one of the area's most prominent citizens. It was the center of a 500-acre farm. From Westport the SFT passed nearby going south to the great camping ground just beyond. The home was briefly used as a hospital during the Civil War Battle of Westport. Now restored, it is administered by the Jackson County Historical Society and open to the public.

K. ALEXANDER MAJORS HOUSE

From the Wornall house, drive west to State Line Road, turn south, and continue to 8201 State Line. Amid the trees on a large lot on the northeast corner of 83rd Street and State Line Road is the Alexander Majors House. As noted in the Lexington section, Majors, along with his partners Russell and Waddell, operated the largest overland freighting firm in the early West. In fact, Majors did some freighting on the SFT before the partnership was formed with Russell and Waddell in 1848. This two-story frame house was built in 1856. Majors died in 1900 and is buried in Union Cemetery at 29th and Grand in Kansas City. Also buried in that cemetery is John C. McCoy, the founder of Westport and discoverer of Westport Landing. The Majors House has been restored and furnished. Behind it are a smokehouse and a large barn (with exhibits), reconstructed on the original foundation. The site, open to the public, is administered by the Alexander Majors Historical Trust and is a certified National Park Service Santa Fe National Historic Trail Site.

ENTERING KANSAS

A little over half of the total length of the SFT fell within the present bound-aries of Kansas. US 56 (and beginning at Kinsley, Kansas, US 56/US 50) gen-erally follows the original route of the trail. US 56 will be your companion as far as Dodge City, Kansas. Scattered along it are nearly one hundred DAR markers and other monuments.

The SFT used five separate routes, evolving over a forty-year span, to enter Kansas (see maps pages 45, 46, and 47). This guide will direct you to Lone Elm Campground by way of the route that utilized the Lower Crossing of the Blue River in the earliest period (1821–1827).The traders passed into Kansas at Nine Mile Point, went on to Flat Rock Creek Campground, and finally Round Grove/Lone Elm Campground south of Olathe.

Drive south on State Line Road past 69th Street. This intersection is about where the SFT, by way of Westport and Wornall Road, crossed into Kansas after 1840. Continue south on State Line to 75th Street. At this loca-tion you are .5 mile north of Nine Mile Point. Turn right (west) here, contin-ue west to Delmar, and turn left to Harmon Park, which can be spotted by its tall water tower. Near the pavilion is a parking lot, southeast of which is a good set of ruts. This is actually on the later route of the trail, after 1840.

From Harmon Park, drive south to 79th Street, turn right (west), and con-tinue past Metcalf several blocks to Santa Fe Drive. Turn south on Santa Fe Drive. At 80th Street and Santa Fe Drive on the northeast corner is a DAR marker, the first one in Kansas.

From the DAR marker continue southwest on Santa Fe Drive to 87th Street. At this point you are about .5 mile southeast of Sapling Grove and .25 mile northeast of the junction of the two SFT routes out of Westport. Sapling Grove was an important rendezvous for SFT traders and Oregon Trail emigrants. If you wish to visit the site, it is in Comanche Park at 83rd Street and Grant.

Drive west on 87th Street, passing Interstate 35, and about 1 mile beyond turn left (south) onto Pflumm. Continue on Pflumm until you pass under the interstate and turn left at 103rd Street. Follow 103rd east for .33 mile and turn left into Flat Rock Creek Park. The Flat Rock Creek Campground was near the small stream (Indian Creek) in the park. In later trail days, this site was called Indian Creek Campground.

Return to Pflumm and drive south to 105th Street. There should be a DAR marker on the west side of Pflumm, moved here from its original loca-tion 1.5 miles north. This is the second DAR marker (Lenexa) in Kansas. From the DAR marker, go south on Pflumm to 119th Street and turn right (west). Go over the interstate, and just beyond turn left onto Renner Road, which becomes Kansas City Road. Continue south on Kansas City Road. This road is directly on top of the SFT from here to 135th Street. (If some places are being skipped, you can drive south on Interstate 35 and take the Olathe exit to arrive at this same location.)

OLATHE

Continue southwest on Kansas City Road toward Olathe. This road becomes Old Kansas City Road as you enter Olathe. Immediately beyond the intersection of Old Kansas City Road and Ridgeway, on the right, is one of the white oval SFT markers of the American Pioneer Trails Association, actually one of several replicas placed along the SFT by Michael Duncan, formerly director of the Mahaffie House.

One block beyond the Ridgeway intersection on the right (1100 Kansas City Road) is the Mahaffie House and Farmstead, a Registered National Historic Landmark. The fine two-story residence was built in 1865 as a farmhouse, but it soon served as the first noon stage stop beyond Westport. It is the only remaining stage station on the SFT that is open to the public.

Continue southwest on Old Kansas City Road about 1 mile to the intersection with Santa Fe Avenue. Turn right (west) four blocks to the Johnson County Courthouse on the left. On the southeast corner of Courthouse Square, is a fine SFT monument. At the top is an oxbow carved in the stone, while below is a bronze plaque with an ox-drawn covered wagon in relief, like the one noted earlier in Penn Valley Park.

In the Kansas Room of the Olathe Public Library, a good collection of SFT materials and maps is available for researchers and trail hounds. Its location is one block east of the courthouse, at Park and Chestnut Streets.

SOUTH OF OLATHE

Several locations of interest can be visited on roads south and west of Olathe. From Courthouse Square in Olathe, drive west on Santa Fe Avenue to Lone Elm Road, also the intersection with KS 7. Turn left (south) on Lone Elm and drive about 4 miles to the intersection with 167th Street. On the southeast corner is the DAR marker for Lone Elm Campground. First known as Round Grove, this site came to be called Lone Elm by 1844 when all the surrounding timber had been cut by travelers for firewood and only a single tree remained. By the end of the decade, the lone elm itself had fallen to the ax. The campground encompassed forty acres behind the marker. Many caravans from

Independence made this place their second stop on the trail. Lone Elm Campground was confused with another campground, Elm Grove, on the same creek until recently. Elm Grove Campground will be detailed in the next chapter.

Return north on Lone Elm

A DAR marker and Park Service trail logo at Lone Elm Campground.

Road (to reach KS 7) to Olathe. This is the last opportunity to make a side trip to Fort Leavenworth. To get to Leavenworth, continue north on KS 7 about 33 miles to the town and fort.

FORT LEAVENWORTH

From anywhere in the Kansas City area, a convenient side trip can be made up the Missouri River to Fort Leavenworth. Established in 1827 by Col. Henry Leavenworth, several branches of the Santa Fe and Oregon Trails crossed its grounds.

There were two principal routes from the fort to the SFT. One followed the Military Road south, crossing the Kansas River at Grinter's Ferry and connecting with the SFT in Lenexa at about present-day 90th and Barton Streets (see maps on pages 46 and 47). The second branch went more directly west and crossed the Kansas River near its confluence with the Wakarusa River in Douglas County, continuing to meet the SFT at Willow Springs near present-day Overbrook. Gen. Stephen Watts Kearny's Army of the West, as well as the celebrated Mormon Battalion, used this route when they marched over the SFT in 1846 to conquer New Mexico.

Border disturbances concerning slavery issues several years before the outbreak of the Civil War disrupted the Westport and Kansas City markets, and many Santa Fe traders began to use the safer protected routes from Fort Leavenworth southwest to the SFT. By the late 1850s and early 1860s, traders and emigrants heading for New Mexico or California increasingly debarked at Fort Leavenworth from Missouri River steamboats and organized caravans for a crossing of the SFT or the Oregon-California Trail. There are two clusters of sites associated with the SFT, one in the town of Leavenworth and another on the grounds of the fort immediately to the north.

THE TOWN OF LEAVENWORTH

Entering the south side of the town of Leavenworth, watch for the junction of KS 7/US 73 with KS 5, which enters from the right (east) along the south side of the large Veterans Administration Hospital. Turn right at this intersection onto KS 5 (which is also Muncie Road) and go two blocks to the entrance of Leavenworth National Cemetery on the left (**A** on the map on page 78). (Note: This cemetery is distinct from the Fort Leavenworth National Cemetery on the fort grounds, described below.)

Here is buried William Sloan, who, as a boy in the 1850s, accompanied his mother Eliza and sister Marian on several SFT crossings. True trail buffs, addicted to Marian Sloan Russell's memoirs *Land of Enchantment*, will want to visit the grave of her brother, who figured prominently in the narrative. He served as a corporal in the Civil War, which entitled him to be buried here, and he died at the neighboring Veterans Administration Hospital in 1917. Sloan's marker is in Section 30, Row 14, Grave 7, near the flagpole. (Directions to his sister Marian's grave west of Raton Pass near Stonewall, Colorado, are given later.)

Back at the cemetery entrance, turn left (east) on KS 5, which quickly curves to the right. Beyond the curve on the left (east), is the gate to Mt. Muncie Cemetery (**B** on the map on page 78). It is .4 mile between the gates of the two cemeteries. Enter and take the first lane to the right. The Fred Harvey family stone, the largest in the immediate vicinity, is on the left about 50 yards up this lane. The Harvey name is on the back of the stone and thus not visible from the road.

Beginning in the 1870s, Frederick Henry Harvey (1835–1901) began developing a chain of famous restaurants and hotels along the Santa Fe Railroad, the successor of the SFT. His splendid company encouraged tourists to travel the "new Santa Fe Trail" by rail. Harvey's name remains legendary in the Southwest, with much written about his career.

Return to KS 7/US 73, turn right, and continue north into Leavenworth. Approaching the center of downtown, turn left (west) on Olive Street and go four blocks to the Fred Harvey House on the northeast corner of Olive and 7th Street (**C** on the map on page 78). The beautiful two-story mansion, once the residence of Harvey, now is an annex to the Leavenworth Courthouse but will be converted into a museum in the near future. The exterior of the structure is well preserved, except for an awful modern door at the entrance. A metal historical sign on the front lawn has a text concerning Harvey.

Again, return to KS 7/US 73 (that is, 4th Street) and turn left (north) toward downtown. On the northwest corner of 4th and Delaware Streets, is a two-story brick building now occupied by the Guarantee Land Title Company. Originally the freighting firm of Russell, Majors, and Waddell, whose association with the SFT is described under "Lexington," maintained general offices here in the late 1850s and 1860s (**D** on the map on page 78). Two plaques are attached to the side of the building facing 4th Street, one commemorating the freight company, the other its famous Pony Express line.

Drive east four blocks on Delaware toward the Missouri River to the Riverfront Community Center, then turn right one block. On your left is a parking lot. This is the site of the Leavenworth Landing, where steamboats docked for the town of Leavenworth (**E** on the map on page 78). It has a nice view of the river and picnic facilities. In addition, there is an interpretive marker near the river, a good round map of the Leavenworth area, and some stylized cement sculptures of covered wagons.

Return to 4th Street (KS 7/US 73) and continue north until it ends at a T at Metropolitan Avenue. Turn left (west) and proceed to the entrance of Fort Leavenworth on the right.

FORT LEAVENWORTH

F. MAIN ENTRANCE
Visitors enter the fort on Grant Avenue. On the right is the information building, where it is possible to obtain maps and a self-guiding tour booklet of the fort. Here, behind the building, is the official Kansas Historical Marker for Fort Leavenworth with reference to the SFT.

G. BUFFALO SOLDIERS MONUMENT
Continue on Grant to the new Buffalo Soldiers Monument on your right, an impressive monument not to be missed. The 10th U.S. Cavalry, or Buffalo Soldiers, was organized at the fort in 1866. These were black soldiers who saw extensive service at various locations along the trail.

H. POST MUSEUM
Go north on Grant past the lakes to Reynolds Avenue and turn right one block to the Post Museum. Here are displayed objects of pioneer and army life, "emphasizing the drama of westward expansion." One of the largest collections of pioneer vehicles in the world can be seen, including a freight wagon and army vehicles of the type that traveled the SFT.

A statue of a Buffalo Soldier in Fort Leavenworth, Kansas.

I. OLD STONE WALL, MORMON BATTALION MARKER, AND MEMORIAL CHAPEL
Continue north on Grant to the intersection of Kearny Avenue. Here in a traffic circle is a statue of President Ulysses S. Grant. Behind it and across the street is a section of the Old Stone Wall, which formed part of the original defense line of the fort. Two plaques are mounted on it, one placed by the DAR. In addition,

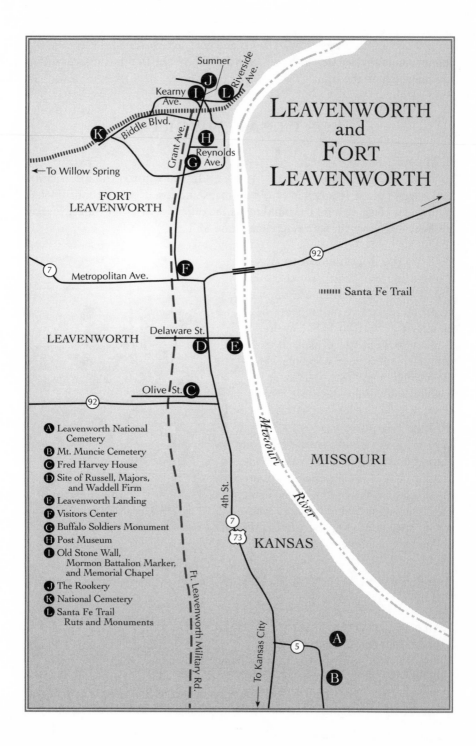

LEAVENWORTH
and
FORT
LEAVENWORTH

Sumner

Kearny
Ave.

Riverside
Ave.

Biddle Blvd.

Grant Ave.

Reynolds
Ave.

←To Willow Spring

FORT
LEAVENWORTH

To Willow Spring

92

7
Metropolitan Ave.

|||||||| Santa Fe Trail

LEAVENWORTH

Delaware St.

Olive St.

92

Missouri River

MISSOURI

Ⓐ Leavenworth National
   Cemetery
Ⓑ Mt. Muncie Cemetery
Ⓒ Fred Harvey House
Ⓓ Site of Russell, Majors,
   and Waddell Firm
Ⓔ Leavenworth Landing
Ⓕ Visitors Center
Ⓖ Buffalo Soldiers Monument
Ⓗ Post Museum
Ⓘ Old Stone Wall,
   Mormon Battalion Marker,
   and Memorial Chapel
Ⓙ The Rookery
Ⓚ National Cemetery
Ⓛ Santa Fe Trail
   Ruts and Monuments

4th St.

Ft. Leavenworth Military Rd.

7
73
KANSAS

To Kansas City

5

Ⓐ

Ⓑ

there is a Mormon Battalion marker at Kearny and Sumner Place nearby. The Memorial Chapel is just to the east of the Grant statue. The walls of this building, made of Kansas stone, are lined with memorial plaques honoring soldiers killed in the line of duty on the western frontier.

J. THE ROOKERY
One block northwest of Grant's statue at 12 Sumner is the Rookery. Constructed in 1832, this is the oldest building in Kansas, in use as the post headquarters during the heyday of the SFT.

K. NATIONAL CEMETERY
Go west on Pope from Grant Avenue to Biddle Boulevard and the cemetery entrance. Civilians and soldiers killed on the SFT were buried here. Near the flagpole is a tall column over General Leavenworth's grave. Another interesting monument is the one for Col. Edward Hatch, once commander of the Department of New Mexico, who pursued Apaches led by Chief Victorio. Graves of Tom Custer (brother of Gen. George Armstrong Custer) and other soldiers killed at the Little Bighorn are also here. Ask at the cemetery visitors' center for the location of individual graves.

L . SANTA FE TRAIL RUTS AND MONUMENTS
Beginning at Grant's statue, follow Riverside Avenue's loop down to the Missouri River. A deep rut running from what was once a boat landing on the river to the top of the hill is the track left by ox-drawn covered wagons. In the 1830s, the river swept along the base of the hill, and the landing was at the location of a present-day warehouse. Stone columns with brass plaques designating the Oregon and Santa Fe Trails are located at the top and bottom of the cut.

After completing a tour of the Leavenworth area, return to Olathe via US 73 and KS 7 and pick up US 56 leading to Gardner.

KANSAS

GARDNER, BURLINGAME, AND COUNCIL GROVE

GARDNER

O n US 56 at 1 mile west of the junction with KS 7 are two houses on the right. The first is a two-story red brick structure and the second a long white bungalow. Just past the bungalow on the right side of the highway is an open field leading down to Cedar Creek, the site of a major SFT campground, Elm Grove. Originally an Indian campground, it was the location of George C. Sibley's "Caravan Grove." Elm Grove was long confused with Lone Elm, but we know now they were two distinct sites (see Crease 1991). The trail wound along the foot of the slope that rises to the present highway.

About .9 mile west of the creek, US 56 curves to the left. Here, 151st Street, really just a section line road, continues straight ahead. In the small triangle formed where the two roads split, is a DAR marker, which has been moved here from its original site 100 feet away.

A. SANTA FE TRAIL MONUMENT

At the main intersection in the center of Gardner, turn right (north) off US 56 onto Elm Street, which has no street sign. Drive one block to the SFT monument in the schoolyard located on the northeast corner of Elm and Shawnee. This handsome marker with a bronze plaque is like the one in Olathe. Continue another block north on Elm to a fine Oregon Trail DAR marker on the right in the schoolyard.

One of the fine Kansas Historical Markers near the location where the Santa Fe Trail and the Oregon Trail split.

B. JUNCTION OF THE SANTA FE AND OREGON TRAILS

Two miles west of Gardner on US 56 there is a small roadside park on the right (north). The historical marker in the park tells the story of the parting of the Santa Fe and Oregon Trails. Just before the park there is a gravel road leading west. Continue on that road for about .25 mile past a farmhouse and row of trees on the right. The actual fork in the trails was about 200 yards to your right on the small rise. The Oregon Trail continued just north of west, while the SFT went west heading for Lanesfield.

C. LANESFIELD DAR MARKER

To find the Lanesfield DAR marker, continue west on the gravel road past the fork in the trails to the next road to your left—Dillie Road. Drive south on Dillie Road for .5 mile to the old Lanesfield School on your left. There is a museum on the south side of the school, a DAR marker in the southwest corner of the grounds, and a patch of land being restored to a tallgrass prairie.

The SFT passed diagonally north of the Lanesfield School grounds from northeast to southwest heading toward the Narrows. Drive south on Dillie Road to the first intersection and turn right (west). Continue to the next corner and go left, returning to US 56 at Edgerton. Then go west on US 56 toward Baldwin City.

BALDWIN CITY

Just east of Baldwin City begins the Narrows, a ridge or divide separating the waters of Wakarusa River on the north from those of the Marias de Cygnes (pronounced locally Mara du Seen) on the south. Scarcely noticeable today, it is nevertheless an important divide since the Wakarusa River leads to the Kansas River, while the Marias de Cygnes flows into the Osage River. The SFT caravans kept to this ridge because it was the easiest way to travel, at least in dry weather. When it rained, wagons sunk to their axles in the deep mud.

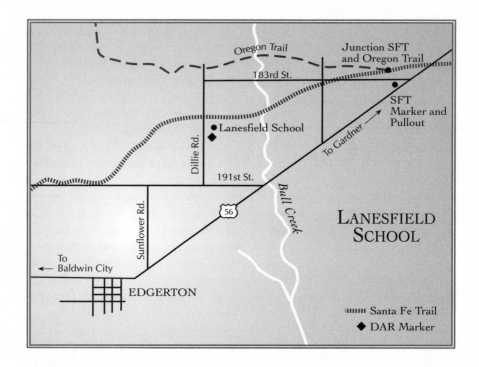

A. IVAN BOYD PRAIRIE PRESERVE

On the south side of US 56 about 3 miles east of Baldwin City is the Ivan Boyd Prairie Preserve, a small roadside park near the beginning of the Narrows. A half circle drive enters from the highway at the east end of the park and exits at the west end. Near the entrance on the left is a Pioneer Meeting House of native logs, a replica dedicated in 1971.

There are three markers here. One, an official Kansas Historical Marker, describes the Battle of Black Jack, a clash that took place .25 mile south of the park. This small clash, which occurred on June 2, 1856, was the first regular battle between free and slave forces, an early prelude to the Civil War. John Brown was the leader of the free-state forces. The second marker, a DAR marker for the SFT, is located nearby. The late Amelia Betts and Katharine Kelley, dedicated women of nearby Baldwin City, painted the worn, incised inscription on this marker (and the other six DAR markers in Douglas County) so that it is easily read by visitors. The third marker is a handsome metal one for "Black Jack Park," with reference to the SFT. If you wish to visit the site of the Battle of Black Jack, continue on the gravel road along the west boundary of the park about .12 mile to the entrance to Battle of Black Jack Park on the right. This park has blow-by-blow markers allowing you to follow the course of the battle.

B. TRAIL RUTS

Enter the gravel road that leads south from the highway along the west boundary of the roadside park. Behind the row of trees along the back of the park is a forty-acre field containing fine traces of the SFT, seen as wide swales and ridges in the sod. They are directly behind the large wooden sign facing the gravel road.

The ease of viewing the ruts depends on the time of year. In April, the dead grass is burned off, and they are clearly visible in the blackened field (see photo in Introduction). Later in the summer when vegetation is thickest they are difficult to see, but on the ridge to the right rear of the sign they show as indentations against the sky. During June, wild strawberries can sometimes be found growing in the depressions. Wagon travelers mentioned their pleasure in collecting the fruit in this area.

The best way to experience this site is to leave your car at the roadside park and walk south over a small bridge, from where you can ascend the hill. At the top are two modern stone monuments commemorating the Sibley survey of 1825, the easternmost with an inscription.

C. OFFICIAL KANSAS HISTORICAL MARKER, "BALDWIN"

This marker, referring to the SFT and local history, is located on US 56 at a turnout on the north (right) side of the highway about 2 miles west of the roadside park as you approach the limits of Baldwin City.

D. OLD CASTLE

On 5th Street, five blocks south of US 56 in Baldwin City is the Old Castle. Built in 1858 during trail days, this three-story native stone structure was the initial building of the first college in Kansas Territory. Now a museum, it is open afternoons. A bronze marker in front has an interesting relief of a SFT wagon.

E. PALMYRA TOWN SITE

On the northern edge of Baldwin City, is the Palmyra Town site. Palmyra, founded in 1854 near the beginning of the Narrows, was known as a "repair stop" during the latter days of the SFT. Here blacksmiths and wagon makers maintained shops for the benefit of travelers. After entering Baldwin City on US 56, turn north (right) on Eisenhower Street (a sign here points to the high school) and go one block to the first intersection. A "Palmyra" sign on the northeast corner indicates the center of the old town. The SFT passed through the grounds of the high school on the left.

At this intersection turn right (east) and go one block, then turn left (north). In the middle of the block on the right, is a modern blue house, the site of Palmyra's Santa Fe Hotel, which burned a few years ago. Continue past

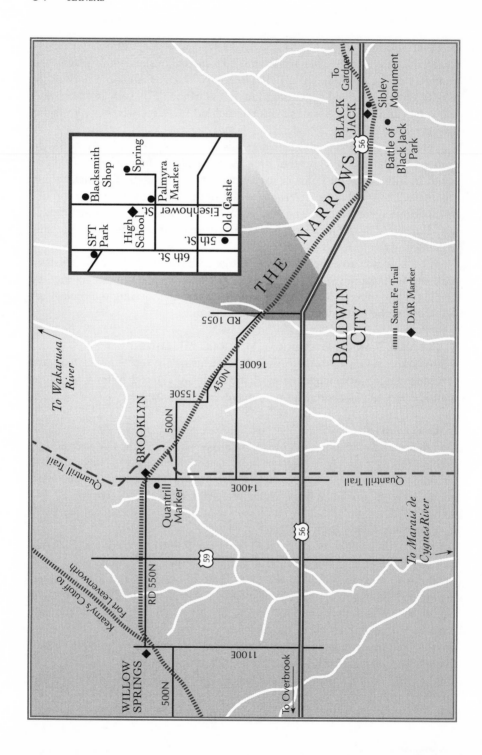

it to the sign on the right marking the Santa Fe Well, a watering place for Santa Fe caravans. The restored well now has a pitched roof over it.

Return to Eisenhower Street and turn right (north). About one-half block beyond the point where the pavement changes to gravel is a wooden sign on the east (right) side of the road indicating the site of the original Palmyra Blacksmith Shop. To view the route of the Narrows from this location, climb the grassy ridge behind the sign and look back toward the southeast, in the direction of the roadside park and ruts visited earlier.

Go back about a block to the high school, and note the markers on the grounds in front of the school. One is a DAR marker, moved here from the site of the blacksmith shop, while another is a Palmyra historical sign, referring to the SFT, installed through the efforts of the late Amelia Betts and Katharine Kelley.

From here at Palmyra the SFT headed in a northwesterly direction to present-day Trail Park. To get there, return down Eisenhower Street to US 56 and turn west (right). Go west on US 56 a short distance to the intersection of 6th Street (also marked County Road 1055). Turn north on 6th and go .75 mile to Trail Park.

F. TRAIL PARK AND DAR MONUMENT

Trail Park is a small park on the west (left) side of County Road 1055 where County Road 358N comes in from the left. Originally the DAR monument here had a fine bronze plaque like the ones in Olathe and Gardner, but it was stolen long ago. In its place, a marble replica of the plaque was put on the monument in 1969 by the local Santa Fe Trail Historical Society. Recently, two new SFT historical signs have also been added to the park. The gravel road that intersects with County Road 1055 and runs along the southwest side of the park is the actual route of the SFT. In dry weather follow this road west about .75 mile to the point where it curves to the left. On the right, just before the curve, is a farm, and in the open areas around it are traces of SFT ruts.

G. BROOKLYN

After the gravel road curves to the left, continue on it about .5 mile, turn right (north) on County Road 1600E and climb the steep hill. Then take County Road N450 coming in from the left (west), and you are now back on the SFT. Then descend into a small valley. At about .5 mile turn right on County Road 1550E and drive .25 mile to County Road 500N, then turn left (west). Continue west for 1.5 miles to County Road 1400E and turn right (north).

Drive .5 mile to an intersection. At this point you are a few hundred feet west of the old community of Brooklyn. Here there is a DAR marker and another for the Quantrill Raiders Trail. On the morning of August 21, 1863, William

Quantrill and a gang of 450 bushwhackers entered Lawrence and spent four hours burning, looting, and killing two hundred men and boys. Quantrill then left for Missouri through Brooklyn, destroying it as well.

From this corner drive west on County Road 550N for 2.5 miles. At 1.5 miles use caution crossing paved US 59. The trail will be on your immediate right as you drive. At a point .5 mile farther west is Willow Springs. Col. Stephen Watts Kearny passed through here in August 1845 on his return from a 2,200-mile trip over the Plains. From here, he decided to head directly back to Fort Leavenworth instead of following the longer route of the SFT. In June 1846, he sent out a party from Fort Leavenworth to blaze this trail in reverse for the use of his Army of the West and the Mormon Battalion, making it the principal Military Road. There is a DAR marker and an information sign.

H. SIBLEY HILL

From Willow Springs drive south .5 mile and turn right (west), then continue 5.5 miles on County Road 500N. At the corner of County Road 1029 and County Road 500N, turn left (south). There is a DAR marker 1 mile after the turn. This is where the SFT crossed the road coming from Willow Springs heading toward Flag Springs.

Continue south to US 56 and turn right at the old Globe Rock Store. From there drive west on US 56 1 mile to a rounded hill with a tall red and white relay tower on your right (north). The deteriorating remains of a house can be seen just east of the hill, back 200 yards from US 56. This is the old Simmons House, built in 1870. Although according to tradition the house was a stage station on the SFT, the SFT had stopped serving this area several years before 1870.

Another mile beyond the Simmons House, on the south (left) side of US 56, is a DAR and interpretive marker. A two-story white farmhouse with white barn can be seen across the highway and slightly to the west of this marker. Here the SFT crossed the current highway from north to south heading toward present-day Overbrook.

OVERBROOK

Continue west on US 56 toward Overbrook. As you approach the town, notice the fine sheet-iron silhouettes on the right side of the road, showing a SFT caravan as it might have looked 150 years ago. Ed Harmison, the local trail expert, is responsible for installing these dramatic images and also convincing the town of Overbrook to change the name of a street to Santa Fe Avenue since it was directly on the old trail.

The trail approached present-day Overbrook on the south side of US 56.

About 1.5 miles east of town was Rock Springs Campground. Another mile beyond that the trail passed through the current cemetery. To get to the cemetery, take the first street to the left as you enter Overbrook, which is Cedar, and go south several blocks. As the street turns left toward the cemetery, there are several houses. Under one of these houses is an old spring used by traders.

A short distance beyond, drive straight ahead after the lane enters the cemetery gate. The graves on the immediate left lie in the faint ruts of the SFT, which heads toward the old spring. At the back of the cemetery where the gravel road turns left, is a 1.5-foot gray wooden post in the ground marking the center of the trail ruts.

From the cemetery return to US 56, and continue several blocks west to the intersection of Overbrook's one main commercial street. Turn left (south) to the DAR marker in front of the town post office. Here the city street called Santa Fe Trail is the route of the trail.

Continue west on US 56 and about 1 mile from Overbrook watch to the right for a tall water tower on legs. Just beyond it cross a bridge. From the bridge and the road just past it, look to the right (north) of the highway to see Flag Spring in a large depression, its location marked by a windmill and cattle tank. Immediately to the west of the windmill is a red barn with a white roof. This spring reportedly was a major watering stop for trail travelers, although no details about its history are available. There is no historical marker here.

SANTA FE TRAIL HIGH SCHOOL

The school is located 5 miles west of Overbrook on the south side of US 56. At the main entrance, there is a large sign attached to a native rock monument with the school's name and above it a metal covered wagon. In front of the monument and sign is a granite marker placed by the Sons of the American Revolution. As far as we know, it is the only SFT marker originating with the Sons, in contrast to the numerous ones placed by the Daughters of the American Revolution. The school grounds lie atop the ruts of the trail.

MCGEE-HARRIS STAGE STATION
AT 110 MILE CREEK

Continue west from the high school on US 56 to an intersection with a sign pointing left (south) to Osage State Fishing Lake. (A cement silo is on the southeast corner.) Drive south .2 mile to SFT ruts in an unplowed field on the left (east), which show as indentations on the skyline. Here the trail, coming from the school grounds, is going toward the crossing at 110 Mile Creek. From here take the road heading west, which goes along the north side of the lake to US 75. As you are about to enter US 75, pause and look northwest across the highway to see the remains of the McGee-Harris Stage Station in the distance. The remains are about .5 mile away.

In the early 1820s, the stream here was known as Oak Creek. When Sibley made his trail survey in 1825, it was determined that the crossing was 110 miles from Fort Osage on the Missouri River (the start of the survey). Consequently, the stream soon became known as 110 Mile Creek, retaining that name to the present day.

About 1854, Fry McGee, who had been over the Oregon Trail and back, settled with his family on the east bank of the creek at the SFT crossing. He farmed, built a toll bridge, and provided overnight accommodations for wagon travelers and stage passengers. The toll was 25¢ per wagon, and in the late 1850s the coach for Santa Fe stopped twice a month.

Subsequently, a Mr. Harris married McGee's eldest daughter, who had the unlikely name of America Puss. Harris then built a residence and store adjacent to his in-laws, and after McGee's death in 1861 operated the stage station until the SFT closed here in 1866 (see Stocking 1971). Today, one major building of stone and frame remains, apparently a residence and station. Ruins of other structures nearby may include the blacksmith shop that was part of the original complex. Traces of the trail are visible at the creek crossing about 100 yards west.

Turn right (north) on US 75, and go a short distance to a DAR marker on the left, surrounded by a steel pipe fence. Continue north to the intersection of US 56 and US 75.

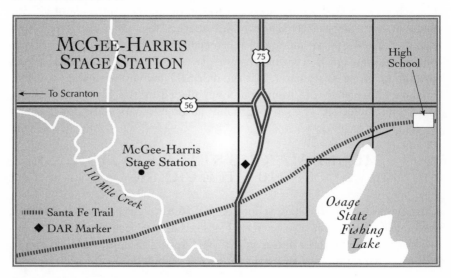

SIDE TRIP TO TOPEKA

From this intersection of US 56 and US 75, a side trip can be made to the state capital of Topeka 15 miles north on US 75. The headquarters of the Kansas State Historical Society is at 6425 SW 6th Avenue. Here SFT buffs will find excellent research materials in the archives, as well as rare books and early newspapers. Superb historical exhibits are on display in this location, including those about the SFT. Featured is the oldest surviving Atchison, Topeka and Santa Fe steam engine, used in the 1880s over Raton Pass. Return to the junction of US 75 and US 56.

BURLINGAME

At 2.5 miles beyond the McGee-Harris Stage Station, US 56 leads to the town of Scranton. The SFT passed through its southern limits, and formerly there was a sign on the outskirts that greeted visitors with the words "Welcome to Scranton on the Santa Fe Trail," but it has long since disappeared. In the center of town, turn left at the first street past the post office (Boone Street) and go one block to Jones Park on the right, which has a DAR marker moved here in the 1970s.

Five miles beyond Scranton, US 56 reaches the edge of Burlingame. Just after the highway passes under a railroad trestle, cross a bridge over Switzler Creek. Here was a major trail crossing. Originally called Bridge Creek, the creek was later named for John Switzler, who built a log toll bridge at this point in 1847. Switzler had married an Indian woman and thus became a member of her tribe, allowing him to circumvent the prohibition on white settlement.

After crossing the highway bridge, Santa Fe Avenue leads two blocks to the center of town. Just past the bridge there is a stone house on the left that was used during trail days. Burlingame claims to be the only town in Kansas whose main street was once a part of the SFT, and on it are numerous businesses named for the trail. The community was founded in 1857 as Council City and later renamed for Anson Burlingame, a famous minister to China and an anti-slavery advocate. It is said blacksmiths here shod thousands of oxen and mules destined for New Mexico. In 1869, tracks of the Santa Fe Railroad arrived here, and Burlingame now calls itself the place where "Trail Meets Rail."

In the center of Burlingame, US 56 reaches a main intersection and turns left (south). Instead of turning, continue straight ahead one block on Santa Fe Avenue (which is also KS 31) to a schoolyard on the left. In the northeast corner of the yard, is a special DAR marker honoring Fannie Geiger Thompson, the woman who initiated the marking of the SFT in 1906.

For the 40 miles from Burlingame to Council Grove, a Boy Scout hiking trail has been established along the original SFT, which lies north of US 56.

The starting point and a base campground are located on the east side of Burlingame at the crossing of the trail and the Santa Fe Railroad. For information and a map, write to: Chamber of Commerce, Burlingame, KS 66413.

From Fannie Thompson's marker, continue west on KS 31 about 3 miles to the bridge over Dragoon Creek. According to Stocking (Stocking 1971), the creek was named by a Lieutenant Fields, who brought a company of dragoons (mounted infantry) over the SFT in 1852. Cross the bridge and go 1.5 miles to a DAR marker, next to a wire fence on the north (right) side of the road, commemorating the nearby Dragoon Creek Crossing. The trail here was actually another branch road leading down from Fort Leavenworth to join the main SFT not far to the south.

From the DAR marker, look across the road to the southeast, and in a field about 100 yards from the pavement you will see the ruins of the Havanna Stage Station. The small community of Havanna was founded by German and French settlers in 1858. In addition to the stage station, there was a store and hotel, both of which have disappeared. To reach the site, return east .2 mile to a primitive road that leads to an old cattle loading chute next to the highway. Park here. Next to the chute is a fence and beyond that a field. Toward the back of the field are the fine limestone walls of the station reaching up to roof level, often obscured by brush and trees in summer. Behind it is a more recent weathered gray barn, and to the left rear is a red barn with a tin roof. Both are easily seen from the road and will serve as landmarks to find the station. The Flint Hills Chapter of the SFTA has placed a nice interpretive marker at the site.

Return to the DAR marker and continue west on KS 31 another .2 mile to a wide highway maintenance pullout that extends along the north (right) side of the road. Recently there have been piles of gravel and dirt and a black portable water tank on legs in this long pullout, but these features can change. At the back of the pullout, in the field just across the wire fence, surrounded by a pipe railing, is the grave of Pvt. Samuel Hunt of Kentucky, who died on the SFT in 1835. The information on the modern gravestone was supplied by the War Department when a new marker was installed a century after Hunt's death.

From Private Hunt's grave you have two choices. You can opt to follow the trail west by way of gravel roads, which are well maintained but require caution if it has rained recently. Or you can opt to return to Burlingame, where you can rejoin US 56 and follow it south, then west until you reach the hamlet of Allen, then go north on Road L to pick up the trail again.

If you choose to follow the gravel-road route, drive west from Private Hunt's grave to the next road, Crawford. Turn left (south) here, and as you head for the crossing of Soldier Creek, the trail ruts should be visible as you descend the hill. At the first corner turn right (west) and cross over Soldier Creek. The trail crossing is immediately to your right after passing over the low bridge.

Continue west (crossing over the Kansas Turnpike) until the road ends in a T. Turn left (south) and proceed .1 mile, then turn west again. Along this road was the once-thriving town of Wilmington, established by H. D. Shepard in 1856. At one time it had thirty houses, two stores, a blacksmith shop, two doctors, a wagon shop, and a hotel. Also, a post office was established here in 1858. All this activity ended in 1880, when the MAB Railroad was built north of Wilmington, and the town's businesses moved north to be near the tracks.

At about .4 mile is the Wilmington School, which opened in 1870 and closed in 1950. It is now owned by the Flint Hills Chapter of the SFTA, which hopes to restore it soon. There is a DAR marker and an interpretive sign in front of the school, as well as a marker for the Boy Scout Trail that passes by here.

After leaving the Wilmington School, turn south. At County Road 400 turn right (west). Continue on County Road 400 about 1.5 miles to an intersection. The SFT crossed the road just south of this intersection. Turn left (south) here and continue .5 mile to the next corner, then turn right on County Road 395, following it west for 3.5 miles. The SFT is almost directly under the road here. Turn left (south) and drive .5 mile, then turn west again on County Road 390. About 1 mile straight ahead is KS 99, where you turn left (south).

At .8 mile there is a DAR marker on your right, before you cross Elm Creek. This is where an Overland Stage Station was established in 1855 by Jacob Hall. Continue past the DAR Marker and then turn right (west) to cross over Elm Creek. As you drive west on County Road 380, you see the William Burch "dug-out" on the right side of the road. In 1874, Burch created a home in the ground here. He first dug a hole and built the walls, then filled in the hole and built a stone arched roof over the dirt, and, finally, excavated the dirt again.

Continue past the "dug-out" to the next intersection and turn left (south). Drive south about .7 mile and take the road approaching from the right on the diagonal. You will come to One Hundred Forty Two Mile Creek, which is the distance from Fort Osage as measured by George Sibley in 1825. In 1854, the original town of Allen was sited on the east side of the creek by Charles Hall Withington. He made six or seven one-room additions to his original cabin, which he rented to travelers along the trail. A saloon and store quickly followed nearby.

Withington must have been proslavery, for the town was robbed and burned by "Free Staters" in 1856. Later, the rebuilt town had a blacksmith shop with ten forges where repairs were made on trail wagons. Here there was once a wooden toll bridge, located about 150 feet downstream from the present bridge, that charged 25¢ per wagon. It is claimed that a primitive sail-driven "wind wagon" crossed this bridge in 1859. Gearing to the wheels of the wind wagon allowed forward movement under a stiff breeze.

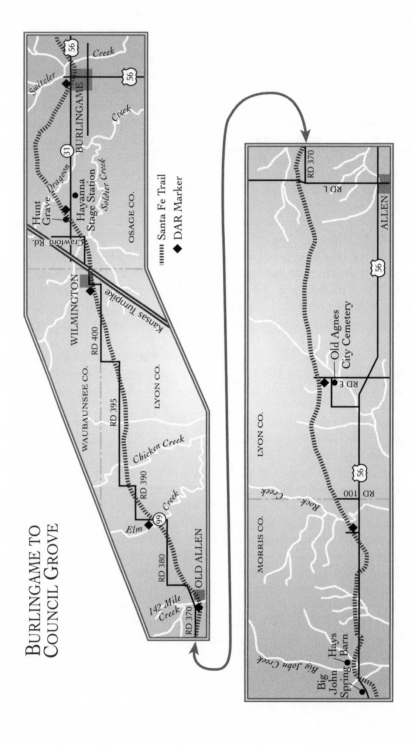

BURLINGAME TO
COUNCIL GROVE

Old Allen moved to its present location on US 56 (2.5 miles south) in 1886 when the railroad bypassed it.

As you leave the site of Old Allen, there is a DAR marker on the west side of 142 Mile Creek. At the next intersection (Road L), turn left (south) and drive to Allen. At Allen, on US 56, turn right (west) and go about 6 miles to Road E. Turn right (north) at Road E and drive about 1.8 miles to the Agnes City Cemetery on your left. A DAR marker is in the cemetery, which is all that remains of Agnes City. Return south to US 56, then turn right (west).

Continue to the next road (Road 200) and turn right again. A short distance on the right (.2 mile) is a another DAR marker. The trail crossed in this vicinity as it headed toward Council Grove. Return to US 56 and turn right toward Council Grove.

On your left along US 56, you will see on the hill black metal silhouettes of "Indians on the Move," placed by the Community Arts Council of Council Grove. All four routes into Council Grove are marked by unique silhouettes. The Flint Hills Chapter of the Santa Fe Trail Association is also very active in locating sites, restoring buildings, and protecting the trail in this area.

Approaching Council Grove, travelers enter the region of the Flint Hills and the prairie grasslands. Here is one of the largest remaining tracts of tallgrass prairie (consisting mainly of bluestem grass) in the Midwest. In trail days leaves of the bluestem grew 3 feet tall, and the seed stems reached 8 feet. In 1846, Susan Magoffin compared the grass to "a waving sea of green" (Magoffin 1982).

At 1 mile from Council Grove, turn off US 56 into the Morris County Fairgrounds. Big John Spring is located under the berm on the south side of US 56 here. The spring, no longer visible, was discovered in 1827 by Big John Walker, a member of the Sibley survey team. The explorer John Charles Fremont stopped here in July 1844 as did Stephen Watts Kearny in 1846.

Continue driving in the fairgrounds until you see a beautiful large, stone barn. Built in 1871 by Seth Hays, Council Grove's first white settler, it is on the National Register of Historic Places. The Flint Hills Chapter of the SFTA is supervising the barn's restoration.

Return to US 56 and continue west toward Council Grove.

COUNCIL GROVE

Council Grove, on the Neosho River, is one of the most historic places on the SFT. It was a natural stop on the route to New Mexico, well-watered with plenty of pasture and timber. Past this point no hardwood trees grew on the plains so spare axles were cut along the Neosho and stored under the wagons for later use. Here caravans also organized their military defenses, for they

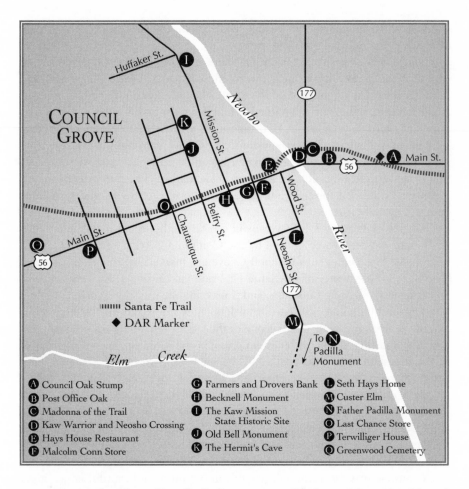

were now on the edge of hostile Indian country. Modern visitors should read Josiah Gregg's description of Council Grove during the heyday of the Santa Fe trade (Gregg 1990).

The site was named by Commissioner George Sibley in 1825 when he made a treaty with the Osage Indians guaranteeing safe passage for wagon trains and providing a right of way to Santa Fe. During the Mexican War, the army built a wagon repair depot here. A few years later, when stagecoach service began on the SFT, the firm of Waldo, Hall and Company operated a station, shops, and corrals.

Much of the traffic on this portion of the SFT ended about 1866 with the building of the Kansas Pacific Railroad 50 miles to the north. From Junction City, the railhead, freight went by wagon to Lost Spring some 20 miles west of Council Grove to connect with the SFT.

The following places can be located on the included map.

A. COUNCIL OAK STUMP
On the right just beyond the junction of Main and 3rd Streets, a jagged stump is all that remains of the famous Council Oak, which blew down in 1958. The tree was purported to be the one under which Sibley signed his treaty with the Osage Indians. The "stump shrine" is now covered by a roof and surrounded by an iron fence. An interpretive historical sign, a special DAR marker, and the Registered National Historic Landmark plaque for Council Grove are also at the site.

B. POST OFFICE OAK
Located on Main Street one and a half blocks past the Council Oak stump on the right (north) is Post Office Oak. SFT travelers are said to have left letters in a crevice at the bottom of the tree, which were picked up and carried back to the States by returning caravans. A nice museum is located behind the stump, all that is left of the Post Office Oak.

C. MADONNA OF THE TRAIL
Kansas's Madonna of the Trail is located in Madonna Park on the right of US 56/Main Street just beyond Post Office Oak and facing the Neosho Bridge. This statue of the Pioneer Mother, placed by the DAR in 1928, is a duplicate of the one already noted in Lexington, Missouri. The park is on part of the old SFT campground at the Neosho Crossing.

D. KAW WARRIOR AND NEOSHO CROSSING
The Guardian of the Grove Statue was recently installed as a companion to the Madonna of the Trail statue across the street, adjacent to the Neosho Bridge. It was created by local artist Mark Sampsel. The original trail crossing is just upstream from the bridge, with the natural rock bed clearly discernible from the bridge. Stands of giant hardwoods, used by early travelers for spare axles and wagon tongues, can still be found on the river both north and south of town.

A statue of a Kaw warrior near the Neosho River in Council Grove, Kansas.

E. HAYS HOUSE RESTAURANT

Hays House Restaurant is located one-half block west of the Neosho Bridge at 112 Main Street. Seth Hays, a great-grandson of Daniel Boone and a cousin of Kit Carson, in 1847 became the first white settler at Council Grove. He established a trading post for the neighboring Kaw Indians, and, in 1857, built this tavern and hostelry to serve wayfarers on the SFT. According to a popular story, he hired a bagpiper to play from the outside balcony of his place to draw customers. The building was also used as a district court, a place for church services, and the site for publication of an early newspaper.

Although it has been remodeled, some of the interior fabric is original, including stone walls and a large walnut beam that can be seen in the basement, and a hand-hewn beam mantelpiece in the dining area. On the wall near the outside entrance, is one of the oval SFT signs of the American Pioneer Trails Association, as well as an ox yoke. The Hays House is a fine restaurant, open six days a week (closed Monday at the time of writing), and a boon to modern travelers on the trail. It claims to be the oldest eating establishment west of the Mississippi.

F. MALCOLM CONN STORE

Across the street from the Hays House Restaurant at the corner of Main and Neosho Streets is the old Malcolm Conn Store. Built in 1858 by a local merchant of that name, it was one of the two most important stores in Council Grove. It has been modified, but the west side of the structure will give you an idea of its original shape.

G. FARMERS AND DROVERS BANK

Across the side street from the Conn Store, on the southwest corner of Main and Neosho Streets, is the Farmers and Drovers Bank. This building occupies the site of Waldo, Hall and Company's log depot and warehouse for its mail wagons to Santa Fe.

H. BECKNELL MONUMENT

At the southwest corner of Main and Mission Streets on the library lawn is the Becknell Monument, a monument and plaque commemorating the 100th anniversary (in 1921) of William Becknell's first pack train to Santa Fe. The monument is not mentioned in local historical guides. Behind it, a large cornerstone set in the library building has an inscription about the SFT Indian treaty of 1825.

I. THE KAW MISSION STATE HISTORIC SITE

From the corner of Main and Mission Streets, drive north five blocks to Huffaker Street. The Kaw Mission is on the right. This beautiful two-story

A small house of the type used by Kaw Indians near Council Grove, Kansas.

native stone structure was built in the winter of 1850–1851, and it first served as a school for children of the Kaw (or Kansas) Indians, upon whose reservation Council Grove was founded. After 1854, it became the school for local white children. As the most imposing building in Council Grove, the mission often accommodated prominent travelers in the later days of the SFT. Now a state museum, it has some trail relics on display.

On the grounds is a stone house built by the government for Kaw families. The house was moved from its original site 3.5 miles southeast of Council Grove on Big John Creek, while other houses and a commissary building for the Kaw Indians are still there. Directions to that site can be obtained at the Chamber of Commerce (212 West Main Street in Council Grove). It is said that the Kaw stabled their horses in the stone houses, preferring to live in their native lodges. Also on the mission grounds is one of the new Mormon Battalion markers.

J. OLD BELL MONUMENT

Go west on US 56, turn right on Belfry, and continue two blocks to the Old Bell Monument. The bell was brought to Council Grove in 1863, and was erected on a tower at this site in 1866. It served as an alarm, school, and church bell for nearly thirty years.

K. THE HERMIT'S CAVE

Two blocks north of Main on Belfry Street, just past the Old Bell Monument is the Hermit's Cave. In this small cave for a brief period in the early 1860s lived a religious mystic, Giovanni Maria Augustini, who was closely associated with the SFT. Born in Italy in 1801, the son of a nobleman, he lived in caves in South America and Canada before coming to Council Grove. In 1863, the hermit approached the wagon train of wealthy merchant Don Eugenio Romero of Las Vegas and asked to be allowed to accompany it to New Mexico, subsequently walking beside the caravan the entire 550 miles over the SFT. (His fate in New Mexico is described later under "Las Vegas.")

L. SETH HAYS HOME
Another interesting building is Seth Hays's residence, located two blocks south of Main on Wood Street, just across the railroad tracks on the right. Built in 1867, this neat brick house is now the museum of the Morris County Historical Society, open in the summer and by appointment. Hays never married, but he did adopt a daughter in 1867. Hays's slave, Aunt Sally, lived in the basement of the residence and cared for the family until her death in 1872. She is buried in Greenwood Cemetery. There is a bronze plaque on the corner of the building.

M. CUSTER ELM
Five blocks south of Main, on Neosho Street at the bridge over Elm Creek is the Custer Elm. At one time the tree was 100 feet high, but it lost its top some time ago, and only the trunk remains. In 1867, George Armstrong Custer camped under this tree while pursuing hostile Indians. Events in Custer's life were associated with the SFT at several locations in Kansas. About the time Custer searched for Indians, he and his wife purchased property near here that was part of his estate at the time of his death.

N. FATHER PADILLA MONUMENT
Go south on Neosho Street from the Custer Elm. After three blocks the road starts up a hill. Halfway to the top of the hill turn right on a small gravel road and go .7 mile. At the third turn in the road, is a gate on the right, and beyond the fence is the tall pyramidal Father Padilla Monument on a hill. A member of the Coronado Expedition of 1540–1542, Father Juan de Padilla remained in Kansas to minister to the Indians but was soon martyred. This is the first of at least five monuments and markers scattered along the SFT to commemorate his passing. Although this monument claims to be the site of his death and burial, the exact site is not known.

O. LAST CHANCE STORE
The Last Chance Store is located on the northwest corner of Main and Chautauqua Streets. A small stone building erected in 1857, and the oldest

The Last Chance Store in Council Grove, Kansas, with interpretive marker in the foreground.

commercial building in Council Grove, it later served as a post office and government trading post. Closed now, its name derives from the fact that for a time it was said to be the last place where supplies could be obtained between Council Grove and Santa Fe. An interpretive historical sign is on the grounds.

P. TERWILLIGER HOUSE
Located at 803 West Main Street, the Terwilliger House was built in 1861 and would have been the last house the SFT traders viewed as they departed Council Grove.

Q. GREENWOOD CEMETERY
The Greenwood Cemetery, established in 1862, is located on West Main Street past the Terwilliger House on the north side of Main Street. After entering the main gate go straight up the lane to a small house. Seth Hays (1811–1873) is buried under a tall white column to the right. Next to his grave is the broken tombstone of Sarah Taylor (Aunt Sally), Hays's ex-slave, who after her liberation remained with his family.

Kansas
Diamond Spring,
Fort Larned, and the Caches

From the Terwilliger House, drive west on US 56 4.4 miles to a DAR marker on the right, about where the trail crossed the highway from the north headed for Diamond Spring. Continue on US 56 about 1.2 miles to County Road 1400. Turn left (south) and drive .6 mile. The trail crossed the road here, and ruts can be seen on the west side. Spring is likely the best time to view them.

Continue south on County Road 1400 .4 mile to the next section road, V Avenue, turn right on V, and continue 4 miles to the village of Wilsey. Drive west on North Street about .5 mile, and a school will be on the right. At the right side of the entrance, is an oval SFT sign. Such signs were placed by the American Pioneer Trails Association at schools along the trail, but this may be the only one in its original location.

Return to US 56 by going west from the school to the next section road, turn right, and then go north 1 mile to the highway.

DIAMOND SPRING

This famous spring, a day's wagon journey west of Council Grove, was mentioned in the accounts of many trail travelers, including Josiah Gregg, Susan Magoffin, and Marian Russell. In 1825, Commissioner Sibley likened the

Attached to a school in Wilsey, Kansas, is one of the last original American Pioneer Trail Association markers placed in 1948.

rushing water to the "Diamond of the Desert," a celebrated spring in Arabia. In 1849, Waldo, Hall and Company built a stage station at the site. Both Kearny's army and the Mormon Battalion camped here on their way west.

To get to Diamond Spring, not to be confused with Diamond Spring Post Office and community shown on some maps, drive west on US 56 3 miles. KS 149 is to your right here, but turn left (south) on County Road 2200 and drive just over 2 miles. There is a road coming in from the right just past the section road that will take you to the Diamond Spring Ranch headquarters. From the entrance of the ranch, drive about 1 mile to a large house, where permission should be sought to visit the spring.

To the right of the house is a barn and a road that turns left in front of it. Just after the turn, on the left, is Diamond Spring and a DAR marker a few feet above it on a knoll under a tree. The spring has been contained in a concrete housing. Kate Gregg in *The Road to Santa Fe* commented on how disappointing it was that the spring was "contained" by concrete and pipes, stating that the most famous spring in Kansas ought to be a state shrine. We can't argue with her. However, the spring is still worth visiting. Given the amount of water flowing from this spring, it is no wonder most travelers commented on it. Sibley wrote:

Six Mile Creek Stage Station ruins west of Diamond Spring, Kansas.

"It is uncommonly large and beautiful, and the water very pure and cold. I have seldom seen so fine a Spring anywhere" (Gregg 1995).

In 1857, when the Government Land Office surveyor came through here he mentioned in his notes that there was a corral immediately to the west of the spring and the Diamond Hotel 100 feet to the north, which would place the hotel just north and west of the present-day barn. The base of a stone corral was visible until a few years ago when it was covered over with dirt.

Return to US 56 and continue west. Past Delavan is a paved crossroad, County Road 2800 that leads south to Burdick. Turn left toward Burdick and go 4.1 miles to a bridge over Six Mile Creek. At .1 mile past the bridge on the left (east), is a DAR marker. Park next to it and walk through deserted farm buildings on a lane leading 150 yards to the SFT crossing of Six Mile Creek. The next stream to the east is Three Mile Creek, and east of that, One and A Half Mile Creek. The names, given by wagon masters, were based on distances from Diamond Spring.

The Six Mile Creek Post Office was established here in 1863, by which time there was already a stage station. In 1865, brothers Frank and William Hartwell bought the station for $2,000. Later, in 1866, Charlie Owens established his Six Mile Ranch here, but two years later a war party of Cheyennes burned it to the ground while he and his wife were absent. If you walk though the ruins and cross the creek, you can see nice ruts to the north of the dirt track.

Return to US 56.

FORT RILEY

Continue west on US 56 to the junction with US 77. From here a side trip can be made 25 miles north on US 77 to Fort Riley and Junction City. One of the functions of the fort, founded in 1853 at the junction of the Republican and Smokey Hill Rivers, was to provide military protection for the SFT to the south. It was named for Gen. Bennet Riley, a Mexican War hero and leader of the first military escort along the SFT in 1829.

Fort Riley remains an active post. An official Kansas Historical Marker, with reference to the SFT, is in a roadside turnout on the grounds. Of chief interest at the fort is the U.S. Army Horse Cavalry Museum, which includes some SFT exhibits. Associated with the museum is the Custer House, dating from 1854. It was long thought that Custer resided in this house, but recent research has shown that he, in fact, lived in a sister house that was later destroyed by fire. Lt. Col. and Mrs. George Armstrong Custer were stationed at the fort in 1866.

Also in 1866, the Union Pacific Railroad reached neighboring Junction City, which then became the railhead and starting point of the SFT for a brief period. The Woolworth and Barton Overland Transportation Line built a large warehouse next to the railroad depot and in January 1867 dispatched its first wagon train to Santa Fe, the shipment destined for the Spiegelberg Brothers. The wagons angled southwest from Junction City to meet the SFT at Lost Spring in Marion County. As the Union Pacific advanced westward across Kansas, the starting point of the SFT moved with it.

HERINGTON

Return to the junction of US 56 and US 77 on the main route of the SFT. Here US 56/US 77 turns south. Before taking it, however, go west on the highway to Herington. When a main thoroughfare (Broadway) crosses the road, turn right (north) on it. Drive .7 mile along Broadway, which has a grass median strip here, past the swimming pool, and before a bridge turn left into Father Padilla Memorial Park. At the back of the circle drive, is a tall sandstone obelisk commemorating the death of Father Padilla (see section "Council Grove" for another Padilla monument).

Return again to the junction of US 56 and US 77, then go south 1.5 miles to a turnout on the right. Here is an official Kansas Historical Marker with text on the Coronado Expedition, which is believed to have followed part of the route of the later SFT.

LOST SPRING

About 5 miles south of the Coronado marker on US 56/US 77, a SFT crossing sign is on the right (west), marking the spot where the SFT, coming from Diamond Spring and heading for Lost Spring, crossed the highway. In the weeds on the left (east) side of the highway, is a DAR marker, while a tall silo with a red and white top is just beyond on the right.

Continue south on US 56/US 77 and cross the railroad tracks. Just beyond them, a sign points to a paved county road leading 1 mile to the modern community of Lost Springs. Turn right (west) on this road, called Chicago. Entering the small community, turn right on the first gravel street (Main) that intersects from the north. Drive one block to the municipal park. On the west side of the park, is a DAR marker with a bronze plaque like the ones noted at Olathe and Gardner.

Return one block to the paved county road and turn right (west). Continue along that street to Berry Street. At Berry turn right (north) and drive several blocks toward the railroad tracks. Just before the tracks, a sign on the left indicates where the SFT crossed the street. Return to the paved county road and again turn right (west).

Go one block to the next intersection (Jefferson), make a right turn, and drive north one block. Here on the northwest corner is a waist-high limestone monument that reads "Santa Fe Trail, July 4, 1908." This is one of three home-made monuments installed in the area on that date by local resident Dan McNicol.

Return to the paved county road, turn right, and go west 2.3 miles to the original Lost Spring on the SFT. Although less renowned in trail days than Diamond Spring, it is now far better preserved, more accessible, and one of the most scenic spots on the eastern leg of the SFT. On the south (left) side of the road surrounded by a pipe railing, is a large DAR-like granite marker, placed there in 1908 by the Marion County Old Settlers. Across the road on the north, is a historical interpretive sign that says erroneously that the Pony Express used this spring.

Behind the marker you can find Lost Spring, which was called "lost" because it would occasionally dry up and disappear. The creek here is named Cress Creek, and the spring enters on the east side of the creek. Early geologists declared that the water originated in the Rockies and followed a fault line to this location. Wagon travelers claimed it tasted like mountain water. In the late 1840s, the army planted watercress and strawberries around the spring hoping soldiers on patrol would eat them as a preventative to scurvy. Although the berries disappeared many years ago, the watercress still grows.

In 1859, George Smith built a stage station, hotel, and tavern here. The station, with its sod roof, was on a knoll southeast of the present county road. Late

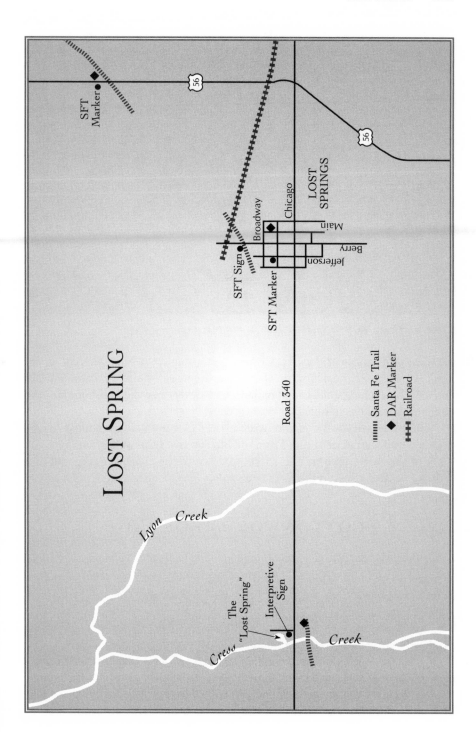

LOST SPRING

Lyon Creek

Cress Creek

The "Lost Spring"

Interpretive Sign

Road 340

Santa Fe Trail
DAR Marker
Railroad

SFT Marker

SFT Sign

SFT Marker

Broadway
Chicago
Main
Berry
Jefferson

LOST SPRINGS

56

56

Cress Creek at the point where Lost Spring feeds it.

the same year, a soldier, Jack H. Costello, returning from New Mexico on the SFT, won the station from Smith in a card game. The place subsequently became a haven for gamblers and outlaws, and eleven men died in shootouts and were buried near the station.

The SFT crossed the county road at the DAR marker and angled southwest down to a creek crossing. From the interpretive sign, walk about 50 yards south of the road to see trail ruts leading down to the creek in a diagonal line with the DAR marker, in the form of a swale.

COTTONWOOD CROSSING

From the Lost Spring site, continue west on the paved county road 2.6 miles to a paved crossroad with a dirt road straight ahead. Turn left (south), and go .7 mile to a marker on the right, behind a barbed wire fence. This marker, although appearing to be a DAR marker, was placed by School District 90. The SFT crossed the road here, and the marker sits in faint ruts extending diagonally toward the trees behind it.

Continue south another .3 mile to an intersection. Then turn west (right) on a gravel road toward Tampa, 5 miles. After a railroad crossing, continue to the next intersection on the edge of Tampa, where the pavement begins. The SFT crossed the road just before the intersection, and faint ruts can be seen in

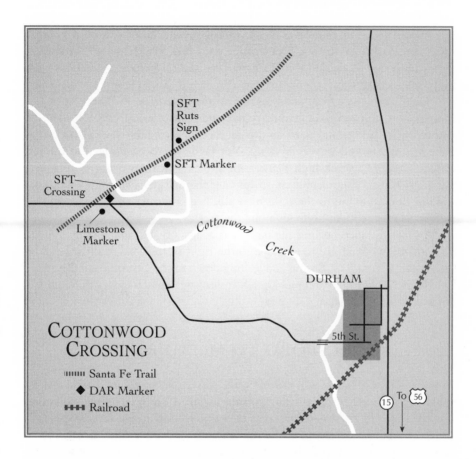

SFT
Ruts
Sign

SFT Marker

SFT
Crossing

Limestone
Marker

Cottonwood

Creek

DURHAM

5th St.

COTTONWOOD
CROSSING

iiiiiii Santa Fe Trail
◆ DAR Marker
▬▬ Railroad

15   To 56

the cemetery on the right. Just beyond on the southwest corner is a large marker with extensive text, which looks like a DAR marker but was placed here by the Marion County Old Settlers.

Continue straight ahead (west) 4 miles to join KS 15, then turn left (south) toward Durham. At 1.5 to 2 miles after entering KS 15, the SFT, coming from Lost Spring and heading for Cottonwood Creek, crosses the highway, marked by a small sign. Long ruts of the trail can be seen in the grassy field on the west (right) side of the highway.

Continue to the small community of Durham, about 3 miles south. Turn right (west) off the highway into the center of town, then take the one paved county road leading west. It begins as 5th Street at the southern end of downtown. As 5th leaves town, it crosses a bridge and beyond turns to the right (north), then left (west), and then right (north) again. You will see Cottonwood Creek to your right along here. Continue until you reach a paved road coming in from the right (east).

At that location there is a DAR marker on the northwest corner and a limestone marker on the south side of the road. The trail crossed Cottonwood Creek immediately behind the DAR marker. Several parties of travelers were hit by blizzards at this spot. Susan Magoffin mentions it at length in her diary.

Turn onto the paved road and continue east to a T. There turn left (north), now a gravel road, and drive over the Cottonwood Creek Bridge. As you cross the bridge and head up the gentle hill, look left to see the approximate area of the old wagon crossing. Not far beyond the bridge, on the left under a tree, is a waist-high marker for the SFT with two bronze plaques, placed by Kansas schoolchildren. In summer the marker is surrounded by poison ivy. Behind it and to the right on a hill, lives a farmer who has plowed up numerous trail relics in his fields along the creek.

A short distance beyond the marker is a sign on the right stating: "Santa Fe Trail Ruts." Behind it on a slope to the right of the road, trail ruts can be seen coming from Lost Spring and leading down to the Cottonwood Crossing.

Return to Durham and pick up KS 15 leading south 10 miles to rejoin US 56, which then goes west.

HILLSBORO TO McPHERSON

At the junction of KS 15 and US 56, a side trip is recommended 1 mile east on US 56 to Hillsboro, one of the tidiest and most energetic small towns in Kansas. Entering the town from the west, watch for the sign directing you to the Adobe House Museum, on the town's south side. A granite marker commemorating the SFT and the Chisholm Trail is in the yard of the museum. The museum contains a small trail exhibit. The Adobe House was built in 1876 by Mennonite immigrants from Russia, who settled this area. The furnished rooms contain splendid examples of their folk culture.

Continue one block past the museum on US 56 and turn left (north) on Main Street. At 102 Main, on the corner, is the Chamber of Commerce offering maps and brochures on points of historic interest. One block beyond on the east side of Main Street is a fine two-story building completed in 1887. Now called Olde Towne, it contains interesting shops. Across the street is a bookshop with a good selection of titles on Mennonite history. If you are interested, check with the Chamber of Commerce for the dates of the annual Folk Festival in late May and Arts and Crafts Fair in September. Return west on US 56 toward McPherson.

At about 9 miles west of Hillsboro, watch for the sign indicating the Marion-McPherson County line. Turn right here to a marker about 50 yards to the north that commemorates the SFT and the Chisholm Trail, which intersected just north of this spot. It includes a very nice map showing the routes of both trails.

At .5 mile beyond the Marion-McPherson County line, the SFT crossed US 56. At 1 mile from the county line, turn right (north) on a gravel road. (This intersection on US 56 is about 2 miles east of Canton.) Go north on the gravel road .5 mile to an abandoned railway bed. Just before that track turn east (right) on a dirt lane (in fair weather only) and go about .25 mile to the Jones Cemetery on a rise surrounded by trees and hedges. This road is now posted, and for entrance you are advised to contact the "Olsons" in Canton (2 miles west of the cemetery). In the center of the cemetery near a large dead tree, is a DAR marker, and next to it the gravestone of eighteen-year-old Ed Miller, a mail courier (not a Pony Express rider) killed on the SFT in 1864 by Cheyennes. Return to US 56 and continue west.

Watch for the Canton junction, with a sign pointing north to Canton. At 5 miles west of the junction, US 56 intersects with paved County Road 307. Turn left (south) and go 2 miles to a tall white brick monument on the left (east). A bronze plaque marks the Running Turkey Creek Campground on the SFT. This was also the site of Fuller's Ranch, the first settlement in McPherson County, established in 1855. Return to US 56.

McPHERSON

Approaching the eastern limits of McPherson, leave US 56 and drive 7 miles north on Interstate 135 to a roadside park located in the wide median of the highway. There are two separate units of the park, one for northbound traffic and the other for southbound. Turn left into the first unit, drive to the rear, and take a small road that leads to the second unit. Here is one of the newly installed Mormon Battalion markers. Also note the trail map, "Historical Kansas," on the building adjacent to the marker.

Return to McPherson and pick up US 56. At Main Street turn left (south). Continue south past the refinery on your right to the stop sign. The crossroad here is the Old 81 Highway (a sign also says County Road 2043). Turn left here toward Elyria. One-half mile from the intersection is about where the Dry Turkey Creek Crossing was located. Drive on to the little community of Elyria. At .5 mile beyond Elyria, on the right (west) side of the highway, is a turnout with a DAR marker for Sora Kansas Creek, the earlier name for Dry Turkey Creek. On the front of the marker is the usual DAR inscription, but on the back is the following: "Sora Kansas Creek. Near this spot August 16, 1825 the Treaty was made with the Kansas Indians for the right of way of the Trail." Unfortunately, this marker is not where it was originally placed by the

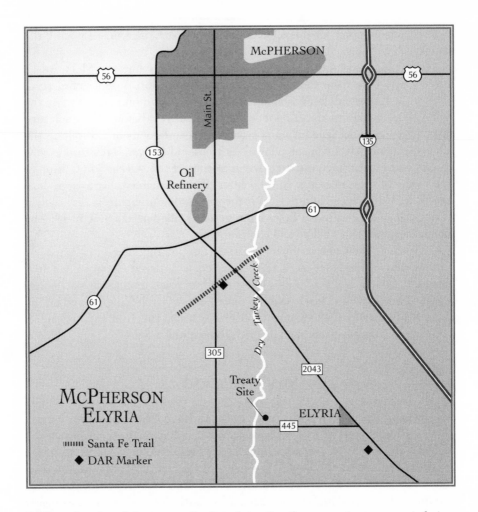

DAR at the site of the treaty signing about 2 miles away. An attempt is being made to return the marker to the treaty site.

To get to the actual site, return toward McPherson. Then as you enter Elyria turn half-left onto County Road 445. After driving about 1.5 miles on County Road 445, the site will be in the field to the right.

Continue on County Road 445 past Dry Turkey Creek to the first section road and turn right on County Road 305 (north). Two miles north is the McPherson DAR marker on the right (east) side of the road. There is also a sign saying, "Santa Fe Trail Crossed Here" on the west side of the road. This road continues north toward McPherson, becoming Main Street. It is easier to turn left at Old 81 Highway, which becomes KS 153, and drive north to meet US 56, west of McPherson. When you reach US 56, head west.

LITTLE ARKANSAS CROSSING

The crossing of the Little Arkansas River was a spot well known to early team-sters and merchants, for although it was comparatively small it had a muddy bot-tom and steep banks. There were actually two crossings about .5 mile apart. The SFT split several miles to the east, drivers taking the fork leading to whichever crossing their scouts reported was in the best condition. A short distance beyond the Little Arkansas the two branches came together to form one trail again. The north crossing, or what we call the Upper Crossing, was the older and more important. In trail days there was no thick lining of timber as now, but there was one large "marker cottonwood" that could be seen far out on the plains that guided wagons to the Upper Crossing. Today, that cottonwood still stands on the east side of the ford, with a huge trunk that forks into two smaller trunks at about the height of a man.

About 1865, a notable landmark, the Stone Corral, was built on the west bank near the Lower Crossing. The structure, which was 200 by 400 feet and had 30-inch-thick walls 8 feet high, not only held livestock but doubled as a fort. Nearby was a stage station and a toll bridge, erected in 1858. In the 1880s, after abandonment of the SFT, local residents hauled away the quarried stone from the corral, and no trace remains today.

To get to the Little Arkansas Crossing, which Stocking described in *Road to Santa Fe*, go west from McPherson on US 56 to Windom (which is actually off to the right .5 mile). A mile beyond the Windom turnoff, paved County Road 443 (Plum Avenue), which is on the county line, crosses US 56. Turn left (south) and drive exactly 5 miles to an intersection. (Note: County roads here are laid out on a grid with intersections 1 mile apart; thus you will pass four crossroads before reaching the 5-mile intersection.) At this point, on the southeast corner, is a DAR marker and sign pointing west to the Stone Corral. This DAR marker is actually the one originally placed at Dry Turkey Creek Crossing south of McPherson but was moved here many years ago.

At this intersection turn west (right) as the sign directs. Go .7 mile to a small dirt road that turns to the left just before the bridge over the Little Arkansas River. A hand-lettered sign on a pipe frame (put up by the property owner) says "Stone Corral" and gives a brief history. However, the corral was not here but across the county road and west of the river. Behind the sign are some depressions reputed to be the remains of trenches dug by troops of Col. George Armstrong Custer when he was here guarding the ford briefly in the 1860s. This is just another location Custer wasn't! Instead, a troop of the 10th U.S. Cavalry (the Buffalo Soldiers) stationed here fought several skirmishes with Indians and maintained what was called Camp Grierson.

Continue down the small dirt road a short distance to a sign on the right:

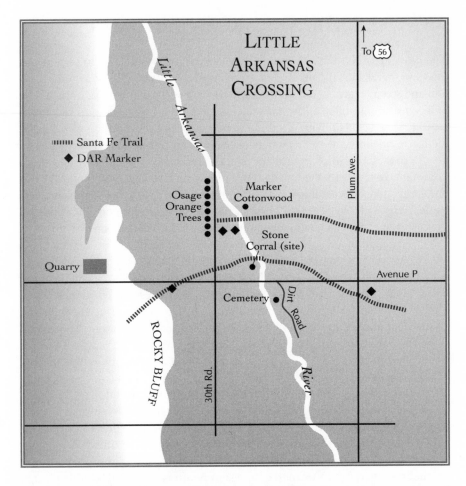

"Cottonwood Grove Cemetery." Depressions behind the sign are remains of graves of soldiers who were killed by Indians while stationed at the crossing. Later their bodies were removed to Fort Leavenworth Cemetery. The small picnic area at the graves is private. For permission to use it, see the farmer whose house is to the east across the fields.

Return to the county road and continue west across the bridge over the Little Arkansas. Just beyond the bridge, on the right, turn onto a new access road leading to a gas well out in the field. To the right toward the river, note a low mound with some small trees on the north end, in the middle of the field. The Stone Corral is thought to have been in the field immediately north of the mound. Stone for the construction of the corral was likely quarried about 1 mile west of the site. When the corral no longer had a use, the corral's rock was sold to locals for a variety of purposes, including the construction of a nearby school.

From the access road, return to the county road and go west to the next intersection. Continue straight ahead .4 mile to a DAR marker on the left (south) side of the road, the "Stone Corral" marker. Past this marker turn left through the first gate leading into pastureland. At .1 mile from the gate, the SFT crosses the road with the deepest ruts to the left (east). A small iron cross is in one of the ruts.

Return to the last intersection and go north to another DAR marker on the right (east) side of the road. It is a replacement for an older marker that had a bronze plaque, which was later stolen. The original marker was placed in 1929 by the Sterling Chapter of the DAR. The plaque eventually turned up at a farm sale and is now preserved in the museum at Lyons. From this point there is another DAR marker .5 mile east, across from the Upper Crossing. Placed in 1929 by the Uvedale Chapter of the DAR, this marker is barely discernible just in front of the cottonwoods. Also from this location you can pick out the "marker cottonwood," which during trail days was used to find the Upper Crossing.

Here on the west side of the road is a line of Osage orange trees. One of the early conditions for homesteading was that the farmer plant such rows of trees to serve as a windbreak and provide firewood.

Return to US 56 and turn left (west) toward Lyons.

CHÁVEZ MARKER

At 9 miles west of the McPherson-Rice County line (where you headed south to the crossings of the Little Arkansas), is 22nd Road. Turn left (south) here, drive 2 miles, turn right (west), and go 2 more miles. Turn left (south) and go about 2.3 miles to a DAR marker on the left (east) side of the road. It may be difficult to locate in the tall grass.

This marker was placed for the Jarvis (Chávez) Creek Crossing, which is .5 mile east on Jarvis Creek. The name Jarvis is a corruption of Chávez. There was also a short-lived town near here called Jarvis View. José Antonio Chávez was traveling east on the SFT with five servants, one wagon, five mules, and a considerable amount of money ($10,000). Fifteen men from Missouri under the command of John McDaniel intercepted Chávez somewhere east of here (likely near the crossing of the Little Arkansas). These bandits had come west specifically to rob Mexican merchants, and after robbing Chávez they marched him west and killed him somewhere near this spot. Most of the fifteen men were eventually apprehended, and two were hanged for his murder.

Return north to the next section road, where you can turn left (west). Continue west 4 miles to the intersection of paved KS 14. Then turn right toward Lyons.

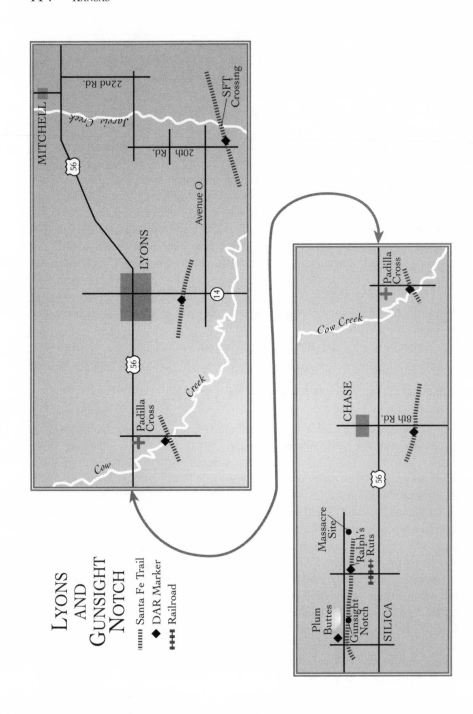

LYONS
AND
GUNSIGHT
NOTCH

▦ Santa Fe Trail
◆ DAR Marker
╊╍╊ Railroad

LYONS

At .5 mile watch for an oversized marker erected by the Sterling Chapter of the DAR, on the left (west) side of the highway and between two large evergreen bushes. Continue north toward Lyons. At the intersection with US 56, turn left (west) and go one block to Courthouse Square.

The Coronado-Quivira Museum is located at 105 West Lyon, one block south of the courthouse. This excellent facility contains exhibits relating, among other things, to the Coronado Expedition and the SFT.

FATHER PADILLA CROSS AND COW CREEK CROSSING

Four miles west of Lyons on the south side of US 56 is a small roadside park with a 30-foot marble cross honoring the Coronado Expedition's well-traveled friar, Father Padilla. Also in the park is an official Kansas Historical Marker with a text describing Coronado's search for Quivira and, next to it, a Rice County Historical Society sign for the Cow Creek Station on the SFT. In the plowed field behind the cross was once a huge Quivira Indian village.

On the east edge of the park is a gravel road running south to Buffalo Bill's Well and Cow Creek. Follow this county road 1 mile to the well-marked site. Next to the well, which is covered by a shelter, is an interpretive sign and a DAR marker. Just beyond, the bridge over Cow Creek is very near the original crossing of the SFT.

Cow Creek marked the boundary between the tallgrass country on the east and the shortgrass prairie stretching westward, the latter being the prize range of the buffalo. Because the site was also on the margin of hostile Indian country, beginning in the 1850s soldiers were often stationed at the crossing to protect passing caravans. Their flagpole is said to have been placed on a low hill just north of the well.

Beginning in the 1850s, Buffalo Bill Mathewson operated a trading post and ranch at the

The Father Padilla Cross on
US 56 near Lyons, Kansas.

crossing. (His grave is in Highland Cemetery, Wichita.) Mathewson built a toll bridge here in 1858, and for a time a youth named William Cody worked for him. Later, when Cody served as a hunter for the Kansas Pacific Railroad, supplying meat for the construction crews, he also took the nickname Buffalo Bill.

In July 1864, this was the site of a five-day siege by Kiowas, which ended when Mathewson discharged a small cannon in their direction.

Return to US 56 and turn left (west). At 4 miles the town of Chase is off to the right of the highway. Turn left (south) here on 8th Road. Drive south 1 mile, and you will see a DAR marker on the west side, directly on the trail. Return to US 56 and turn left (west).

PLUM BUTTES

Midway between Cow Creek and Fort Zarah was the Plum Buttes noon stop. The so-called buttes were really sand hills surrounded by plum thickets. About 100 feet higher than their surroundings and easily noted by travelers, they could be seen shortly after the crossing at Cow Creek. Wagons paused here for lunch, even though there was no water or firewood. Today, the buttes are still in evidence, although difficult to recognize.

Four miles west of Chase on US 56, a blacktop road crosses the highway. Approaching the intersection, a sign points south (left) to the town of Raymond. At the intersection is a small white sign pointing north to Salem Methodist Church. Here, turn north (right) on the blacktop. At about .25 mile cross a railroad track, and after another .5 mile watch for a small sign on the right reading: "Original Santa Fe Trail Crossed Here." Beautiful ruts in the form of a deep swale are visible on the east (right) side of the road. They have been carefully preserved by the owner, Ralph Hathaway. There is a new DAR marker at the site.

It was on the Hathaway farm that the famous Huning, or Plum Buttes, Massacre occurred in September 1867. Franz Huning of Albuquerque was traveling west on the trail escorting his mother-in-law and others to New Mexico. Apparently, the train was a single column caravan traveling through tall grass when Indians attacked, cutting off the last four wagons, murdering Huning's mother-in-law and her son, and taking mules, which they packed up with stolen goods. As they left they set fire to the prairie, forcing Huning's remaining wagons to flee. Huning knew of the danger here and had requested an escort from the Buffalo Soldiers stationed at the Little Arkansas Crossing, but he had been turned down.

Continue straight ahead (north) to the next intersection. Turn left (west) and go 1.5 miles to a high point in the road. The trail is visible to your left along this road. From this high point you can see "Gunsight Notch" to the left, which David Clapsaddle of Larned believes is the route of the trail as it skirted the buttes. This high point may be on one of the remnants of the Plum Buttes, unmarked but recognizable as low sand hills. Originally, the buttes were over 100 feet high, with no timber to obstruct the view as is the case now. Look for the wild plum bushes still growing along the road and at the base of the buttes.

Drive to the next intersection, where you will see a DAR marker on the northeast corner, returned to this site in 1996. Turn left (south), continuing 1 mile past a grain elevator, to rejoin US 56. Turn right (west).

FORT ZARAH AND WALNUT CREEK CROSSING

The next town after Plum Buttes is Ellinwood. Two blocks past its one traffic light is a DAR marker on the right. This site is very near the trail, on the route from Plum Buttes to Fort Zarah.

Continue west on US 56 about 5.5 miles to a road just west of the point where KS 156 comes in from the right (north). Turn left here, cross the rail-road tracks, and drive to the next intersection. It may be possible to continue a short distance straight ahead, depending on the road condition. Off to the right was the first Fort Zarah, established in 1864 and abandoned in 1866. The Allison-Peacock Trading Post was to the southeast of that point. The SFT crossing is almost due south. A toll bridge over Walnut Creek was established here in 1863. All of these sites can be found on a map produced by Bob Button and published in Franzwa's *The Santa Fe Trail Revisited*. Return to US 56 and turn left (west).

Continuing west on US 56, cross a highway bridge over Walnut Creek about 2 miles east of the town of Great Bend. Just past the bridge on the right (north) side of the highway is a spacious roadside park commemorating Fort Zarah and Walnut Creek Crossing. Near the entrance is an official Kansas Historical Marker, "Fort Zarah," with reference to the SFT.

This was the second Fort Zarah, established in 1866 and located in the field across the creek from the park. For a brief period (1864–1869), the fort guarded one of the most dangerous sections of the SFT. In those years Barnum, Veil, and Vickery, which operated a stage line and held the govern-ment mail contract between Kansas City and Santa Fe, built a fortified stage station and corral at the Walnut Creek Crossing. Fort Zarah troopers provided escorts for the stagecoaches. However, no trace of the sandstone fort or station remains today.

GREAT BEND

The SFT joined the Arkansas River at its great bend, sometimes called the north bend, and followed its broad valley toward the southwest and Pawnee Rock. The present-day town of Great Bend was not founded until 1872, after the SFT had closed in this area. The trail ran through the grounds upon which the courthouse now stands downtown. Entering Great Bend from the east on US 56, a DAR marker can be seen on the left side of the road, next to some evergreens adjacent to the Economy Inn.

Continue to the center of Great Bend. At Main Street (US 281), turn right (north). Drive to the courthouse, where there is a DAR marker on the west side of the building, moved here from the railroad depot in 1993. The trail came directly through the courthouse grounds.

Return south on Main Street, crossing US 56 and going past the railroad and the Arkansas River to the Barton County Museum on the right. The museum contains extensive displays of Fort Zarah and the Allison-Peacock Trading Post. Return to US 56 and turn left (west). Continue west toward Pawnee Rock.

Note: On the west side of Great Bend, US 56 has a stop sign. At this point US 56 turns left. The turn is easy to miss.

PAWNEE ROCK

Pawnee Rock, the most famous natural landmark along the SFT in Kansas, was well known to all trail travelers and described by almost everyone who wrote about the trail. Merely a small hill with a rock face, it would pass unnoticed anywhere but on the flat plains of Kansas.

Modern visitors with a copy of Susan Magoffin's diary should read her description of the place in the entry for July 4, 1846. As many other passersby, she carved her name here, but those priceless inscriptions were lost in later years when Pawnee Rock was heavily quarried for building materials. Now it is a state park and protected.

Entering the small community of Pawnee Rock on US 56, turn right (north) at the sign in the center of town which points to the historic site. Go about .5 mile to the park entrance. On the right side of the gate, almost hidden by a lilac bush, is a DAR marker.

The road passes through the gate and leads to the base of Pawnee Rock. Embedded in its face are two bronze plaques. One shows William Becknell's first pack train of 1821 in relief. This plaque, and an identical one at Wagon Mound, New Mexico, were designed and cast by Harold Rosner of Larned and placed in 1971. The Becknell plaque here erroneously claims that he passed by Pawnee Rock. In fact, Becknell traveled along the south side of the Arkansas River on both of his trips. The second plaque at Pawnee Rock commemorates the SFT. Inscriptions seen on the rock are from post-trail days.

The road makes a circle to the top of the rock, where there are a stone shelter and a tall white marble SFT monument with inscriptions on four sides. This is the only marker we know of on the trail that mentions the women as well as the men who ventured forth on the SFT. Look south across the town to the line of trees marking the Arkansas River. The SFT ran about 100 yards south of the rock, which had a caravan campground at its base.

Return to US 56 and turn right toward Larned. Leaving the western outskirts of the community of Pawnee Rock, stop at an official Kansas Historical Marker in a roadside park on the left. The text gives a brief history of Pawnee Rock and recounts a bogus story about a youthful Kit Carson making his first trail trip and shooting his own mule on night guard duty here.

About 1 mile past the roadside park, look to the right (west) of the highway about .25 mile to a long ridge. The feature is most conspicuous at this point, although it extends all the way from Pawnee Rock to Ash Creek, paralleling the trail. It might well be called Kirwan's Ridge, after Pvt. John S. Kirwan, 4th U.S. Cavalry. In 1859, he was with a small patrol from Fort Riley operating on this section of the SFT. Escorting a party of eastbound Pike's Peakers (returning Colorado gold seekers) and their families, the patrol encountered hostile Indians, who the day before had attacked the Santa Fe mail coach, killing the driver and conductor. Kirwan says in his journal: "Pretty soon we came in sight of the Indians scattered along the bluff as far as we could see, moving up and down the sides of the slope. They did everything possible to draw us on, and away from the wagons, but Lt. Otis gave positive orders that we were not to fire . . . and under no circumstances to leave the wagons. The women were brave and even the children were plucky" (Kirwan 1955). The strategy was successful, and the wagon train escaped without a fight. Several farm structures can be seen on the low bluff. Try to imagine the same scene with menacing Indians, as Kirwan and his companions saw it in 1859.

THE WET AND DRY ROUTES

The route of the SFT from Pawnee Rock to Dodge City has been researched thoroughly by the Wet and Dry Routes Chapter (W/DRC) of the Santa Fe Trail Association. This group, led by David Clapsaddle of Larned, has placed well over one hundred attractive limestone markers at important sites along the several branches of the trail. The serious trail buff should head for the Santa Fe Trail Center in Larned for a copy of the book *Wet and Dry Routes Self-Guided Auto Tour*, which is very useful for finding the SFT in this area.

One branch, the Wet Route or sometimes called the Water Road, stayed close to the Arkansas River, approximately the route of today's US 56. This route was the primary one until the early 1830s, when a shortcut was developed that was about 10 miles shorter than the Wet Route. This shortcut, the Dry Route, left the Wet Route southwest of present-day Larned and went directly to the Caches west of today's Dodge City. As its name implies, this route was devoid of water most summers during the travel season but nevertheless remained the road of choice until the mid-1840s.

A later variant of the Dry Route developed after the establishment of the Hall and Porter Company mail station in 1859. This station was on the south bank of Pawnee Fork west of present-day Larned. After 1859, the eastern terminus of the Dry Route moved to a point just north of Larned, where wagons headed southwest for Fort Larned, which was established in 1860. By 1866, a third variant left the Wet Route as before (north of Larned) but went along the north bank of Pawnee Fork, crossing it just west of Fort Larned. (For a complete description of the Dry Route, see Clapsaddle 1999.)

Just as the eastern ends of the Dry Route changed, so did the western end. From its terminus at the Caches in the 1830s, it retreated to a point 1 mile east of Fort Dodge. In 1867, the SFT in the Larned area ended service because the Union Pacific Railway (Eastern Division) had reached Hays City, Kansas. From the railhead, a new road was developed connecting Fort Hays and Fort Dodge, meeting the trail at the latter location. However, even the Fort Hays–Fort Dodge Road was short-lived, as railheads were established farther west on the Union Pacific, and later, on the Santa Fe Railroad as it laid tracks up the Arkansas Valley.

THE LARNED COMPLEX

In the vicinity of Larned, are a variety of SFT points of interest, probably enough to warrant designating the area a complex. The only complex formally established thus far is the Clayton Complex comprising a cluster of trail sites in eastern New Mexico. At Larned a fairly substantial river, Pawnee Fork, flows from the west and joins the Arkansas River on the southern edge of town. The crossing of Pawnee Fork was an important one, and many a wagon train had to wait here for high waters from sudden cloudbursts to subside. The first settlement was at the crossing, and it was near here that George Sibley's survey team camped in 1825.

The complex consists of the following sites:

A. ASH CREEK CROSSING

Just over 3 miles past the above roadside park in Pawnee Rock, an unmarked gravel road crosses US 56. Turn west (right) and go 2 miles to the Ash Creek Crossing, about 50 yards past the second bridge. Immediately to the right (north) of the road is the tree- and brush-filled bed of Ash Creek, usually dry. Here there is a Kansas sandstone marker at the site inscribed "Ash Creek Crossing," placed by the W/DRC.

Across the creek due north, is a white farmhouse and a silo with a silver dome. Wagons coming from Pawnee Rock crossed here (if you know where to look you can see the line of trees marking Ash Creek from the top of Pawnee Rock) and camped in the plowed field just to the south of the road. Although the creek has been diverted here, resulting in the cut-bank being filled in, a fine photo of the original cut can be seen in the Pizza Hut restaurant in Larned, near the stoplight where US 56 turns left.

In the context of trail history, this unspectacular crossing is significant because it was here that young Susan Magoffin's carriage turned over. She was thrown to the ground unconscious, resulting in injuries that caused her to have a miscarriage later at Bent's Fort. Read the account of the incident in her journal.

B. DRY ROUTE AND WET ROUTE JUNCTION (POST 1859)

Continue from the crossing to the next road (about .5 mile) and turn left (south). At about .5 mile on this road, there is a W/DRC marker indicating the junction of the Wet Route and the Dry Route after 1859. Following the establishment of the mail station and the fort, this became the preferred way for the Dry Route. At this point the Wet Route continued toward the Lower Crossing, while the Dry Route angled southwest toward the Upper Crossing of Pawnee Fork. From here continue south until the road meets US 56 on the eastern edge of Larned.

This small city was founded officially in 1872 as the Santa Fe Railroad pushed up the Arkansas Valley. We will return to Larned after visiting sites west and southwest of town.

C. LARNED CEMETERY ROUTES

Continue on US 56 (also KS 156 here) to the first traffic light at Broadway. Go straight, leaving US 56 and continuing on KS 156 for 2 miles to a paved road coming in from the left. Turn left (south) and drive .5 mile to the cemetery. Continue past the entrance on the paved road to the southeast corner. There is a W/DRC trail marker just inside the fence labeled "Dry Route Crossed Here." The wagon trains came this way headed for the crossing of Pawnee Fork about 1 mile ahead. If you look closely under the fence, you can see the faint undulations of the several tracks of the trail. And from the cemetery you can see Jenkins Hill, which is close by the crossing. Return to KS 156 and drive west.

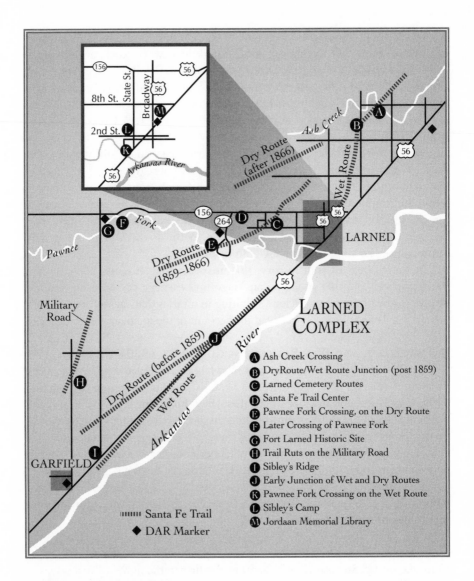

A Ash Creek Crossing
B DryRoute/Wet Route Junction (post 1859)
C Larned Cemetery Routes
D Santa Fe Trail Center
E Pawnee Fork Crossing, on the Dry Route
F Later Crossing of Pawnee Fork
G Fort Larned Historic Site
H Trail Ruts on the Military Road
I Sibley's Ridge
J Early Junction of Wet and Dry Routes
K Pawnee Fork Crossing on the Wet Route
L Sibley's Camp
M Jordaan Memorial Library

Santa Fe Trail
◆ DAR Marker

D. SANTA FE TRAIL CENTER

On the south side of KS 156 at 2.5 miles west of Larned, is the Santa Fe Trail Center. Built in 1974, the beautiful center interprets both the trail story and Kansas pioneer history with a series of fine exhibits. For researchers there is a small but growing library and archive. In addition, various trail-related special events are held during the year. One of the Mormon Battalion markers is located near the northeast corner of the building. This center is one of the high points of the modern trail. It also is the headquarters of the Santa Fe

Trail Association. Information about this important association and its many chapters along the SFT can be obtained at the center.

Serious trail buffs will want to join the Fort Larned Historical Society, which established the center and issues a newsletter called *Trail Ruts*. Requests for information can be addressed to: Director, Santa Fe Trail Center, Route 3, Larned, KS 67550.

E. PAWNEE FORK CROSSING ON THE DRY ROUTE

At .5 mile beyond the Santa Fe Trail Center, turn left (south) off KS 156 onto KS 264 and drive 1 mile to the Larned State Hospital. Entering the hospital grounds, Jenkins Hill, surmounted by a large water tower, can be seen on the right. In 1860, the army considered placing a fort on the hill's summit but instead chose a location 3 miles up the Pawnee Fork.

Take KS 264 to a T, turn right, and follow the road a short distance until it begins to curve left at the foot of Jenkins Hill. On the right at the curve, is a DAR marker designating the Dry Route Crossing of the Pawnee Fork. The W/DRC also has a marker here. The river is through the trees immediately behind and below the markers. The cutdown is evident if you walk around to the right and look down through the second-growth trees lining the creek.

In 1865, Samuel Parker established a ranch just south of this crossing. The first Parker Ranch was built in 1864 in Larned near the Wet Route Crossing of

Two soldiers commemorative marker and two other markers near the Pawnee Fork Crossing in Larned, Kansas.

Pawnee Fork. In 1868, the ranch at the Dry Route Crossing was acquired by A. H. Boyd, who built here the first permanent civilian buildings between Fort Union and Council Grove. The site became known as "Boyd's Crossing," and soldiers from Fort Larned patronized the saloon for drink and entertainment.

Just past the DAR marker is a red brick building, boarded up. On its south side, a dirt lane leads right, off the paved road down to a cement bridge over the Pawnee Fork. It is best to walk down to the bridge. If you continue across the bridge and take the left fork in the dirt road, you will soon come to a W/DRC marker for "Boyd's Ranche" (the spelling at the time).

F. LATER CROSSING OF PAWNEE FORK

Return to KS 156 and turn left (west) toward Fort Larned. At 2.5 miles from the Santa Fe Trail Center is a junction. Here, turn left (south) and drive .8 mile. Across a field to the right, a line of woods marks the course of the Pawnee Fork. The tallest tree is near where a wooden bridge was built in 1859–1860. In 1864, it was burned by Kiowas, who ran off some horses and mules, and was never replaced. The crossing was used primarily by military forces at Fort Larned. Once across, the trail continued along the bank of the river about .5 mile to a civilian mail station, built by the firm of Hall and Porter, which had the mail contract in the 1850s. About .1 mile beyond the station was Fort Larned, which was established after the mail station was built. Return to KS 156.

G. FORT LARNED HISTORIC SITE

Located west on KS 156 about 6 miles from Larned is the Fort Larned Historic Site. The first military establishment in this immediate area was called Camp on Pawnee Fork, built in 1859. In February 1860, its name was changed to Camp Alert, followed by the permanent Fort Larned in May 1860. The fort's function was to protect caravans, stagecoaches, and travelers on the eastern leg of the SFT.

Today, the nine surviving stone buildings around the parade ground have been restored and contain military and SFT exhibits. Books pertaining to the SFT are sold at the information desk, and a film about the trail is shown in the theater. Also ask for the brochure entitled *Fort Larned History Trail*, which provides directions for a walking tour of outlying points of interest, including the site of the stage station mentioned above. Moreover, special historical events are scheduled periodically. Direct inquiries to: Superintendent, Fort Larned National Historic Site, Route 3, Larned, KS 67550–9321.

At the fort entrance alongside KS 156, is a roadside park containing a National Park Service interpretive sign, a DAR marker, and a SFT map. Turn left at the west edge of the park on a road that crosses the Pawnee Fork and enters the fort.

Restored officers' quarters at Fort Larned, Kansas.

H. TRAIL RUTS ON THE MILITARY ROAD

Go west from the Fort Larned entrance on KS 156 .25 mile to a paved county road that intersects from the left (south). Drive 4 miles, then go right (west) 1 mile, then left (south) on a gravel farm road .5 mile to a well-marked parking area on the left. From the small, elevated observation booth out in the field, visitors can observe excellent SFT ruts that have been preserved in an undisturbed forty-acre pasture. The ruts were carved by wagons on the Military Road that connected Fort Larned to the Wet Route southwest of Garfield. An interpretive historical sign is in the booth. A sharp eye can also discern shallow oval depressions about 6 feet in diameter, which are old buffalo wallows where the big animals rolled in the dust seeking relief from biting flies. The ruts are now administered as a detached unit of Fort Larned.

I. SIBLEY'S RIDGE

From the Military Road site, continue south to the small town of Garfield, where you rejoin US 56. Turn left (back toward Larned) and drive about 1 mile to where US 56 runs adjacent to a small ridge on the north (left) side. (The road that intersects US 56 here goes north to Fort Larned.) This ridge should be called Sibley's Ridge. The Sibley survey team passed by this point, and George Sibley climbed this ridge to get a better view of the surroundings. His account included the following statement: "The Waggons passed round the point, still keeping in the bottom about half a mile from the River. I rode upon the ridge, from the top of which I could distinctly trace the course of the Pawnee River for a great distance by the fringe of trees along its banks" (Gregg 1995). There is a W/DRC marker on the southwest corner on the hill.

**J. EARLY JUNCTION OF WET AND
DRY ROUTES (PRE-1859)**

Continue north on US 56 from Sibley's Ridge 5.1 miles to a marker on the left. This is the junction of the Wet and Dry Routes called the Forks in Santa Fe Road during the earliest period. From here wagons angled off to the southwest toward the Caches. This route began in the early 1830s and was in general use until the late 1840s. A W/DRC marker is on the west side of the road.

K. PAWNEE FORK CROSSING OF THE WET ROUTE

Continue towards Larned until you reach the bridge on the edge of town. Just past the bridge turn left into the nearby park. There are four markers here. The first and second (both placed by the W/DRC) are for the "Pawnee Fork Crossing," although the actual crossing was about 500 yards downstream from this point. The last two markers are the gravestones of Pvt. Robert Easley and Pvt. Arthur Hughes, soldiers who died during the Mexican War.

L. SIBLEY'S CAMP

From the park drive toward downtown Larned and turn left (north) at State Street. Continue on State to the intersection with 2nd Street. On the northwest corner is where George Sibley and his survey team camped the nights of September 1 and 2, 1825. The site has been purchased by David Clapsaddle, Bob Rein, and Mildon Yeager, who are planning to restore it and have already placed an information sign on the north side of the property. The original Parker Ranch (see "E" above) was located two blocks west of this site.

M. JORDAAN MEMORIAL LIBRARY

From Sibley's Camp, go back to US 56 (2nd Street intersects US 56 if you go east on it). Continue on US 56 until it turns left at Broadway. To the right at this corner is the old railroad station, with a DAR marker directly in front. At 8th Street and Broadway, is the Jordaan Memorial Library, which contains excellent materials on local history and the SFT.

LARNED TO DODGE CITY

Retrace your route southwest on US 56 to Garfield. A DAR marker is in the northeast corner of the town park, on the right side of the highway near the grain elevator opposite the post office. From this marker continue on US 56 .9 mile to Coon Creek Crossing on the Wet Route of the SFT. Approaching the highway bridge over Coon Creek, a faint dirt road turns right into a field, with a tree at the junction. Stop under the tree after entering the road. There is a

W/DRC limestone marker on the fence line for "Coon Creek Crossing-Wet Route." The field behind the marker was the site of a wagon campground. To the left, is the crossing where the Military Road from Fort Larned approached the Wet Route. To reach it, you must cross a fence. Just beyond, several indentations in the cut-bank are wagon ramps leading down to the crossing.

About 400 yards past Coon Creek on US 56 at the right, you can see a set of ruts visible at times, depending on the condition of the grass. This was where the Military Road from Fort Larned met the Wet Route. There is a pullout with a W/DRC marker on the right.

Continuing on US 56 4.3 miles past the bridge over Coon Creek, there is a W/DRC marker on the left for "Plain Camp," which is across the railroad tracks and closer to the Arkansas River. This campsite apparently lacked any defining characteristic, hence its name.

At 7.4 miles past the Coon Creek Bridge on US 56 is a DAR marker on the right, between mile markers 162 and 163. There is also a W/DRC marker here for "Love's Defeat." Lt. John Love's company was attacked here in 1847 by 300 Comanches, resulting in a loss of five soldiers and 130 oxen.

At 4.8 miles past the last marker, turn left to the marker on the left side of the road. On June 18, 1848, the famous Battle of Coon Creek took place here. Lt. William Royball's detachment was attacked by some 700 Comanches and Apaches, but he was able to rout the Indians without losing a single soldier. There is a W/DRC marker at the site.

Continue on to Kinsley. The state of Kansas has placed an interpretive marker, "Battle of Coon Creek," on the south side of the Arkansas River along US 50 3 miles east of Kinsley. Since the actual battle site, as noted, was on present-day US 56, this marker can be ignored.

On the western limits of Kinsley, back on US 56, is a large roadside park, where a DAR marker stands beside a black railroad engine, moved here from its original site. The Sod House Museum is also in this park.

Continuing on US 56, at 4.7 miles from the roadside park is a pullout on the left side of the highway with another DAR marker. Three miles beyond is the town of Offerle. On the west side of the town and to the right of the highway, is a small park with a DAR marker. There is also a W/DRC marker there with interpretive text.

The early Dry Route crossed US 50/US 56 at about Offerle. We left the Wet Route at Kinsley, and it is now about 10 miles to the south following the Arkansas River floodplain. Since there is no easy way to follow either route in this area we will continue southwest on US 50/US 56 to its intersection with US 283, just beyond the hamlet of Wright.

On the northeast corner of this junction, is a large roadside park with an official Kansas Historical Marker "Road to Santa Fe." Its interpretive text on the SFT is one of the most detailed of any found in Kansas, although unfortunately the explanations for the names Wet and Dry routes are incorrect.

SIDE TRIP TO LOWER CROSSING

Go south on a paved county road that leaves US 50/US 56 at the intersection with US 283. Continue 4 miles to join KS 154. At this point you are on the Wet Route, only a few hundred yards east of its junction with the Dry Route. We will turn here and briefly go east down the valley of the Arkansas River but return to this junction later.

Drive east on KS 154 (away from Dodge City) about 9 miles. There is a large feedlot on the left, and KS 154 curves to the right. As it curves take the paved county road entering from the left. After .5 mile the paved road turns left (north) but continue straight ahead on the gravel road about 1.2 miles.

In the vicinity of a windmill on the left, you will see some excellent SFT ruts. These are the "Riegel Ruts," and there is a W/DRC marker near the windmill. The Wet Route left the river bottom just east of here because of sandy terrain. A short distance before the brick farmhouse, the trail crosses the county road and goes into a field on the right.

Return to KS 154 and turn right (north) to the entrance of the Ford County Feed Yard. About .7 mile after meandering through the feedlot you will see a W/DRC marker describing the point where the traders using the Lower Crossing left the Wet Route to ford the Arkansas River at Mulberry Creek. Return to KS 154, and immediately south of the highway intersection there look for another W/DRC marker identifying the "Mulberry Creek Ford." Travelers crossed the Arkansas River behind the marker. Sibley's survey team camped here September 6 to 9, 1825.

Drive east here on KS 154 over the Arkansas River then south toward the small town of Ford. Once off the bridge on the south side, stop and look west across an open field. A line of trees about .5 mile away marks the course of Mulberry Creek as it approaches its confluence with the Arkansas. This Lower Crossing was used in the early trail period, but its use declined as other fords developed farther up the Arkansas. It is about a half-hour hike across the wide field to the mouth of Mulberry Creek, but due to thick trees and brush the actual trail cannot be located here. Return on KS 154 to the feedlot.

Turn toward Dodge City on KS 154. At about 1 mile past the bridge (just after a large house on the right), the Wet Route descended from the high ground back to the Arkansas River floodplain. Five miles beyond the Mulberry Creek marker on the left is the W/DRC marker for "Jackson's Island." This was a commonly used campsite on the Wet Route and the scene of an 1843 confrontation between Capt. Philip St. George Cooke and a group of raiders from

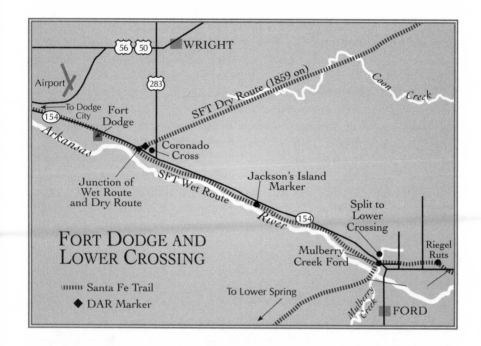

Continue west on KS 154 about 5 miles to the junction with the road from Wright, where you first joined KS 154. About .25 mile west of the junction, there is a small park on the right. Behind it on a hill is the large Coronado Cross, a 38-foot cross of prestressed concrete erected in 1975 as a bicentennial project. It commemorates a religious service believed conducted in this vicinity on June 29, 1541, by Father Padilla after the Coronado Expedition successfully crossed the Arkansas River.

At .3 mile west of the park, on the right side of the highway, is a W/DRC marker telling about the western terminus of the Dry Route as it merged with the Wet Route. There is also a DAR marker here. Looking up the hill and slightly to the right, you can see ruts leading down toward the marker, a trace of the Dry Route. The deep depression is not part of the trail but a "dirt silo."

Drive west 1 mile to the Fort Dodge Soldiers Home. Just west of the entrance is a marker on the south side describing Fort Dodge as the western terminus of the Fort Dodge–Fort Hays Road. That road came down the hill from the north to meet the Wet Route.

Fort Dodge was established in 1865 to provide protection for this section of the SFT. Its location was well chosen as it was close to the junction of the Wet and Dry Routes. Because the place has been adapted to modern use, little remains among the remodeled structures to suggest the primitive life of frontier days. Of greatest interest is the Custer House (turn right on Custer Street a couple of blocks inside the entrance), once the post headquarters. Although Custer may have passed through Fort Dodge, he was not stationed here. The house is now a white two-story structure with pitched red roof and a columned porch across the front. It is a private residence not open to the public. Further, the building in the southeast corner of the fort is an original barracks, although greatly modified. In addition, the post hospital and quartermaster's warehouse date from trail days.

From the fort drive west on KS 154 to Dodge City, 5 miles away. (Note: If you follow this side trip, you will miss an official Kansas Historical Marker, "Dodge City, the Cowboy Capital," which refers to the SFT. It is located on US 50/US 56 3 miles east of Dodge City at an overlook of a giant cattle feedlot and stockyards. The turnout for the sign is on the south side of the highway.)

DODGE CITY

Dodge City is much more interested in its Wild West image of cowboys and shootouts than it is in the SFT. However, there are some points of interest in the area for trail buffs. From Fort Dodge continue west on KS 154 to the edge of Dodge City, where KS 154 intersects US 56 at a stoplight. At this intersection continue straight ahead. This is Trail Street and is directly on top of the SFT. In the center of town, turn left at 2nd Street and go south one block to a DAR marker just inside the entrance of Wright Park on the right. This park was named for Robert M. Wright, who donated the land. An early freighter on the SFT, he also contracted to supply hay to the army posts. In addition, Wright served as mayor of Dodge City and wrote a book, *Dodge City: The Cowboy Capital*, which contains useful trail information. A monument to him is in the center of the park.

Return north on 2nd Street, cross the railroad tracks, and turn left on Wyatt Earp Boulevard. On the northwest corner of 3rd Street and Wyatt Earp, is the Visitors' Information Center/Convention and Visitors' Bureau, which provides a great variety of information about Dodge City and the surrounding area. Behind and to the west of the Visitors' Information Center is Boot Hill. Front Street, at the foot of Boot Hill, is Disneyesque but does commemorate Dodge City's heyday in the mid-1870s when it was a shipping point for cattle driven up from Texas. The Boot Hill Museum at the west end of Front Street has excellent exhibits relating to the SFT, Fort Dodge, and Fort Mann.

Santa Fe Trail Park is located two blocks east of 2nd Street on Wyatt Earp Boulevard next to the railroad tracks and adjacent to the depot. Although some-

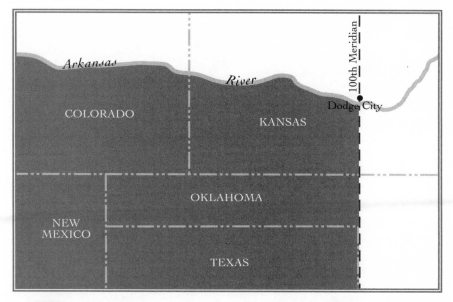

SPANISH TERRITORY 1819–1821• MEXICO 1821–1846
State Boundaries

what run-down, it commemorates the trail but more importantly the 100th meridian, which passes through it. When the early traders arrived at this point, Mexico began beyond the meridian south of the Arkansas River. From here on west, traders looked across the Arkansas into Mexican territory, until the Mexican War pushed the international boundary far to the south.

Modern trail travelers may also find it useful to visit the Kansas Heritage Center at 1000 2nd Avenue, which has a variety of historical publications and services provided by a very friendly and helpful staff. One of the center's books is *West by Southwest: Letters of Joseph Pratt Allyn, a Traveler Along the Santa Fe Trail in 1863*, edited by David K. Strate.

Another point of interest in town is the modernistic metal statue *The Plainswoman*, erected in 1972 on the campus of Dodge City Community College to honor early pioneer women. To reach the campus, drive west on Wyatt Earp Boulevard and turn north on 14th Avenue. After approximately 1 mile the campus is on the left. After turning left into the campus, the statue is at the end of the road.

Returning south on 14th Avenue, watch for a major intersection with traffic lights. Turn left (east) here on Comanche and go about five blocks to Chilton Park. Turn left (north) on Manor Drive and proceed two blocks along the east side of the park, watching for a 6-foot-high light-colored stone monument in

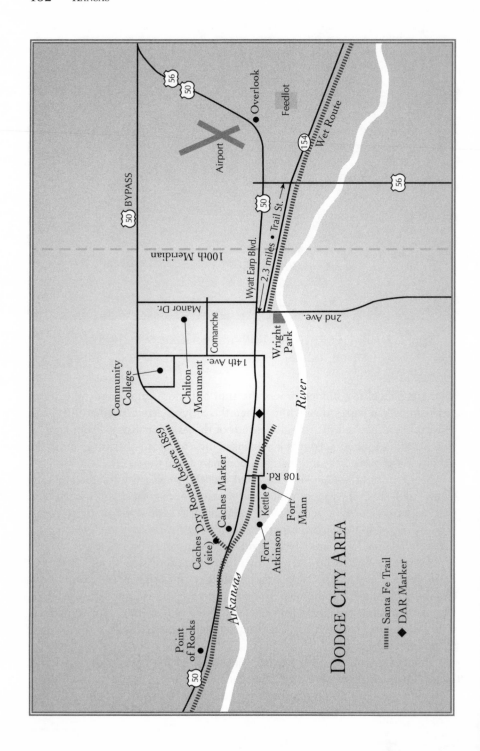

DODGE CITY AREA

⁏⁏⁏⁏ Santa Fe Trail
◆ DAR Marker

the center. The inscription on it honors Maj. Robert H. Chilton, commander of Fort Atkinson, which was located on the SFT just west of Dodge City. In 1853, Major Chilton presided over a large council with the Comanches, Kiowas, and Apaches designed to provide safe passage for travelers on the trail. A vivid description of the event is given by Sgt. Percival G. Lowe in his book *Five Years Dragoon* (Lowe 1965).

Return to Wyatt Earp Boulevard and turn right (west) headed out of town. At about 1 mile, there is a roadside turnout with a DAR marker and an official Kansas Historical Marker, "Dodge City, the Cowboy Capital." The text refers to Fort Mann, Fort Atkinson, and to the SFT.

From the above marker, drive 1 mile west on US 50 and turn left (south) on 108 Road just beyond the point where the US 50 Bypass comes in from the right. Drive .2 mile (one block) and turn right on Kettle Way Street. At .6 mile is the W/DRC marker for Fort Mann, which was located .4 mile south of the marker. Established in 1847 as a wagon repair depot during the Mexican War, Fort Mann was abandoned in 1850.

Continue west .4 mile on Kettle Way to a W/DRC marker for "Fort Atkinson," which lies at the end of the road but may be difficult to find because of weeds. Originally established as Fort Mackey in 1850, its name was later changed to Fort Atkinson. The fort was built of sod and housed regular military troops, who called it "Fort Sodom." It predated Fort Union, New Mexico, by a year and was abandoned by 1854.

Go back to US 50 and turn left 1 mile. At the intersection of a dirt section line road, there is a large white monument for the Caches. Turn right just beyond the monument on the dirt road and go .2 mile. A W/DRC marker for the Caches is on the left (west) of the road. This spot was where the earliest Dry Route joined the Wet Route. The Caches are named for some pits dug near here by the Baird-Chambers party in 1823. The party had left Missouri late in 1822 and was hit by a blizzard at this spot. The men lost most of their pack animals and hid (cached) their trade goods in the pits. Then they continued to Taos, New Mexico, purchased mules, and eventually returned to retrieve their goods.

Return to US 50 and continue west 2 miles to a W/DRC marker on the right side of the highway, "Point of Rocks." This is the first of several such features by that name on the trail. All that remains is a low hill, the rocky point having been destroyed when the local Highway Department widened the road in 1981. It is here we leave the series of W/DRC markers.

Two of the earliest trading expeditions, the Cooper party on its way to Santa Fe and the Fowler-Glenn party returning from Santa Fe, met here on June 12, 1822. Until 1846, individuals standing on top of Point of Rocks could look south across the Arkansas River to Mexican territory on the other side since there was at that time no timber along the river. However, today its banks are marked by a line of trees seen to the left of the highway.

Four and a half miles beyond Point of Rocks is a fine and well-marked set of SFT ruts. The trail left the flat floodplain here and climbed the hill. The ruts are on the right side of the highway, near a sign that reads: "Historic Point of Interest." At the site is a turnout and parking area. These ruts are being protected by the Boot Hill Museum in Dodge City. There is also a DAR marker.

The SFT swung up this hill and made a 2-mile arc before once again returning to the valley farther west. The splendid set of ruts seen here, perhaps the longest and best preserved in Kansas, are part of that arc.

RIVER CROSSINGS

Continue west on US 50 to the town of Cimarron. At the traffic light and main intersection, turn left (south) on KS 23. Four blocks south, just before the bridge over the Arkansas River, is the entrance (on the right) to Cimarron Crossing Park. The park is one of the most pleasant spots on the SFT today in western Kansas. Just inside the entrance on the right is a large red granite marker with text and map showing the two branches of the SFT. Behind the marker stands a white brick pavilion and beyond it a new official Kansas Historical Marker, "The Santa Fe Trail." Its extensive text includes reference to William Becknell's inaugural trip. To the right of this marker is a covered wagon. In viewing the Arkansas River directly south of the park, you can get a feel for what a crossing of that river would have entailed.

The Cimarron Crossing of the Arkansas River was a major landmark for trail travelers since it was the midpoint of the journey, roughly halfway between Independence and Santa Fe. Here the SFT split into two great divisions—the Cimarron Cutoff, or Desert Route, and the Mountain Route, also called the Bent's Fort Cutoff. The Cimarron Cutoff forded the river here (or at other crossings 6 miles up the Arkansas River as far as present-day Ingalls) and continued in a southwesterly direction 50 miles across the waterless desert (or Jornada), which ended at the Cimarron River. In addition to the lack of water, there was a constant threat of attack from Comanches and Kiowas. However, since this was the shortest route to Santa Fe it was preferred by most traders.

This area of the river was called the Middle Crossing, and the fords here were those most frequently used. The Lower Crossing (the least utilized) was downriver at present-day Ford, Kansas (14 miles east of Dodge City), while the Upper Crossing was near modern Lakin (roughly 60 miles upriver from the town of Cimarron). All the crossings eventually led travelers to the Cimarron River.

The Mountain Route did not cross the river in Kansas but continued up the north bank of the Arkansas to Bent's Fort in southeastern Colorado, where it forded the river and then headed for Raton Pass. Although it was about 90 miles longer, there were fewer concerns about water and Indian attacks along the Mountain Route. After the mid–1830s, there was also the attraction of Bent's Fort, which offered travelers a welcome stopover. The two branches finally converged at La Junta (present-day Watrous), New Mexico, with a single route continuing the last 75 miles to Santa Fe.

Continue west on US 50 up the Arkansas Valley to Ingalls. The old railroad depot two blocks south of the railroad tracks on the left has been converted into the Santa Fe Trail Museum. Although there are good displays of pioneer artifacts, none actually relates to the trail. There is a DAR marker in front of the museum and another directly across the street to the west on the corner in a small park. All the towns along this stretch were established as the railroad advanced and the SFT was closing down.

GARDEN CITY

Approaching the eastern limits of Garden City, a roadside park is on the left (south) side of US 50, just beyond the overpass for alternate US 50, which you do not want to take. In the park is a DAR marker and an official Kansas Historical Marker, "The Indian and the Buffalo," with an interesting text.

Enter Garden City on Business US 50 and proceed to the intersection of US 83 in the center of town. There turn left (south) on US 83 (which is also Main Street) and drive three blocks to Maple Street. Turn left (east) on Maple and go two and a half blocks along the north boundary of Finnup Park to a DAR marker in the park on the right. Continue past the marker to Maple and 4th, then turn right (south) into the park.

On the right is the Finney County Historical Society Museum, which contains exhibits and a small research library with items pertaining to the SFT. The facility is open afternoons only.

Return on Maple to US 83, turn left (south), and drive about 2 miles to the bridge over the Arkansas River, which is dry here much of the year. Just beyond the bridge on the right is the information office for the Garden City Buffalo Refuge. Operated by the Kansas Fish and Game Commission, it contains the largest buffalo herd in the state. Late in the last century, a local resident, C. J. "Buffalo" Jones, helped save these animals when they were on the verge of extinction.

Return to the center of Garden City and continue north until you rejoin US 50. In the center of town, note on the left side of the street the imposing four-story Windsor Hotel, built in 1887. Although constructed after the close of the SFT, it is interesting. On the courthouse lawn behind the Windsor Hotel, is a statue of Buffalo Jones.

The next town west of Garden City is Holcomb. The highway now bypasses the town, so you must turn left off US 50 and continue to the center of town. Just past the elementary school is a DAR marker on the right, set directly on the SFT.

TO LAKIN

Continue west on US 50 to the small community of Deerfield. Turn left (south) at the main intersection and drive five blocks to a park on the right. A DAR marker is on the southeast corner of the park, almost directly on the original trail.

Back at the main intersection, go 3 miles west on US 50 to a highway bridge, where you will see a sign advising you of a "historical marker." At a small pullout

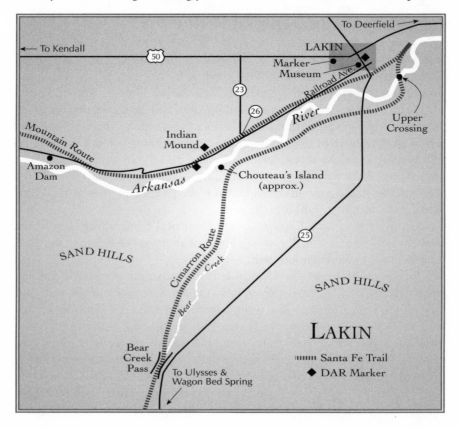

on the right, is the site of "Charlie's Ruts," which should not be missed. This land was donated to the local Kearny County Historical Society by Paul Bentrup of Deerfield. Charlie's Ruts are named for Paul Bentrup's father Charlie, who preserved them. Here you can walk across the small dam and experience the ruts close up. There are some very pronounced ruts behind the marker.

Drive on to Lakin and the intersection of US 50 and KS 25. Turn left (south) on KS 25 and go two blocks to the Kearny County Courthouse on the left, where there is a DAR marker on the lawn.

Continue south two blocks to Waterman and turn right (west) two blocks to Buffalo Street. The Kearny County Historical Museum, a complex of five buildings, is on the left. Turn left on Buffalo and go one block to the entrance, which faces the railroad tracks. This excellent museum has a number of trail-related exhibits, including one of the finest original Conestoga freight wagons to be seen anywhere. In addition, superb railroad memorabilia is displayed in the restored Atchison, Topeka and Santa Fe depot. If you only stop at one museum, this should be it.

Lakin was in the vicinity of the Upper Crossing of the Cimarron Cutoff. There may have been several places used for crossings. Paul Bentrup tells us that even today you can drive a pickup truck across the river at a point just downstream from the bridge. Another likely crossing point was Chouteau's Island upstream from Lakin.

Motorists wishing to follow the Cimarron Cutoff should continue south on KS 25 to Ulysses and the Wagon Bed Spring site, picking up US 56 beyond at the town of Hugoton. This guide, however, will continue west, following the Mountain Route to Springer, New Mexico, and then return to Lakin and describe the Cimarron Cutoff.

THE MOUNTAIN ROUTE
CHOUTEAU'S ISLAND, BENT'S FORT, AND CIMARRON

TO CHOUTEAU'S ISLAND

From the Kearny County Historical Museum, drive west on Railroad Avenue (this road is on the south side of the museum). At approximately 5 miles is a pullout on the right, with a path over a bridge and continuing up to the summit of a hill. This small hill, rising conspicuously above the Arkansas floodplain, was known to traders as Chouteau's Mound, or later, Indian Mound. On the summit is a DAR marker, although sand-laden winds have nearly obliterated the inscription.

In trail days, Indian Mound was a prominent landmark since it denoted the location of Chouteau's Island immediately to the south. From the mound's summit, look south and slightly east to the tree-lined Arkansas River. The approximate location of the island was in a bend of the river, but with changes in the river, the island has long since disappeared. It was named after Auguste Chouteau, who with a band of approximately twenty trappers was returning from the Arkansas River in 1816 when the group was attacked by two hundred Indians near here. They took refuge on the island and held off the Indians with the loss of only one man.

During the summer of 1829, Bvt. Maj. Bennet Riley and two hundred infantry soldiers camped here after escorting the annual westbound caravan, captained by trader Charles Bent, to this point. The troops did not have permission

The Indian Mound with DAR marker west of Lakin, Kansas.

to cross the Arkansas River into Mexico. Instead, they waited at the ford, fending off Indian attacks, until the wagons returned from Santa Fe.

In the plowed field between the railroad tracks and the river, was the Bluff Stage Station, of which no trace remains. Trees along the river are now mostly dead due to a drastic fall in the water table in recent years.

Wagon caravans taking the Cimarron Cutoff either crossed the Arkansas several miles east at present-day Lakin and then followed the south bank of the river to Chouteau's Island or crossed the river here at the island. These two crossing points were considered the Upper Crossing of the Arkansas. The traders left the river at this point and started due south through a wide band of sand hills via Bear Creek Pass, which was merely a shallow valley whose level floor offered an easy route of travel.

Once out of the pass and through the hills, the caravans were on flat prairie for the next 35 miles to the Cimarron River. This section, called the Jornada, was much feared since there was no water for those 35 miles and no clear landmarks to follow. By the early 1830s, the Cimarron Cutoff was the preferred route because it was faster and avoided the rugged Raton Pass. Those wagon trains using the Mountain Route stayed on the north bank of the Arkansas and passed between Indian Mound and Chouteau's Island as they ascended the valley.

(Note: If you followed the route above, you missed an official Kansas Historical Marker, "Chouteau's Island," which is located 1 mile west of Lakin on US 50.)

Leaving Indian Mound, continue west on Railroad Avenue. The road here is almost directly on the SFT, which was at the very edge of the floodplain and next to the bordering hills. About 2 miles from Indian Mound, there is a DAR marker on the left (south) side. Continue west toward Kendall. Those who do not wish to drive on this gravel road should return to US 50 and turn left (west) on US 50 to Kendall.

At approximately 6 miles from Indian Mound, the Amazon Diversion Dam is on the left. Just before the dam traders left the floodplain and climbed the hills since the river and the hills here prevented easy passage. The trail returned to the floodplain after 1 mile. Continue on the gravel road to Kendall, where there is a DAR marker directly across the road as you turn right toward US 50. Kendall was originally named Aubry in honor of famed SFT freighter and long-distance rider Francis X. Aubry, but the Post Office Department later forced the change to Kendall because a town with a name similar to Aubry already existed in eastern Kansas. Aubry is noted for his record-breaking 780-mile trip from Santa Fe to Independence in 1848, which took only five days and sixteen hours. Thereafter, he was called the "Skimmer of the Plains." Return to US 50 here.

West of Lakin and Chouteau's Island, at high points on the highway, modern drivers can look south across the Arkansas Valley and see long, undisturbed vistas that were familiar to wagon travelers. In this vicinity you first get the sense that the crowded East has been left behind and that the spacious West has been reached.

About 8 miles west of Kendall on US 50 and 1 mile south of the highway, are traces of the remains of Fort Aubry, a temporary post used to guard the SFT in 1865–1866. However, the site is on private land and not accessible to the public. In this vicinity, a secondary branch of the SFT, known as the Aubry Cutoff, left the Arkansas and led southwest to Cold Spring (Oklahoma) on the Cimarron Route.

Continue west on US 50 to Syracuse. Approaching the one main intersection in the center of town, note the Hamilton County Museum on the right, housed in an old commercial building. The museum contains nothing of interest about the SFT except the DAR marker in front. Beyond Syracuse there is a sign reminding travelers that the highway here lies on top of the SFT for 5 miles.

The next town, 15 miles farther, is Coolidge, the last place in Kansas. Note the fine two-story stone building on the right, which lies immediately to the west of the post office. One block beyond, on the left (south) side of the highway, is a DAR marker, the last in Kansas on the Mountain Route.

At the state line on the right (north) side of US 50, on the northeast corner of an intersecting dirt road, is the first DAR marker in Colorado. The marker is below a "Prowers County" sign. The word *Kansas* is incised on the east side of the base and *Colorado* on the west side. The Colorado markers are of gray granite, in contrast to the red ones in Kansas.

HOLLY TO GRANADA

In Colorado, Holly is the first town on US 50. At the intersection of Main Street, turn left (south) three blocks to the railroad tracks and depot. Straight ahead, and 100 feet beyond the tracks, is a large white limestone barn in beautiful condition with a fine arched opening in the loft. According to local lore, the barn was erected in the late 1860s during the SFT era. The small square openings along the sides, it is claimed, are portholes used by early settlers in fending off Indian attacks. From the barn look west up the driveway of a large two-story stone house. On the right side of the drive, there is a DAR marker in front of a lilac bush.

Return to the junction of Main Street and US 50 and continue west. At 4.3 miles from the junction, take the road coming in from the right. On the right at 1.1 miles is the Amity DAR marker, almost directly on the trail.

Return to US 50 and turn right (west). Soon you cross the Arkansas River to its south side, leaving the SFT on the north bank. Just past the bridge over the Arkansas on the left are several silos and buildings. This was the site of Old Granada. On July 4, 1873, the Santa Fe Railroad reached here, and the new town of Granada grew up around the terminus. Within weeks two mercantile firms moved to this site (Chick, Brown, and Co. and Otero, Sellar, and Co.) and began sending goods by wagon to New Mexico. Soon three restaurants, two hotels, and three grocery stores were built. By 1875, however, the town was in decline because the railroad had extended its line to La Junta. Fred Harvey bought much of the nearby land here in the 1880s and raised beef for his many Harvey Houses.

If you leave the highway and drive past the silos, you can see several decaying buildings, one of which, in the center, is an original building from trail days.

From here, the new SFT route was called the Granada to Fort Union Military Road or sometimes the Two Buttes Branch. Although the route is unmarked, you can see a swale of this branch if you turn left .4 mile past the railroad bridge at Road 27. At about 1 mile south on this road, ruts can be seen to the right (west). Return to US 50.

Laid out by the army, the Military Road was used by freighters going to Fort Union and Santa Fe. There was much traffic on it from 1873 to 1875, when Granada as a short-lived railhead was the actual beginning of the Santa Fe wagon road. The Military Road went southwest, passed near modern Folsom, New Mexico, and joined the Cimarron Cutoff in the vicinity of the Rock Crossing of the Canadian River. You will have an opportunity to view a part of this route if you choose to take a side trip from Trinidad described below. A good description of the route is provided by Stocking in his *Road to Santa Fe*.

Before rejoining the SFT, it is worthwhile driving 1.1 miles west of modern Granada on US 50 to Camp Amache, which was the only World War II

Japanese-American internment camp in Colorado. At one time there were as many as 7,000 Japanese-Americans interned here. Many of the foundations are still in place. The camp is named for Amache Ochinee Prowers, a Cheyenne Indian who met and married John Prowers in 1861.

GRANADA TO LAMAR

To rejoin the original route of the SFT (left where US 50 crosses the Arkansas east of Granada), take US 385, which goes north from the center of Granada. At just over 2 miles, the highway crosses the Arkansas River. At .4 mile beyond the bridge, is a DAR marker on the right. Continue 1 mile north on US 385 to a junction and turn left (west) on CO 196. At 5.5 miles from the junction, is an intersection with a sign for Road 19. Turn left (south) off CO 196 and drive .2 mile toward the river to a DAR marker on the left (east) side of the road. Good SFT ruts existed in the field behind the marker until 1968, when they were silted over by a flood that covered the Arkansas Valley. Return to CO 196 and turn left (west). At 6 miles is an intersection, with a DAR marker on the northwest corner. After another 5.3 miles, you intersect with US 50 in Lamar.

SIDE TRIP TO SAND CREEK MASSACRE SITE

Currently, the National Park Service is charged with locating and documenting the site and events of the Sand Creek Massacre. The site is approximately 8 miles north of Chivington, Colorado, which can be reached by driving north from Lamar on US 287, then east on CO 96. It can also be reached from Granada by driving on US 385, then west on CO 96. When the site is developed, it will be well worth visiting.

The massacre at Sand Creek involved the Third Colorado Volunteer Cavalry Regiment under the command of Col. J. M. Chivington, who had enlisted his volunteers, called "hundred dazers," in Denver for short-term service. He led his regiment south to New Fort Lyon, then marched to Sand Creek and on November 29, 1864, attacked the sleeping Cheyenne encampment at dawn. About two hundred Cheyennes were killed, most of whom were women and children. The Cheyennes had believed that they were under the protection of the U.S. Army.

Following the massacre, Chivington was hailed as a hero when he returned to Denver, and the event had a strong impact on the SFT. For years afterwards, travel on the trail proved very dangerous for traders and others since the outraged Indians retaliated.

LAMAR

At the intersection of US 50 and CO 196, turn left (south) and drive across the Arkansas River into the center of Lamar. On the east side at the corner of Main and Beach Streets is Colorado's Pioneer Mother statue, or Madonna of the Trail. The statue is just past the railroad tracks, and there is a Colorado Welcome Center in the nearby depot. An inscription on the statue's base refers to the "Big Timbers," a 45-mile-long grove of cottonwoods extending up and down the Arkansas Valley. The grove served as a popular campground for Plains Indians and was a familiar landmark to SFT traders and mountain men since it was the first significant stand of timber on the trail west of Council Grove.

Return north on US 50 (Main Street) and recross the Arkansas River. Just past the bridge watch for a pullout on the right side of the highway, where there is a DAR marker. Just beyond the pullout, US 50 curves to the left (west), but continue straight ahead to the large red brick building housing the Big Timbers Museum. To the left of the museum's main door, is a metal historical plaque with extensive text. The facility is open afternoons only.

Traveling west on US 50, a little over 4 miles from the river bridge and DAR pullout watch for a huge stone barn about .5 mile south of the highway, clearly visible across tilled fields. Now part of a private ranch, this structure was built in 1891 with sandstone hauled from the ruined walls of Old Fort Lyon a few miles upriver. The keystone in the giant arched door on the west end is inscribed: "1st Cavalry 1860." Part of the tin roof is missing, and the building is rapidly deteriorating.

BENT'S NEW FORT

At 7.5 miles from the Arkansas River at Lamar, US 50 crosses the Bent-Prowers County line. One mile beyond the line is a gravel crossroad, County Road 35. Turn left (south) and go 1 mile, where the road ends in a T. From here look straight across the field directly ahead to a stone monument barely visible on a hill—the site of Bent's New Fort.

To get to the fort, turn left (east) at the T, drive .2 mile to the first road intersecting on the right (south), and follow it .5 mile to a wire gate on the right. Park at the gate, cross the fence, and hike .2 mile to the site, aiming for a telephone pole on top of the hill. Around the monument are the stone foundations of the fort, and a few feet north is a fine DAR marker.

The original Bent's Fort, completed by the Bent brothers and Ceran St. Vrain in 1833, was located about 30 miles west up the Arkansas River. In 1849, it was abandoned by the one surviving Bent, William, who in the winter of

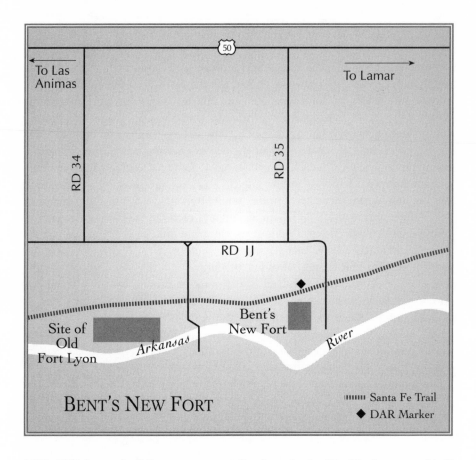

BENT'S NEW FORT

1852–1853 began building a new stone fort here in the Big Timbers on a bluff overlooking the Arkansas.

Like the earlier fort, the new one also served as a way station for SFT travelers, as well as a trading post and Indian agency. In 1860, William Bent leased his fort and surrounding land to the army, which soon built a new post on the bottomland between the present monument and the iron bridge over the Arkansas just to the west. The army first called its establishment here Fort Wise, in honor of the governor of Virginia. In 1862, it was renamed Fort Lyon after Nathaniel Lyon, the first Union general killed in the Civil War. Following a flood in June 1867, this site was abandoned and Fort Lyon moved 20 miles upstream to its present site.

Return to the T and go straight ahead (west) to the first intersecting road from the left. Take it and start south toward the iron bridge over the Arkansas. At about .25 mile, an irrigation ditch crosses the road. Stop just beyond it, and in the distance to the left (east) you can see the monument at Bent's New Fort.

Fort Lyon was to the right (west). Across a plowed field about 200 yards, a slightly elevated pasture, resembling an island of grass, can be seen from the road. Extensive foundations of the fort remain in that area, including a row of eight buildings in line with the irrigation ditch, and between them and the ditch a string of low mounds representing the sites of sentinel boxes or stations. The SFT passed along the north edge of the fort, just above these stations. Stone bases of other buildings are in evidence to the south, extending down to the fringe of trees along the river bottom.

Return to US 50 and continue west about 4 miles, watching for the McClave junction. At that intersection, CO 196 goes right, and gravel County Road 34 turns left (south). Hud's Campground is on the northwest corner. Turn left (south) on County Road 34, and at 1.9 miles, where the road curves right and starts down toward the bridge over the Arkansas, watch for a DAR marker on the left in an open field near prominent SFT ruts. Return to US 50.

RED SHIN'S STANDING GROUND

At the community of Hasty, turn left (south) off US 50 on CO 260 leading to John Martin Reservoir. Although the reservoir, completed in 1948 with the damming of the Arkansas River, has destroyed sections of the SFT, one patch of ruts is preserved.

At 1.8 miles south of Hasty, CO 260 forks to the left and continues to the dam and a campground. At the fork (with a wooden "Welcome to the Reservoir" sign in the middle of the Y), a dirt road goes straight ahead (the right fork of the Y). Follow it, and a short distance beyond a dirt road intersects. Turn right (west) and drive .1 mile to a small access road entering from the left (south). A wooden sign here calls attention to the SFT ruts. Turn left (south) and follow the access road .2 mile to a fenced area with a turnstile at the entrance. Inside, there is a DAR marker on faint SFT ruts. This site is not kept up very well by the John Martin Dam personnel, who, however, assure us that the site will not be abandoned and visitors are welcome.

Return to the Y and turn right .5 mile toward the dam on the paved road. Just before that road starts across the top of the dam, another road, leading to the picnic and camping area, intersects from the left. Take this road, which descends below the dam. Near the bottom where it makes a curve to the left, note on the left a toadstool-shaped rock formation with a flat top, a prominent trail landmark known as Red Shin's Standing Ground. In his *The Old Santa Fe Trail*, Stanley Vestal tells how the rock got its curious name (Vestal 1996). In 1833, Cheyennes were camped on the river below. A warrior named Red Shin got in an argument with some of his tribesmen over a woman. The quarrel

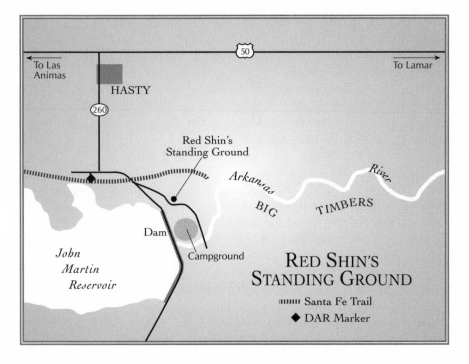

became violent, and taking his weapons Red Shin fled to the top of the flat formation behind camp. Although his foes attacked him furiously, he successfully drove them off, and ever after the rock was known as Red Shin's Standing Ground. From a pullout, you can climb to the top and stand on the same spot where the Cheyenne warrior made his stand.

This interesting site narrowly missed destruction when the John Martin Dam was built immediately to the west. In fact, the location of Red Shin's rock had been lost until recently, when Paul Bentrup identified it as this formation.

Return to US 50 at Hasty and continue west.

NEW FORT LYON

At the intersection of CO 183 with US 50 (6 miles east of Las Animas), is a sign pointing left (south) to Fort Lyon, now a Veterans Administration hospital. At mile .5 on CO 183, is a gray granite DAR marker on the right (west) side of the road, just past a faint intersecting dirt road leading west into a field. (In summer it may be hidden by weeds.)

At 1 mile from US 50, is the fort entrance gate. Drive straight through extensive grounds and turn left at C Avenue. That street leads east. The fort parade ground is on the right, while a row of two-story houses on the left comprises the original officers' quarters, now considerably remodeled, some of which date to the late 1860s. The middle house, in line with the flagpole in the center of the parade ground, was the commanding officer's house. Continue straight ahead past a main building with columns on the right. Behind this building is the Kit Carson Chapel. The small structure with steeple added was originally the residence of the post surgeon. An ailing Carson was brought here from his nearby home at Boggsville and died on May 23, 1868. The upper two-thirds of the building was dismantled in 1957 and the stones used to rebuild it in the form of a chapel, so the structure now has little historical integrity. An explanatory sign is on the outside wall, and an inscribed stone brought from the site of Old Fort Lyon downriver is located to the left of the entrance.

Return to the junction of C Avenue and the entrance road (called Gate Street). Turn left (south) on Gate and follow it past the west side of the parade ground until it curves left to become A Avenue. To the right (south) of A Avenue, are two large buildings of cut limestone, the best-preserved original structures still standing. The one on the east (or left as you face south), Building 19, housed the Commissary Department. It has an incised stone in the west gable reading: "Capt. E. B. Kirk, 1867." The building on the west (right), Building 17, was the quartermaster warehouse. Note: At this writing, plans are afloat to convert the Fort Lyons hospital to a Colorado correctional facility. If that occurs, the site will no longer be accessible to the public.

Return to US 50 and continue toward Las Animas. About 2 miles west of the US 50 and CO 183 junction is a paved crossroads, County Road 13, marked by a small green street sign. On the northeast corner is a DAR marker.

Continue west. Near the eastern limits of Las Animas (at the intersection of US 50 and CO 194) there is a motel on the left called Bent's Fort Inn. In the parking lot of the motel there is another DAR marker.

BOGGSVILLE

Just past Bent's Fort Inn and before the bridge over the Arkansas River, CO 194 turns off US 50 to the right and goes 15 miles west (along the north bank of the Arkansas) to Bent's Old Fort. Before taking that road, however, continue south on US 50 across the bridge and down the main street of Las Animas. At the end of the street, US 50 curves right and a block later intersects with CO 101. There are signs directing you to the Boggsville National Historic District. Turn left (south) on CO 101 and go about 1.2 miles to a Y. The left fork is CO 101, but drive straight ahead on a paved road that goes .5 mile south to the entrance of the Las Animas Cemetery on the left.

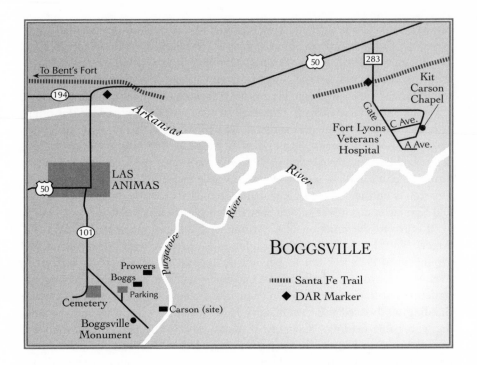

At the right-hand (southeast) corner of the cemetery, at the junction of the lanes marked 6th Street and South Drive, is a stone column with an urn on top marking the grave of William Bent (May 23, 1809–May 19, 1869), one of the most prominent men associated with the SFT. From this point go north on 6th Street one block to the next intersection. On the right at the corner is the tall marble monument, also with an urn on top, for the grave of John Wesley Prowers (1837–1884), who freighted for William Bent on the SFT and was later a station agent for Barlow, Sanderson and Company.

From the cemetery go back .5 mile to the Y and take the other fork, continuing south on CO 101 another .6 mile to a tall concrete monument, titled "Boggsville," on the left (east) side of the highway. Thomas O. Boggs, long associated with the Bents and Kit Carson, settled near here in the early 1860s with local pioneer John Wesley Prowers. The monument provides information about the history of the place.

Return a few yards from the monument and enter the parking lot at Boggsville Visitors' Center. By 1871, Boggsville had a school and served as the county seat for Bent County but declined due to the western expansion of the railroads. In 1873, when the Kansas Pacific built a branch line south from Kit Carson, Colorado, to the new town of West Las Animas Boggsville quickly lost its importance.

The restored Boggs House at Boggsville near Las Animas, Colorado.

The Boggsville site is now being restored by the Boggsville Revitalization Committee and is one of the most interesting areas along the trail. Both the Boggs and Prowers Houses are registered historic sites, open to the public, during summer at least. Maps are available for a worthwhile walking tour of the site. The U-shaped adobe house belonged to Boggs. Behind that is the two-story house of Prowers, once a stage stop on the SFT. Furthermore, Kit Carson and his family lived in a primitive house, now gone, several hundred yards to the east, along the small Purgatoire River. It was there that Carson became ill in 1868 and was taken to nearby Fort Lyon, where he died. Tom Boggs took the Carson children to live in his own house and was the executor of Kit's will. It is said that Boggs himself planted the huge cottonwoods that still grow around the house.

The recently restored Prowers House at Boggsville near Las Animas, Colorado.

Return to the junction of CO 101 and US 50 on the south side of Las Animas. From here, one option is to turn left (west) and follow US 50 to La Junta on the south side of the Arkansas. About midway there, at the Bent-Otero County line, is a roadside park on the left (south) side of the highway containing an exhibit with extensive text on the "Big Timbers" and referring to the SFT.

However, if you travel this route you will miss Bent's Old Fort, the pearl of the SFT. Therefore, it is preferable to turn right at the above junction on US 50 and follow it to the north side of Las Animas, where you can pick up CO 194 and follow it west to the fort. It is at the Bent-Otero County line on this route that traders had their first glimpse of the Spanish Peaks to the southwest.

BENT'S OLD FORT

Bent's Old Fort was the most renowned landmark on the Mountain Route of the SFT. Many travelers wrote about it, and its history has been ably presented by David Lavender in his book *Bent's Fort*. The place was a private, not a military, post and served as a center for the Indian and fur trade. Established by Charles and William Bent and Ceran St. Vrain in 1833, it was called Fort William by many traders because William Bent largely directed its operations. Faithfully reconstructed in the mid-1970s by the National Park Service, it is now a Registered National Historic Landmark and one of the most exciting points of interest on the entire SFT. Here one can feel the pulse of trail days.

The site of the fort was chosen for several reasons. First, it was on the north bank of the Arkansas and thus in United States territory rather than in Mexico. Second, it was a natural trading area. In 1821, Jacob Fowler reported from a location just upstream that his camp was among seven hundred lodges representing the Comanche, Arapaho, Kiowa, and Cheyenne tribes (Coues 1965).

Approaching the grounds from the east on CO 194, the first entrance gate (now closed) is seen on the left (south), a large stone arch with "Bent's Old Fort" at the top. One DAR marker is at the left of the gate, and a second, with a map of the fort, is under the gate. Continue west to the present entrance marked by a National Park Service sign.

At this point the imposing fort can be seen to the south in a loop of the Arkansas River. To preserve the historical atmosphere, visitors must leave cars in a parking lot near the entrance and walk a long path to the fort's front gate. Transportation is available for those unable to make the walk.

Approaching the main gate, the path passes the Fort Cemetery, containing a historical marker. The only gravestone is that of Edward Dorris (d. 1865), but the plot contains twelve other unidentified graves. The cemetery was used after William Bent's abandonment of the fort and while the place was a stage

Bent's Fort on the Arkansas River.

station. Close to the fort's gate notice the marshy area to the left of the path. The Arkansas River flowed through here during trail days. The river was forded directly in front of the main gate as the traders headed for Timpas Creek and Raton Pass.

Inside, the storerooms, shops, and living quarters all have period furnishings. The Susan Magoffin Room is furnished with the type of things she carried in her wagon and installed for her comfort during a brief stopover here in 1846, when she suffered a miscarriage. A freight wagon is on display, a Mexican *carreta* can also be seen at the entrance to the fort. Used in New Mexico during the trail period, the turning wheels of these vehicles were so loud that they could be heard for miles. In summer individuals in period clothing give demonstrations, and a mountain man rendezvous is held in the spring. In addition, a sales shop offers publications on the fort and the SFT.

LA JUNTA

From Bent's Old Fort, drive 8 miles west on CO 194 to La Junta and pick up US 50 on the east side of town. (Note: This La Junta is not to be confused with the historical La Junta at Watrous, New Mexico.) Passing through the center of town, at the railroad station (which will be on the right) turn left (south) on Colorado Avenue and go two blocks to 3rd Street. On the northwest corner is an unusual DAR marker on the Otero County Courthouse grounds.

From this marker go south to the Koshare Indian Museum located at 115 West 18th Street (at the corner of Santa Fe Street). This is the home of the famous Koshare Boy Scout dancers. The museum contains excellent exhibits of Plains Indian materials, some from the era of the SFT. The trail entered La Junta on its eastern edge, went up the slope, and passed just south of the Koshare Kiva before continuing southwest toward Trinidad.

LA JUNTA TO TRINIDAD

On the west side of La Junta, pick up US 350, which runs almost 80 miles to Trinidad. This is a desolate stretch of road, but the country looks much as it did in trail times. (There are no gas stations along the way, and the only privy is at the Timpas Picnic Area.) The earliest wagon road stayed close to Timpas Creek, a short distance to the right (west) of the present highway. Susan Magoffin had much to say about this route. A later stagecoach road followed parts of the highway or paralleled it on the left (east), while another route, the Purgatoire Stage Road, coming from Boggsville, was 10 or more miles to the east. There are some remains of stage stations along the latter route (described by Margaret Long in *The Santa Fe Trail*), but unfortunately much of the country east of US 350 has been condemned by the army for military use, and thus the station ruins are not accessible to the public.

A little less than 4 miles from La Junta, there is a DAR marker against the fence on the right (west) side of US 350. It is on the spot where the trail crossed the present highway from east to west heading toward Timpas Creek, and ruts lie behind it. From this point on, watch for trail ruts to the west. Along here is a good view of the famed twin Spanish Peaks (Wahatoya [Two Peaks] in Ute) on the far horizon to the front right, about 70 miles away—a guiding landmark for trail travelers. Most traders would have reached this point in July when the peaks would still have been covered with snow, providing the hot, weary travelers with a refreshing sight.

At 13 miles from La Junta, CO 71 comes in from the right. Turn here and drive .5 mile to the Sierra Vista overlook. This area is in the Comanche National Grasslands, and the rangers have built this overlook to give visitors a sense of trail. The trail is marked here, and hikers can walk a 3-mile section of it to the Timpas Picnic Area, the next stop.

Go back to US 350, turn right, and drive about 3 miles to the Timpas Picnic Area on the right (west). Traders used this route because in Timpas Creek they could always find water, which was foul but wet. Park at the picnic area, where there are informative signs, and walk the .5-mile nature trail, which begins on the west side of the fenced grounds. The trail goes to Timpas Creek and past a DAR marker. Interestingly, this site was homesteaded until drought drove the farmers out.

Approaching the ghost town of Timpas on US 350, observe the Three Buttes (really three pointed hills) to the left (east) of the highway. The stage route of the SFT passed through a gap between them and the adjoining hills on the west side. Deeply eroded ruts ascend the gap. A stage station was thought to be in this area, but recent research has provided no such evidence.

About 4 miles from Timpas a gravel road leading left from the highway is

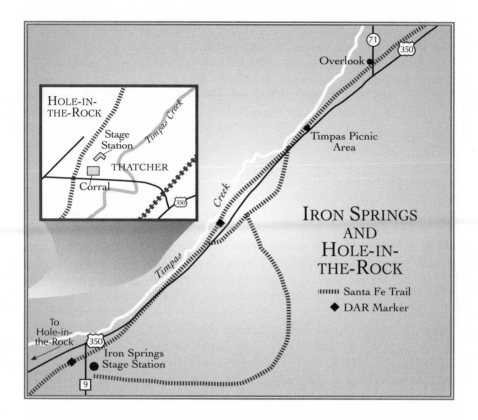

an alternate trail route to Iron Springs but becomes a private road and thus is not open to the public. Another mile past this road, there is a DAR marker located on the west side of US 350. Near mile marker 47 you will begin to see limestone marker posts on your right between the highway and the railway. These are in the ruts of the SFT. The trail eventually crosses the highway and heads for Iron Springs.

At 11 miles beyond Timpas, County Road 9 turns off US 350 to the left (south). This is a well-marked corner advising you of the Iron Springs Historic Area. Turn here and drive .4 mile to the marker on the right, which is located on the trail. There is a DAR marker 200 yards to the right. Continue another .6 mile to the parking area, close to the Iron Springs Stage Station site. In the parking area is a very good interpretive marker. Trail ruts can be seen just west of it, and beyond individuals with good eyes can see the DAR marker in the distance. It is an easy walk to it and the ruts through low grass.

Leave the parking lot, turn right (east) on the county road, and cross over a small bridge. Just past it on the left are two low stock tanks. To the right of them is a concrete box which caps the original Iron Spring. Water from the box goes underground to one of the tanks. Near it is the stone foundation of what was once the station's small fortified barn.

The adobe station itself is marked only by a very low mound of dirt around which are fragments of colored glass. Stubs of cedar fence posts to the left of the stock tank outline the original rectangular stage corral. A protective wall was built around the station soon after its establishment in 1861, but that did not prevent hostile Cheyennes from burning the place in 1864. This site is about .5 mile east of the main SFT, but an alternate route reportedly came down to the station through the saddle at the end of the high bluff seen in the distance behind (north of) Iron Springs.

Return to the highway and continue toward Trinidad to the nearly deserted town of Thatcher, about 45 miles from La Junta. At the only real intersection in the center of Thatcher, turn right (west) on a gravel road, cross the railroad tracks, and go .6 mile past a two-story deserted school. Just beyond the school you will drive across the dry bed of Timpas Creek.

Stop in the creek bed and look .25 mile north down it to the mouth of a rocky canyon, the site of the major SFT landmark Hole-in-the-Rock, a deep hole filled with water available even when the creek was dry. Susan Magoffin had much to say about the hole, which is now filled with sand.

The site of the Barlow, Sanderson and Company's Hole-in-the-Rock Overland Stage Station was west of the creek and north of the corrals. To reach the location, drive past the creek bed, and before the corrals you see a barbed wire fence with a sign warning you not to gather artifacts. There is a gate you can open and enter, but remember to close it behind you. This property was donated to the Archaeological Conservancy by Bob Jones of La Junta, hence the warning signs. Drive or walk straight ahead past the corrals, and in about 100 yards you will see the remains of the station. Although today it is basically a hole in the ground, the station was made of rock, and the basic outline of the foundations are still visible. The corrals near the road were there during trail days, noted in the original government survey of this area in 1869.

Further, early railroad maps show three pools, one south of the road crossing the creek and two north near the canyon. In addition, Margaret Long, who interviewed old-timers in the 1950s, speaks of a "fort" just north of the corrals that must have been the stone stage station (Long 1954).

Return to the highway and continue to Trinidad, keeping an eye on the looming Spanish Peaks just as wagon travelers once did. At 4.5 miles past Thatcher, there is a DAR marker on the right (west) almost across from the entrance to the U.S. Army's Piñon Canyon Maneuver Site. Straight ahead you will also see Fisher's Peak, which looms over Trinidad.

One-half mile past Model (59 miles from La Junta) turn right at County

Road 52, a gravel road but one that should be avoided if it has recently rained. At 2.5 miles a DAR marker is on the right, and some very nice swales are on the left.

TRINIDAD

From far out on the highway northeast of Trinidad, flat-topped Fisher's Peak (originally called Raton Peak) is visible. With Trinidad lying at its foot, it rises just to the left (east) of the entrance to Raton Pass and therefore served as a pilot point bringing wagon caravans to this important crossing of the mountains.

US 350 enters town from the east and becomes Main Street, the actual route of the SFT, at least when it was part of the stagecoach route. The earlier trail route stayed on the west side of the Purgatoire River, where the swales west of Model were located.

Approaching the edge of downtown, observe a two-story adobe house on the left at the southeast corner of Main and Chestnut Streets. This is the house of Don Felipe Baca, a rancher who was the principal founder of Trinidad in 1862. Dating from 1869, in the trail era, the Baca House is now a museum containing furnishings recently brought from New Mexico. It was originally built for John Hough, who moved here from Boggsville and later in 1873 sold it to Felipe Baca. Directly behind it is the interesting Santa Fe Trail Museum in an adobe building that was once the Baca servants' quarters. On exhibit is a hunting coat reportedly given to Kit Carson by a Cheyenne chief.

Behind the Santa Fe Trail Museum on the southeast corner of the intersection of Chestnut and 1st Streets is a 1930s WPA building reportedly constructed to resemble Bent's Old Fort, although the resemblance is minimal.

Continue west on Main Street two blocks to the intersection with Commercial Street. On the northwest corner is the old Colombian Hotel, which has on the outside wall near the door, facing Commercial, a splendid metal plaque with an extensive text on the SFT.

Go one more block on Main Street and turn right (north) on Convent Street. This street leads down to the railroad tracks and just beyond, after a curve, to a bridge over the Purgatoire (or Purgatory) River. It was about here that the early trail crossed the river. Just before passing under the interstate, at University and Nevada Streets, is the Colorado Welcome Center, which has a wealth of information about southern Colorado. Continue under the interstate, turn right (north) on State Street, and follow it about six blocks to Kansas Street. Turn right (east) and go two blocks to Kit Carson Park.

At the park entrance at the intersection of San Pedro and Kansas is a fine archway. In addition, on the hill in the center of the park is a magnificent equestrian statue of Kit Carson showing the scout in mountain garb peering toward Raton Pass. Nearby is the largest DAR marker on the SFT in Colorado.

SIDE TRIP TO STONEWALL

Individuals who have been following the SFT journal of Marian Russell will want to make a side trip from Trinidad to her grave. Go west on CO 12 up the Purgatoire Valley about 40 miles to the small community of Stonewall. Ask directions to the local pioneer cemetery at the one store on the left. Entrance to the cemetery is through an unmarked wire gate (with a crosswire overhead) on the right (north) side of CO 12 about .5 mile past the Stonewall store, just beyond the western limits of the community. The dirt road, which crosses an irrigation ditch just inside the gate, is merely two tire tracks leading up a hill .5 mile to a pine clearing. All the Russells are buried in this inspiring place.

At Trinidad you have a choice of routes. You can either continue south over Raton Pass, the original trail route, or you can take an interesting, but longer, side trip to Tollgate Canyon and follow an alternate route to Raton, New Mexico.

SIDE TRIP TO TOLLGATE CANYON

From Trinidad (or Raton, New Mexico, in reverse) an interesting side trip can be made to visit parts of the Granada to Fort Union Military Road, a late and little-known section of the SFT. From Trinidad go back on US 350 about 6 miles to the junction with US 160. Take US 160 east 39 miles to its junction with CO 389. Turn right (south) on CO 389 at the junction and continue to the hamlet of Branson.

One mile beyond Branson is the New Mexico State line. This low exit is called Emery Gap or Cimarron Pass. The Military Road came to this point from the northeast after leaving the Arkansas River at Granada. The Jacob Fowler party passed nearby in 1822, and in 1820 Maj. Stephen Long went through the gap on his search for the Red River. A wagon road was not established until 1867 or 1868 by Madison Emery. As you pass south through the gap, note that Emery's route went down Gleason Canyon, which is 2 miles east of the highway. You can see faint ruts to the left of the highway leading to the canyon.

Freighters first used this trail in 1868, but its real importance dates from March 1870, when the Kansas Pacific Railroad reached Kit Carson, Colorado. A new freighting road was established south from the railhead to Fort Lyon, where it connected with the Military Road going south to Emery Gap. Here traders

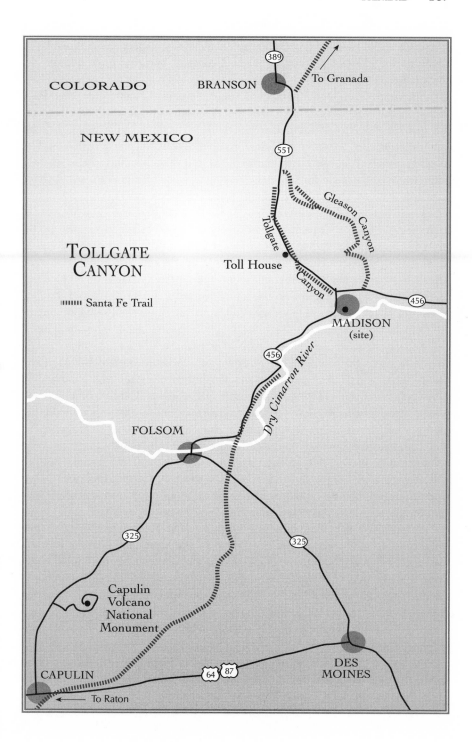

encountered the road already established by Madison Emery. In summer 1873, the Santa Fe Railroad reached Granada, Colorado, and that town became the new trailhead.

The route down Tollgate Canyon was opened in the same year when Basil (Missouri Bill) Metcalf cleared a road there. Eventually, his toll road was easier and quicker than the Gleason Canyon road to the east, but it was a difficult route to construct, prompting Metcalf to charge tolls to recoup his costs. The roofless stone toll house is on your right as you descend the canyon, about 5 miles south of the state line. For the complete story of this road, see Richard Louden's article "The Military Freight Road" (Louden 1993).

At the bottom of the canyon, NM 551 intersects NM 456. You are now in the valley of the Dry Cimarron River, likely first used by wagons in the 1850s. In 1851, Francis X. Aubrey had pioneered his cutoff from near Syracuse, Kansas, southwest to the Cimarron Cutoff near Cold Springs, Oklahoma. There caravans could turn west and continue up the Cimarron Valley. They would have passed this point on the later Military Road and followed the Dry Cimarron by the present-day village of Folsom and on to the Rock Crossing of the Canadian.

Turn right at the junction onto NM 456 and continue 1.2 miles. There, on the left are the remains of the town of Madison, named for Madison Emery. Emery arrived in 1862 and shortly thereafter established his town. In trail days, this was a thriving community with a gristmill, ruins of which can still be seen, a store, a saloon, a blacksmith shop, and a post office. From the road you can see some stone ruins about 200 yards toward the river. Since the site is on private property, you can only view it from the road.

Continue on NM 456 up the Cimarron Canyon, and at 3.5 miles Folsom Falls is on the left. Between the falls and the town of Folsom, ruts can be seen along the road. Mostly on the right side of the road, they are particularly evident in open fields as you reach the top of the canyon.

At the town of Folsom continue south on NM 325 toward Capulin. The Military Road is now several miles to the east, but continue on to the Capulin Volcano National Monument and drive to the summit of the cinder cone. From the east side of the paved road ascending the cone, you can get an aerial view of the ruts of the Military Road several miles to the east. They came down the distant creek before turning west toward Capulin (see map for help locating the ruts). The monument is worthwhile visiting even if you cannot spot the ruts.

Return to NM 325 and drive to the hamlet of Capulin. The Military Road passed through here and then headed south to the Canadian River. From this point drive to Raton by way of US 64/US 87.

RATON PASS

From Trinidad take Interstate 25 south over Raton Pass. This route, now an easy twenty-minute drive, was a major obstacle for the wagon trains. It took the caravan in which Susan Magoffin traveled five days to get through the pass. Her comment on the road was: "worse and worse the road" (Magoffin 1982). The trail followed Raton Creek (on your right as you drive south), purportedly crossing it fifty-three times in the ascent. At Exit 6 (Gallinas), is a DAR marker, just behind the exit sign—accessible only from the southbound lane of Interstate 25.

Several miles beyond, just past the Wootton Exit, watch for a little valley that opens on the right (west) side of the interstate. A billboard facing the highway, placed by the Santa Fe Railroad, reads: "Dick Wootton Ranch and Old Santa Fe Trail." In 1865, "Uncle" Dick opened a toll road for wagons over the pass. His ranch had a stage station as well as a tollgate, although the present owner of the ranch claims that none of the original Wootton buildings remain. In 1878, Wootton's toll road was purchased by the Santa Fe Railroad, and the tracks were laid on the road for much of its route. The entrance to the ranch has a gate across it, and the present owners do not want visitors.

Follow Interstate 25 to the summit, take Exit 460, and proceed to the right of the weigh station. At a small pullout behind the weigh station, is a stone marker indicating a National Historic Landmark, Old Raton Pass. The actual Old Raton Pass is about .5 mile west of this location, but the Highway Department moved the marker to this spot. If you look back towards the northwest, you have a fine view of the Spanish Peaks.

While facing the marker, look to your left to see a bridge over Interstate 25. You may want to drive across this bridge and turn left on the frontage road to view a four-panel interpretive display on the SFT. To get back on Interstate 25 south bound, retrace your steps to the weigh station and take the Interstate 25 south ramp towards Raton, New Mexico.

As you enter the interstate you have a fine view of flat-topped Tinaja Peak ("water tank" or "water jar") and to its right Eagle Tail Peak. The trail is now on your right, and just past mile marker 459 you will see a welcome sign and then an informal turnout. From the turnout, looking back to your right you will see a valley coming in from the northwest. The trail came down this valley and followed the present route of the train tracks into Raton.

RATON

Leave the interstate at Exit 454, cross the tracks, and follow the highway (Business Interstate 25) into Raton. On the northern outskirts of town, watch for a Texaco

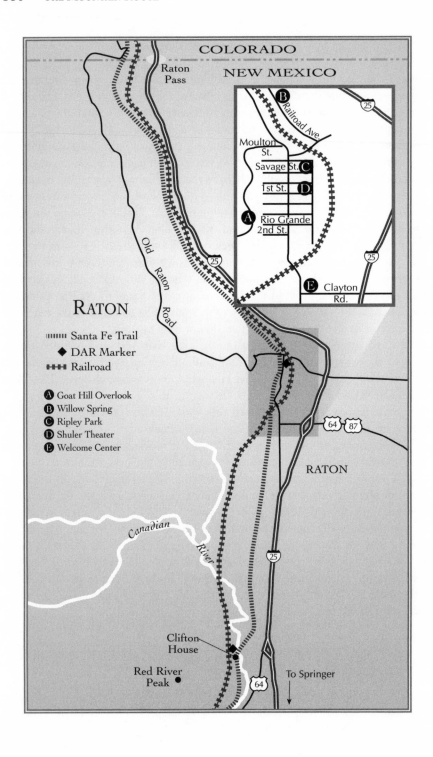

COLORADO

Raton
Pass

NEW MEXICO

25

Railroad Ave.

Ⓑ

Moulton
St.

Savage St. Ⓒ

1st St. Ⓓ

Ⓐ Rio Grande
2nd St.

25

Ⓔ Clayton
Rd.

RATON

⫘⫘⫘ Santa Fe Trail
◆ DAR Marker
╫╫╫ Railroad

Ⓐ Goat Hill Overlook
Ⓑ Willow Spring
Ⓒ Ripley Park
Ⓓ Shuler Theater
Ⓔ Welcome Center

Old Raton Road

25

64 87

RATON

Canadian River

25

Clifton
House

Red River
Peak ●

64

To Springer

station on the right, and a block beyond is Moulton Street. Turn right here to follow the Old Raton Pass Highway, the principal auto highway in 1905. Although this road only goes 5 miles now, it is worth following at least as far as Goat Hill. As Moulton Street climbs toward Goat Hill, motor courts associated with the old highway are on the right. The overlook at Goat Hill provides an excellent panorama of Raton and surroundings, from which you can see the route of the SFT approximately along the railroad tracks. The City of Raton is preparing to develop a new SFT park just to the east of the tracks near the old train terminal. Brave individuals may want to continue up the old highway to get a feel for turn-of-the-century roads. Nancy Robertson, a Raton historian, reports that young men in Raton would offer to drive cars over the pass for the fainthearted. Five wrecked cars at the bottom of one ravine are evidence of the dangers involved.

Returning to the corner of Moulton Street and Business Loop 25, turn right, and drive one block, then turn left and go under the railroad tracks. After passing under the tracks, take the first left turn and drive along the east side of the tracks to 545 Railroad Avenue, a building on the site of the Willow Spring forage station established in 1860. Stagecoaches began stopping here the following year when the U.S. Mail was rerouted over the Mountain Route from the Cimarron Cutoff. By 1870, the stage station and ranch house was a four-room, flat-roofed log building. A portion of that structure is said to be incorporated in the present building, which is a private residence. Behind it, the old Willow Spring, later dug out as a well, is capped and still flows.

Go back under the railroad to East 2nd Street, turn left, drive one block, and then turn left again on Savage Street. On your left is Ripley Park, where there is a DAR marker on the southwest corner. Although unrelated to the SFT, there are two other historical features in this park: a pair of Civil War cannons brought from Rock Island, Illinois, in 1911 and an air porthole, installed in a stone monument, from the battleship *Maine*, whose sinking in 1898 led to the Spanish-American War.

Go east toward the railroad tracks and turn right on 1st Street. As you drive this street, you are passing through the oldest part of Raton built just after trail days. There is a beautiful Mission Revival-style railroad depot and other buildings, including a museum with a few items relating to the SFT. Turn right on Rio Grande Street, go one block, then turn right again on 2nd Street, continuing north to the Shuler Theater on the right side. Inside the entrance of the Shuler Theater, near the ceiling of the lobby, is a series of murals painted by Manville Chapman for the Public Works of Art Project in 1933–1934 that depict scenes related to the SFT, including the Wootton Toll Gate, Willow Springs Ranch, Clifton Stage Station, and Maxwell's Mansion in Cimarron. If the lobby is not open, go to the Old Pass Gallery next to the railroad depot, and the proprietors can let you in the theater.

From the Shuler Theater go back south on 2nd Street. Turn left at Clayton Road and then left again into the Raton Welcome Center's parking lot. The center has information about northern New Mexico, as well as numerous photos of early Raton. The Chamber of Commerce is also in this building.

CLIFTON HOUSE

Return to 2nd Street and drive south to rejoin Interstate 25. Leave the interstate at Exit 446, which is the intersection with US 64 to Cimarron and Taos. Leaving the intersection, just past the frontage road on the right, stop at a turnout, where there is an official New Mexico Historical Marker for Clifton House, an important way station on the SFT.

The site of the Clifton House is on private land, about .75 mile to the west of the turnout. To visit it, you need to request a guided tour at the Welcome Center in Raton. The Clifton House is on the far side of the Canadian River beyond the open field and a row of cottonwood trees seen from the turnout. At the location are a DAR marker and scattered foundation stones, all that remains of the historic structure.

Located where the SFT crossed the Canadian River on its way to Cimarron, the three-story adobe Clifton House with promenade balconies around the upper levels was built between 1866 and 1870 by rancher Tom Stockton. Barlow, Sanderson and Company soon leased most of the building for a "home station" where its passengers could get meals and stay overnight. Barns, outbuildings, and a blacksmith shop were installed nearby. The food and lodging here were considered the best along this section of the trail. With the establishment of the railroad in 1879, the stage line was abandoned and the Clifton House closed down. In 1885, the fine mansion, with woodwork and windows that had been freighted over the SFT from Fort Leavenworth, was gutted in a fire believed to have been started by hoboes.

From the turnout look west past the Clifton House to the highest mountain on the horizon, which is Red River Peak, a well-known landmark for all SFT travelers.

CLIFTON HOUSE TO CIMARRON

A couple of miles beyond the Clifton House pullout on US 64, the highway crosses the Canadian River then goes under a railroad trestle. Just beyond on the right begin the grounds of the National Rifle Association (NRA) Whittington Center. From this point to Cimarron, identifying trail traces is difficult. There are several abandoned railroad beds along here that once served various coal mines. Also, the old highway, which was parallel to the present one, has left its marks: culverts, bridge abutments, and roadbeds.

Continue on US 64 to the entrance of the Whittington Center, and at the gate tell the guard you wish to view the SFT ruts. About .5 mile past the gate, you will see the ruts cross the road. Here there is a pullout with a New Mexico State Historic sign "Santa Fe Trail." There is also a nice marker for the trail consisting of a small New Mexico boulder with a bronze plaque attached, surrounded by four smaller stones brought from each of the other four trail states. A bronze, life-sized replica of SFT wagons, animals, and traders is being commissioned by the NRA. When completed, this sculpture will be placed at the crossing.

Return to the highway and turn right. At high points along the highway in this vicinity watch to the left front for occasional glimpses of the silhouette of the Wagon Mound on the far horizon, 60 to 70 miles away. At 8.7 miles from the Clifton House pullout, is the Hoxie Junction, a mere Y in the highway on the bald prairie. The left fork, old US 85, continues to Maxwell and rejoins Interstate 25. The right fork, US 64, goes to Cimarron.

The Mountain Route of the SFT divided in this area. The right fork stayed close to the foot of the ridge of mountains seen on the north and headed for Cimarron. Continuing west on US 64, ruts of this fork can be detected from time to time on the right. The left fork struck off across the rolling plain in a direct line for a point below Rayado, a small community south of Cimarron. From the air these two forks are plainly visible, as well as a number of crossovers connecting them at various points. The trail can be seen about 100 yards to the right as you approach the Y. The actual location where the Mountain Route split is past the Hoxie Junction near a relay tower on the right. The trail can be seen to the left of the highway just as you pass the tower.

The next point of interest on US 64 is at the crossing of the small Vermejo River. Approaching two bridges here—one concrete, the second steel—a paved road enters from the right (north). Take this Vermejo Creek Road and at .9 mile is a trail crossing marked with the new Santa Fe Trail crossing signs. If you continued up this road, it would lead to the now-closed coal mining town of Dawson. Return to US 64 and turn right. Past the second bridge and just across the railroad tracks on the right are the remains of the ghost town of Colfax. At this crossing there was also a stage station, the adobe ruins of which are in the center of the Colfax site.

Beginning at about mile marker 319, you may see buffalo on both sides of the highway since the local rancher has a very large herd. If you look carefully, you can see the electrified fence that keeps them where they belong.

CIMARRON

Settlers, including Kit Carson, first entered this area in the mid-1840s. Later Cimarron became the home of frontiersman Lucien Maxwell and headquarters for his 1.7 million-acre Maxwell Land Grant. He acquired the grant through his father-in-law Charles Beaubien, who had been an associate of the Bents. In 1870, Maxwell sold the grant to a group of investors. Afterward Cimarron became an outlaw hangout and the center of the bloody Colfax County War (1875–1878).

As early as the 1850s, Cimarron was an important stop for wagon and stage traffic on the Mountain Route of the SFT. A dozen buildings and sites associated with trail days can be visited. The Cimarron River divides the community into a new town and old town, with the trail sites all in the latter, a National Historic District.

Entering from the east on US 64, there is a pullout with an official Scenic Historic Marker. One side describes Cimarron, the other the Colfax County War. Continue toward the center of Cimarron to the junction with NM 21. Just before the junction are two official New Mexico highway markers referring to the SFT, both on the left side of US 64. Approaching this junction a sign reading "National Historic District" points left (south) on NM 21 to old Cimarron. Before following that route, however, turn north one block off US 64 and view a concrete enamel-painted statue of Lucien Maxwell in a park next to the small City Hall.

At the intersection of US 64 and Lincoln, is the bright yellow Chamber of Commerce Visitors' Center. The staff can provide you with information about Cimarron and maps of a walking tour of the historic district.

Go south an NM 21, crossing the rushing Cimarron River to the old part of town in the National Historic District. Find the St. James Hotel, which is on your left (east) after you enter old town, and park somewhere nearby. The SFT sites, all clustered within a small area, are listed below. The Historical Society has provided very nice informative signs at these locations, which can be visited by referring to the accompanying map.

1. SITE OF THE MAXWELL MANSION
The entire block across from the St. James Hotel to the north was once the location of Lucien Maxwell's huge mansion, which was built about 1858 and burned down in 1885. Today, part of the site is occupied by a brown frame dwelling. Maxwell's mansion faced the west side of the plaza and had two sections, divided by an inner courtyard. Adobe and stone walls surrounded the rear section, where the cooking was done and the many employees fed. A remnant of the original stone wall foundation can be seen at the southwest corner of the

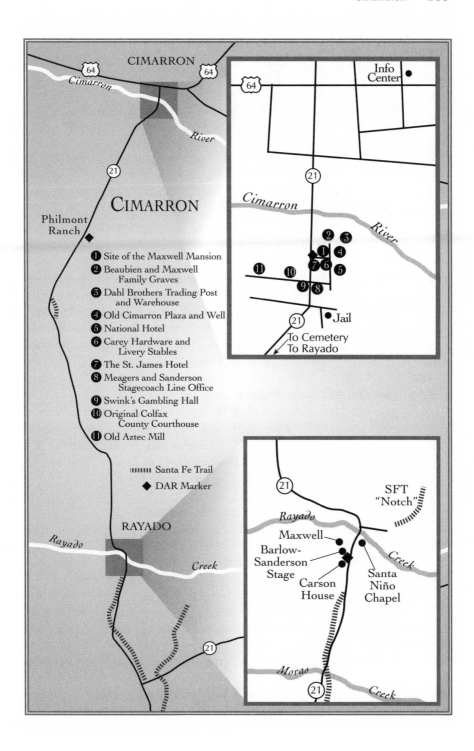

CIMARRON

Philmont
Ranch

CIMARRON

1 Site of the Maxwell Mansion
2 Beaubien and Maxwell
   Family Graves
3 Dahl Brothers Trading Post
   and Warehouse
4 Old Cimarron Plaza and Well
5 National Hotel
6 Carey Hardware and
   Livery Stables
7 The St. James Hotel
8 Meagers and Sanderson
   Stagecoach Line Office
9 Swink's Gambling Hall
10 Original Colfax
   County Courthouse
11 Old Aztec Mill

|||||||| Santa Fe Trail
◆ DAR Marker

RAYADO

Rayado

Creek

Info
Center

Cimarron

River

Jail

To Cemetery
To Rayado

SFT
"Notch"

Rayado

Maxwell

Barlow-
Sanderson
Stage

Carson
House

Creek

Santa
Niño
Chapel

Moras

Creek

*Lucien Maxwell Mansion, Cimarron, New Mexico. Neg. No. 102576,
courtesy Museum of New Mexico.*

property, opposite the St. James Hotel. Luxurious furnishings for the mansion,
freighted over the SFT by Maxwell, included two grand pianos as well as gam-
ing tables and wheels. Maxwell's dinner table was open to all, and trail travelers
took advantage of his hospitality. Many Santa Fe traders knew Maxwell or did
business with him. Before construction of the Clifton House, his mansion was
called the "first civilized stop on the trail in New Mexico."

2. BEAUBIEN AND MAXWELL FAMILY GRAVES
From the Maxwell Mansion site, walk to the east and then north at the corner.
There are two graves here of interest to trail buffs. Behind an iron fence lie
Pabla Lovato Beaubien (d. 1864), wife of Charles and mother-in-law of Lu-
cien, and Verenisa Maxwell (d. 1864), little daughter of Lucien. This site was
originally a part of the Lucien Maxwell property on the south.

3. DAHL BROTHERS TRADING POST AND WAREHOUSE
This long building is immediately east of the graves and runs along the north
side of the plaza. Allegedly begun in 1847 or 1848, the structure has been
extensively remodeled so that it is difficult to get any idea of its original character, despite the fact that it contains some of the original adobe walls.

The history of the place is murky. Some sources claim that Maxwell first
had a commissary on the site. Later, it seems to have been occupied by the Dahl
Brothers Company, which owned two hundred teams of mules and oxen. The
firm made two wagon trips yearly between Cimarron and Westport. At various
times sections of the building served as a post office, jail, stage depot, and office
for the old *Cimarron News*. Near the end of the nineteenth century, fire
destroyed part of the original complex. Just behind the present-day building
(now a private residence) is a well-preserved dugout in the riverbank reputed to

have been built by Maxwell's father-in-law, Charles Beaubien. According to local tradition, it was the first structure built on the site of Cimarron.

4. OLD CIMARRON PLAZA AND WELL
The SFT crossed the Cimarron River about 50 yards northeast of the plaza. Perhaps as early as the 1870s over the river there was a log bridge, which later burned. Wagons entered the open east end of the plaza, in the center of which was a well, said to have been dug in 1871. It is now covered by a white well house with a red roof. A SFT sign is nailed to an adjacent tree.

5. NATIONAL HOTEL
Located to the south of the plaza behind the St. James Hotel, the National Hotel reputedly dates from 1858. It is thought to have become a hotel sometime after 1871, and if so, trail travelers would have stayed there. It also served as home office for Maxwell Land Grant officials. Today, it is a well-kept white building with bright blue trim used as a private residence.

6. CAREY HARDWARE AND LIVERY STABLES
Constructed in 1872, this building also housed the *Cimarron News*.

7. THE ST. JAMES HOTEL
Formerly called the Don Diego Hotel, this two-story structure was built in the 1870s by the French immigrant Henri Lambert, who was once a chef for

The St. James Hotel in Cimarron, New Mexico. Note the DAR marker near the sign.

General Grant and President Lincoln. For a while it was a hangout for out-laws, including the notorious Clay Allison. Pancho Griego was one of Allison's shooting victims in the hotel. In the room that served as a saloon, twenty-six bullet holes still show in the pressed-tin ceiling. In addition, Buffalo Bill may have been a guest, and a room is named for him. The hotel and restaurant are open for business. A DAR marker is on the northwest corner of the block facing NM 21.

8. MEAGERS AND SANDERSON STAGECOACH LINE OFFICE
To the south of the St. James Hotel, this building recently served as a store but is now closed. We can find no historical reference to Meagers, but Jared Sanderson was of the stagecoach firm of Barlow, Sanderson and Company, which operated the Southern Overland Mail line on the SFT. In 1870, the firm is known to have maintained a station with a stock tender at Cimarron. Then it was the last major stagecoach company in the country.

9. SWINK'S GAMBLING HALL
Across the street from the stage station, Swink's was the most notorious gam-bling hall and saloon in northern New Mexico. Originally built as a brewery in 1854, it served as a gas station in recent years but is now closed. An interesting bronze plaque giving a brief history is attached to the front of the building.

10. ORIGINAL COLFAX COUNTY COURTHOUSE
Located on the right as you approach the Old Aztec Mill, this one-story build-ing, constructed in 1872, now houses a Masonic Hall. It served as the local courthouse from 1872 to 1882.

11. OLD AZTEC MILL
A noted SFT landmark, the Old Aztec Mill was operated as a gristmill by Lucien Maxwell between 1864 and 1870. Trail travelers bought flour here for the last push to Santa Fe, and Ute and Jicarilla Apaches were issued gov-ernment flour rations purchased from Maxwell. The building is now owned by the CS Cattle Company, which allows the Cimarron Historical Society to operate it as a museum. The museum opens in early May on Saturday and Sunday only, but is open from Memorial Day through Labor Day from 9:00 A.M. to 5:00 P.M.

Two more sites related to the SFT can be seen as you leave town to the south on NM 21. At the first road beyond the old stagecoach office (8 on the map), turn left and then right into a little lane. On your left is a stone building with a pitched roof, originally the county jail. Return to NM 21 and turn left.

As you leave town, look for a sign directing you to the Mountain View

A few buffalo just east of Cimarron, New Mexico.

Cemetery to the right. Established in 1870, it contains the grave of Rev. F. J. Tolby, who was assassinated in 1875 during the Colfax County War.

From Cimarron a side trip can be made 55 miles across the Sangre de Cristo Mountains via US 64 to Taos and its SFT sites. However, since the excursion requires an entire day, the trip is better made from Santa Fe, after completion of your main tour.

From the Cimarron Historic District, go south on NM 21 toward the Philmont Boy Scout Ranch. Watch to the left of the road for ruts of the Cimarron to Rayado section of the SFT. In the open pasture to the right (west) of the road, you may catch a glimpse of the Philmont's large buffalo herd, or occasionally antelope.

NM 21 goes through the center of the ranch headquarters. The huge Mediterranean mansion, Villa Philmonte, once owned by Waite Phillips, who donated the ranch to the Scouts, can be seen on the left (east). Just past it, also on the left, is the library and museum named in honor of famed naturalist Ernest Thompson Seton, a founder of the Boy Scouts of America, whose collections are housed here. The exhibits are open to the public. A DAR marker is in front of the facility near the road.

Just beyond Philmont, NM 21 climbs a hill and makes a curve to the left. Below the check dam on the inside of this curve (to the left) are deeply eroded trail ruts. Continue on to the hamlet of Rayado, about 10 miles from Cimarron.

RAYADO

This small community was begun in 1848 by Lucien Maxwell and others on land belonging to his father-in-law, Charles Beaubien. Kit Carson also had a farm and house here. In 1850, a small military post was established at Rayado (using Maxwell's buildings) to escort caravans along the SFT between Raton Pass and Las Vegas. Later, the community was designated a "home station" by Barlow, Sanderson and Company.

Deeply eroded SFT ruts sweep into Rayado from the northeast. To see the cut through which they came, turn left on the ranch road just before Rayado Creek. At about 200 yards, you can observe the cut on the left. When early stagecoaches came over this ridge, the driver blew a bugle signaling the station ahead as to the number of passengers so that enough places could be set at the table.

Entering Rayado from the north, note the small, private Santo Niño Chapel on the left (east). Directly across the road on the west is Lucien Maxwell's long adobe house with white wooden posts and railing on the veranda. Constructed in the early 1850s, it originally had a flat roof. Late in the decade Maxwell moved north to Cimarron, where he built his larger mansion on the plaza. Afterwards, the Rayado house came into the possession of Jesús Abreú, another son-in-law of Beaubien.

Just past the Maxwell House on the right, facing the road, is a restored building of brown stucco with a red pitched roof. This was the combination stage station and store operated by Jesús Abreú. Several hundred yards beyond, also on the right (west) side of the road, is the restored house of Kit Carson with a DAR marker in front. The large building with interior courtyard incorporates some of the walls of the original, but the plan and design bear little resemblance to what Kit built. The place is operated as a museum by the Philmont Scout Ranch and is usually open only in summer. Inquire at the Seton Museum and Library back at the ranch. Inside are a stagecoach and covered wagon, as well as other exhibits relating to the SFT. The wagon is reputed to have been used on the SFT by Ceran St. Vrain, a partner of the Bents.

About 1 mile south of the Carson House, NM 21 crosses Moras Creek. Looking to the right (west), note that a wide canyon forms a bay in the mountains. This is the gap mentioned by Commissioner George Sibley in 1825 as the one through which a "trace," or rough trail, passed then ascended Grulla Mesa and crossed the mountains to Taos. Pack trains heading for Taos rather than Santa Fe left the Cimarron Cutoff of the SFT at the Rock Crossing of the Canadian River, about 30 miles to the east, and steered for the Moras Gap, visible in the distance.

Continuing on several miles, the road makes a sharp turn to the left (east), while a gravel road continues straight ahead. The gravel road, closed now, eventually becomes a primitive jeep road. That is the route of the SFT as it threads its way around mesas to the Ocaté Crossing and eventually on to Fort Union. We will pick up this route later at the Ocaté Crossing.

At this corner you can look back toward Rayado and see deep ruts just to the east of NM 21. Continue east here on what is now NM 199, until, at .3 mile, you can see more ruts to the right of the highway. This is the branch of the trail we left at Hoxie Junction.

Stay on NM 21 about 20 miles to Springer.

SPRINGER

Near the center of Springer on US 85, two blocks north of its junction with US 56, is the Santa Fe Trail Museum, in the historic old Colfax County Courthouse. The museum's first floor is dedicated to the SFT.

To continue on toward Wagon Mound, go south on US 85 to the outskirts of Springer and pick up Interstate 25. The convergence of US 85 and US 56 at Springer brings together the Mountain Route and the Cimarron Cutoff, at least for modern highway travelers. Originally the trail's arms at this point were still some miles apart, moving across country toward a union at La Junta (present-day Watrous).

Here we drop back to the parting of the trail in western Kansas and describe a motor tour of the Cimarron Cutoff from Lakin through the Oklahoma Panhandle to Springer.

THE CIMARRON CUTOFF
WAGON BED SPRING, McNEES
CROSSING, AND WAGON MOUND

WAGON BED SPRING

From Lakin, Kansas, on the Arkansas River, go south on KS 25 toward Ulysses. Just after crossing the Arkansas River Bridge you are on the flood-plain. One local branch of the SFT passed here, continued upriver to the crossing at Chouteau's Island, then turned south to head for Lower Spring on the Cimarron River. The traders followed Bear Creek until they climbed out of the sand hills at Bear Creek Pass, about 11 miles from the Arkansas River crossing on KS 25. Ruts can be seen here to the right of the highway. Continue another 17 miles to Ulysses.

At the intersection of KS 25 and US 160, turn left (east) about three blocks to the Grant County Museum, a large white building set back on the left. It has excellent SFT exhibits with special reference to the nearby Wagon Bed Spring site.

From Ulysses continue south on KS 25 another 7.5 miles to a point where the highway veers slightly left. Here there is a sign directing you straight ahead to Wagon Bed Spring.

Continue south on that road about 3 miles and turn right on a dirt road to Wagon Bed Spring, about 1 mile from the turn. The road to the spring site is just before the ford at the Cimarron River. There is a small parking lot at the

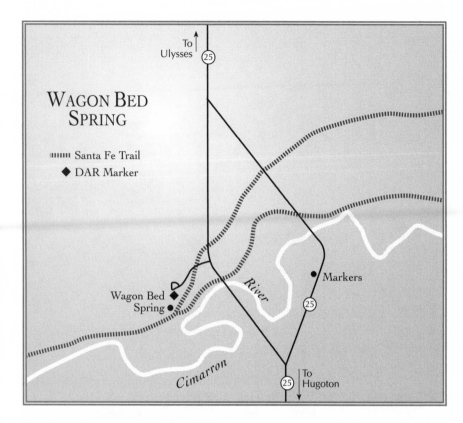

location of the spring. Initially called Lower Spring, it was the first reliable water source after leaving the Arkansas River. The stretch between Lakin and the Cimarron represents part of the infamous Jornada, the waterless section of the SFT that caused so much trouble for early caravans. Most travelers mentioned it in their journals in doleful terms. Today, with all the farms supported by deep-well irrigation, it is difficult to visualize the country when it was considered an uninhabitable desert, a place to be gotten through quickly.

At the site is a DAR marker, near the river enclosed by a white railing, as well as a Kansas State Historical Marker reading "Wagon Bed Spring." It was near here that famed mountain man and explorer Jedediah Smith died in 1831. He was scouting for water for a wagon train and ranged out ahead to find the Cimarron River. Comanches attacked him while he was digging in the river's sand for water. There is a monument to Smith, as well as a Kansas Historical Marker for Wagon Bed Spring and a Mormon Battalion marker on KS 25 where it crosses the Cimarron.

The name Wagon Bed Spring came into use in 1847 when someone sank a wooden wagon bed in the spring to collect water and serve as a holding tank.

The Cimarron River at Wagon Bed Spring, Kansas—a rare sight with considerable water flowing in the river.

Before that it was commonly referred to as the Lower Spring and was the first in a series of three in the valley of the Cimarron River. The next, the Middle Spring, was on the SFT upriver about 36 miles, and the Upper Spring beyond that another 18 miles. These springs were crucial because in this area the river itself seldom had water in summer, and when it did the water was bitter with alkali.

MIDDLE SPRING

From Wagon Bed Spring the SFT followed the Cimarron River on its north bank. Since it is not possible do that, it is necessary to make a detour to Middle Spring.

From Wagon Bed Spring, return to the gravel road, turn right, and in dry weather ford the Cimarron River to reach KS 25. However, if any water is running in the riverbed (a very rare occurrence), return north to pick up the highway. If you wish to see the monument to Jedediah Smith and the marker for the Mormon Battalion, you will have to return to KS 25 where it crosses the Cimarron River.

At Hugoton, the next town going south, rejoin US 56, which was left in Dodge City. Go southwest on US 56 to Elkhart on the Oklahoma border. As

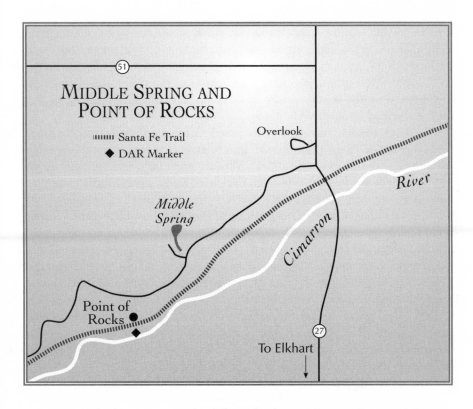

MIDDLE SPRING AND
POINT OF ROCKS

|||||||| Santa Fe Trail
◆ DAR Marker

Overlook

Middle
Spring

River

Cimarron

Point of
Rocks

To Elkhart

you approach the town, on the left is the large Morton County Museum, which has excellent SFT exhibits. The highway passes along the east side of Elkhart and at the one traffic light intersects with Morton, the main commercial street. Turning right here will take you through downtown on the way to Middle Spring.

Before proceeding to Middle Spring, however, go beyond the intersection on US 56 for another few blocks past the white grain elevator to a turnout on the right. Here is the last official Kansas Historical Marker, for Point of Rocks and La Jornada, whose text focuses entirely on the SFT. Point of Rocks is a prominent landmark that juts out into the valley near Middle Spring.

From the turnout, return to the intersection with Morton and take that street several blocks through the business district. Just past a park on the right, Morton Street ends in a T at Baca Street. Turn right on Baca and join KS 27 headed north toward Middle Spring at Point of Rocks. At 8 miles cross the Cimarron River. Here you will see the many limestone markers on either side of the road indicating the route of the trail. At .5 mile beyond the bridge, a dirt road intersecting from the left (west), with a yellow cattle guard, leads to Middle Spring.

Before taking this dirt road, however, continue straight ahead on KS 27 another .5 mile to the crest of the ridge that is the edge of the Cimarron Valley. There on the left (west) is a dirt road leading to a pullout and overlook. At the site is a Cimarron National Grassland marker with extensive text on the SFT. From this location, you have a good view of the valley, the open grassland beyond on the south, and Point of Rocks, several miles to the west. Go back to the road leading to Middle Spring.

At about 2 miles after leaving the paved highway and cattle guard, a small road intersects from the right (north). Immediately after turning on it is another yellow cattle guard and just past it the Middle Spring historical sign with excellent text. Immediately behind the sign the spring forms a pond surrounded by a grove of trees, where there are several picnic tables and restroom facilities.

Return to the main dirt road and turn west again toward Point of Rocks. You can see more limestone SFT markers along here. At about 1.5 miles from Middle Spring, the road divides at a Y. Take the left-hand fork a short distance to the top of Point of Rocks. At the parking area are several interpretive markers. The SFT passed between the foot of the bluff and the river. From the parking area, you have an excellent view of the Cimarron River snaking southwestward about 5 miles, where it clips the extreme corner of Colorado before continuing into Oklahoma. It is possible to hike a steep trail from the parking area downslope toward the river to a DAR marker. Rededicated here in 1997, the marker had been moved to nearby KS 27 before it was returned.

Return to Elkhart and rejoin US 56 leading to Boise City (pronounced Boyce), Oklahoma.

THE OKLAHOMA PANHANDLE

Soon after entering the present state of Oklahoma, the SFT crossed to the south bank of the Cimarron River at a well-known site called Willow Bar, which got its name from a stand of willow trees growing on a sandbar in midstream. At that point the trail left the river, but for approximately the next 20 miles it remained in the Cimarron "breaks," the rough country composed of hills and mesas lying in the wide valley of the river.

The next campsite after Willow Bar was Upper Spring (or Flag Spring), followed by Cold Spring and then Fort Nichols. About 5 miles beyond Fort Nichols, the trail entered what is today the state of New Mexico. Unfortunately, all of these sites are on private ranch land and not easily accessible. However, several good markers and some fine trail ruts can be seen.

In the center of Boise City, is the Cimarron County Courthouse. On the grounds on the north side is a Mormon Battalion marker dedicated in summer 1983. From here follow US 287/US 385 north and stop at the museum that is part of the Heritage Center, on the left with a large metal dinosaur in front. The museum has some SFT exhibits. But, more importantly, the museum staff can give you directions and permission to visit fascinating Autograph Rock, an important stopping place on the SFT where many travelers carved their initials in sandy cliffs. Continuing north on US 287 at about 9.6 miles is a pullout on the left (west) with a historical marker commemorating Joseph C. Brown, the surveyor for the Sibley party of 1825.

The SFT crossed the highway here, and ruts can be found on both sides of the road. Excellent ruts begin directly behind the pullout; walk west beyond the railroad tracks to view them. Also, look northeast, across the highway, and observe prominent Wolf Mountain, around both sides of which branches of the SFT passed angling up from Willow Bar on the way to Upper Spring. Upper Spring is about 1.5 miles due west of this location, only a thirty- to forty-five-minute walk, although individuals unfamiliar with the country are apt to miss it.

Return to Boise City, and on the west side of Courthouse Square pick up a paved state road that leads to Kenton. At 15 miles, the paved road to Wheeless intersects from the left (south). This is the road that goes to New Mexico, but for the moment continue straight ahead another mile where the highway makes a sharp turn to the right (north). At about 3.5 miles from the curve, is a pullout on the left (west).

Here is one of the choicest spots on this section of the SFT, with no fences and unspoiled prairie stretching toward the western horizon. The trail crosses the highway coming from Upper Spring and Cold Spring heading for Fort Nichols, 7 miles to the southwest. An official Oklahoma Highway Marker refers to the founding of the fort in 1865 by Kit Carson. During its few months of existence, it guarded this section of the trail from hostile Indians. A second handsome marker refers to Sibley's surveyor Joseph C. Brown. Behind the markers, thick vegetation in the trail ruts appears as a discoloration in the prairie.

Return 4.5 miles to the Wheeless junction, then go south 1 mile and turn right. The New Mexico State line is 12 miles from this point. As you turn onto this road, ahead to your left you will see the distant Rabbit Ears, the first elevations of any prominence that traders saw on the Cimarron Cutoff.

McNEES CROSSING

At the New Mexico State line, the Wheeless Road makes a sharp left turn. At this turn is a new DAR marker. The SFT passed directly over the marker site and into New Mexico. You can see the swale to the west just behind a sign on a fence stating "Santa Fe Trail Ruts, New Mexico." After turning left at the DAR marker, drive about 1 mile south on the state line and then right again,

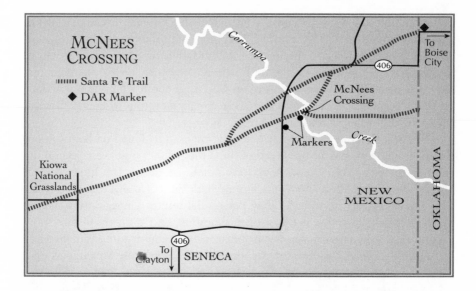

entering New Mexico. Straight ahead is the distant mountain Sierra Grande, another familiar trail landmark. At 2 miles inside New Mexico, is an intersection and stop sign. Here go west toward Clayton on NM 406.

At the intersection with NM 406, you can see the SFT in the fenced pasture on the east (right). It is represented by a wide swale, or cut, that makes a conspicuous indentation on the horizon. Following this trail takes you back to the DAR marker previously noted in Oklahoma. In late summer, because of extra moisture, the trail depression is marked by a thick stand of bright green rabbit weed.

From the high ground at this intersection, the renowned trail landmark Rabbit Ears can be seen in the distance to the southwest. They are a mountain and a butte of unequal size lying close together, but from certain places on the trail they vaguely resemble a pair of rabbit ears. According to one story, however, they did not get their name from their appearance but from Chief Rabbit Ears of the Cheyennes, who was killed in the vicinity by the Spaniards. In any case, all travelers on the Cimarron Cutoff were familiar with the twin peaks, which remained in sight for many days. The main SFT passed along their north flank, while a less-used branch skirted them on the south.

From the intersection go west toward Clayton, noting ruts on the left of the road, then curve south on NM 406 for 2.4 miles to the highway bridge over the usually dry North Canadian River (called locally Corrumpa Creek). At .8 mile past the bridge, is a wire gate on the left (east) side of the highway. About 100 yards past the gate, there is a marker, "McNees Crossing," which is right on the SFT. Looking toward the western horizon, traces of the trail can be seen disappearing in the distance.

The cut-bank heading up from the McNees Crossing of Corrumpa Creek.
The trail is in the center foreground.

The gate gives access to a two-track ranch road leading east across an open cow pasture .5 mile to McNees Crossing. This is private land, but the current owner allows entry, provided you CLOSE THE GATE BEHIND YOU, since there are livestock inside. From the gate a windmill can be seen near the end of the ranch road, and to the right of it the white monument marking the crossing.

Go to the end of the ranch road past the windmill and right up to the large square monument. The road is okay for passenger cars in dry weather, but in summer the center is high with weeds. Immediately to the southeast of the monument, a dirt ramp (the original trail) leads down to the crossing of the North Canadian. Both upstream and downstream the bed is loose sand, but at this one spot is a rock shelf in the bottom of the riverbed, making a natural crossing for wagons. On the east and west banks are traces of caravan campgrounds.

From the monument or ramp, look east across the North Canadian, where tracks of two branches of the trail can be seen coming down to converge at the crossing. The beginning of this short split is approximately 8 miles back, in the vicinity of Fort Nichols, Oklahoma.

At this crossing, in autumn 1828 two young traders named Robert McNees and Daniel Monroe rode ahead of their eastbound caravan, stopped to take a nap, and were shot by Indians. When the caravan arrived, McNees was dead and was promptly buried on the spot. The wounded Monroe was carried on to the Cimarron River, where he died. These deaths contributed to the clamor for military escorts, the first of which was Major Riley's in 1829. Josiah Gregg records an Independence Day celebration here on July 4, 1831, the first such observance

The monument at McNees Crossing commemorating a Fourth of July celebration noted by Josiah Gregg.

in New Mexico. The white monument was placed by the American Legion in 1921 to commemorate that event.

Return to NM 406 and continue south toward Clayton. The highway makes a sharp right and continues for about 3 miles, where it turns left. Instead of following the highway at this point, continue straight ahead (west) on the gravel road 3 miles, then turn right and go 1 mile to an intersection, which is at the corner of the Kiowa National Grasslands.

This is a good place to get out and walk the ruts. At the northwest corner of the intersection is a parking lot, and you can enter the walking area through a gate. Once inside the gate, there are fine ruts coming from right to left. You can also drive north from here down the arroyo and up the other side through a gate on the right, continuing for about .25 mile. This is also Kiowa National Grasslands property, and you can walk the trail here as well. Moreover, in the arroyo to the right, about .5 mile from where you parked, are many large exposed rocks, and on one there are some dinosaur tracks. Return to NM 406 and turn right toward Clayton. At 1 mile you will see the deserted Seneca School on your left. This part of New Mexico was homesteaded early in the 1900s, and this school served the homesteaders' children, at one time accommodating ninety-eight youngsters.

THE CLAYTON COMPLEX

In 1964, New Mexico State Senator William Wheatley of Clayton was instrumental in having the Clayton Complex designated a Registered National Historic Landmark. It includes an assembly of SFT campsites and geographical features beginning at McNees Crossing and extending for about 35 miles southwest along the trail to Round Mound. (A description of the various sites is supplied by William E. Brown in *The Santa Fe Trail*, 1988.) Unfortunately, several sites like Turkey Creek Camp and Rabbit Ears Creek Camp, are on private land and not easily accessible to the public.

From Seneca School follow NM 406 south to its junction with US 56 4 miles east of Clayton. There turn right (west) on US 56. At .1 mile on the right (north) is a pullout with an official New Mexico Highway Marker, "Rabbit Ear Mountain."

In the center of town is the old Eklund Hotel, founded in post-trail days by a Swedish-born Clayton pioneer, Carl Eklund. Although it is closed as a hostelry, the dining room has been restored in grand Victorian style and serves splendid meals.

One-half block east of the Eklund Hotel take US 64/US 87, which leads northwest toward Raton. At the city limits just beyond the Holiday Motel (one of only three in town), in a pullout on the left (south) side of the highway, is an official New Mexico Highway Marker, "Clayton," with reference to the Cimarron Cutoff.

One mile farther is the Union County Feed Lot (on the right) with plenty of cows. Just past it is another official New Mexico Highway Marker, "Rabbit Ear Mountain," with a text about the SFT that differs from the one east of Clayton with the same title. This location offers a good view of the Rabbit Ears just to the north.

At 18 miles from Clayton, US 64/US 87 goes through the small community of Mt. Dora. The large, round mountain from which the town takes its name lies to the right (north) of the highway. The SFT coming from McNees Crossing passed along its north side and then headed southwest to intersect the highway straight ahead.

Five miles beyond Mt. Dora is a roadside park with picnic table on the right (north). Here, alongside its tracks, the Colorado and Southern Railway has erected a SFT marker (a bronze plaque set in a white monument) designating the place where the trail crossed the tracks and the highway. Directly to the south and slightly west is Round Mound (today often called Mt. Clayton), a major trail landmark recognized by all wagoners, who often scaled the summit for a view of the surrounding country. In Josiah Gregg's *Commerce of the Prairies*, there is a lithograph showing the view from the top with a wagon train passing below.

From the park and railway marker, rejoin US 56, which is some 20 miles to the south. The longest way, but safest if the weather is bad, is to return to Clayton and pick up US 56 on the west side of town. In good weather you can continue ahead on US 64/US 87 another 3.5 miles to the nearly deserted community of Grenville. There dirt NM 453 intersects on the left (south) and leads 22 miles south to US 56. After a period of rain or snow, the road, although dried out, may remain badly rutted. After turning onto NM 453, Round Mound is straight ahead.

At 2.5 miles from Grenville the road turns sharply to the right (west). At this point the SFT is off to the left of the road between you and Round Mound. The trail can be seen from the top of the mound, but if you stop and look carefully you can see it from the road. Those wishing to make the climb should park here. Allow at least half a day, as the distance across the flat prairie to the base and the height of the mound are deceiving.

Two miles from the first turn is a second one to the left (south), which goes along the west side of Round Mound. Soon after the second turn, the SFT crosses NM 453 headed southwest toward the next major landmark, Point of Rocks. The crossing of the road is unmarked, however, and we have not located ruts. Continue south to the junction of US 56, located 29 miles west of Clayton, and turn right (west) toward Springer.

TO POINT OF ROCKS

At about 18 miles west of the above junction, US 56 crosses the western boundary of Union County into Colfax County. From this point look north to a long sloping mountain in the far distance. This is 8,720-foot Sierra Grande, which first became visible to wagon travelers as they crossed the Oklahoma Panhandle and remained a prominent landmark for many days thereafter.

From the same location also look north and west (to the front right of the highway) at the corner of a mesa jutting onto the plains. This is the dark outline of New Mexico's Point of Rocks, which caravans used as a guide as they traveled westward after passing Round Mound. There was a fine spring at the site, but it was also a place Indians used for ambushes.

Point of Rocks, New Mexico.

At 31.5 miles from the aforementioned junction (US 56 and NM 453), is a roadside park on the right (north) and an official New Mexico Highway Marker, "Point of Rocks."

A gravel county road, County Road 52, intersects with US 56 at the east end of the park, while a power transmitter is on the northeast corner. Look north and a bit east of County Road 52 to a cluster of ranch buildings and trees about 5 miles away on the plain. The round mountain (behind and to the right of the ranch) with the mesa at its base marks Point of Rocks.

For a closer look, drive (in dry weather only) north on County Road 52 about 7 miles. Between 6 and 7 miles the deep swale of the SFT crosses the road. The Soil Conservation Service has placed low earth dams across the swale to check erosion. At 7 miles turn right (east) at the intersection onto County Road 53, go 2 miles, then turn left (north) 1 mile toward a ranch house near the base of Point of Rocks. This is the Gaines Ranch, and the owners welcome visitors. A toilet is available for site visitors, and there is a mailbox with trail information that will show you the way to the historic grave and the spring. The main SFT stuck to the flat plain about 1 mile to the south, but many caravans made a swing here because of the availability of water. Return to the park and continue west on US 56.

ROCK CROSSING OF THE CANADIAN

At 14.5 miles from the Point of Rocks roadside park, look for an old, abandoned stone house that is a partial dugout with a weathered shingle roof, on the left (south) side of US 56, with a telephone pole directly behind it. In this vicinity, the SFT coming from Point of Rocks crossed from the right to the left side of the highway, although the ruts are not in evidence close to the road. (They can be seen, however, at another point .25 mile down the highway to the left.) There are some new SFT crossing markers here. This location is also near the junction of the Cimarron Cutoff and Grenada to Fort Union Military Road.

To see the well-known Rock Crossing of the Canadian, look southwest past the house and down a natural trough between the mesas about 2 miles away. The mesas form the edge of the Canadian River Valley, while the river itself is at the bottom of the trough, marked by a line of trees. The SFT led down the trough to the river. Here was the famed Rock Crossing of the Canadian (El Vado de las Piedras). A natural rock bottom at the ford (similar to the one at McNees Crossing on the North Canadian) aided the passage of wagons. Below this point was the impassable Canyon of the Canadian, and above it the river bottom was of sand.

Once past the crossing, the SFT forked. The left branch, the main trail, continued in a southwesterly direction to the Wagon Mound. The right branch, merely a pack trail, went due west to the vicinity of present-day Rayado, where it crossed the mountains to Taos.

The actual site of the Rock Crossing is on a private ranch, accessible only by a jeep road. Thus visitors will have to settle for this distant view. Hobart Stocking gives a historical sketch of the site in *The Road to Santa Fe*.

Continue 8 miles on US 56 to Springer, where today's Cimarron Cutoff, via the paved highway, rejoins the Mountain Route of the SFT.

NEW MEXICO

FORT UNION, LAS VEGAS, AND SANTA FE

WAGON MOUND

From Springer, Interstate 25 goes almost due south 26 miles to Wagon Mound. About halfway there, at the Colmor exit, the silhouette of the Wagon Mound becomes clearly visible on the horizon to the left of the highway. Early Santa Fe traders thought the mountain's shape resembled a high-top shoe. Later someone decided the profile looked more like a covered wagon pulled by oxen, so the feature became known as the Wagon Mound. The last great landmark on the westward journey across the plains, it was as renowned as Pawnee Rock and the Rabbit Ears.

To the right (west) of the Wagon Mound, are two elevations known to trail guides as the Pilot Knobs. The left one is a narrow flat-topped butte, while the right one is a wider mesa. In former days the term pilot knob was applied rather indiscriminately to any natural feature serving wagon masters as a point of reference. The Rabbit Ears and Round Mound, for example, were both referred to by some diarists as "pilot knobs." The SFT, like today's Interstate 25, threaded a narrow pass between the foot of the Wagon Mound and the Pilot Knobs.

Although from a distance the Wagon Mound appears to rise isolated from the plains, nearer one sees the small town by the same name that hugs its base. Approaching the community's one interchange, look right (west) from the highway up Santa Clara Canyon, a deep indentation in the edge of the plains that stretches westward. At the head of this canyon, about 2 miles away, is Santa Clara Spring, now covered over and serving as the source of the town's water supply. Since there were several smaller springs about where the town is now, it is likely that few traders climbed the mesa to use Santa Clara Spring.

After exiting, turn left (east) and drive under the overpass. Immediately beyond on the left behind the service station note the marshy pond, which shows that water is close to the surface and probably accounts for traders utilizing this area instead of Santa Clara Spring on the mesa.

Continue straight ahead one-half block on NM 120 to the junction of old US 85. In front of the service station on the northwest corner facing US 85 in a small park area, are two plaques set in a low red sandstone monument. One is a bronze marker designating the Wagon Mound as a Registered National Historic Landmark. The other shows William Becknell's first pack train over the SFT with the Wagon Mound in relief in the background. Made by the same sculptor who created a similar plaque for Pawnee Rock, it was installed in 1971 on the 150th anniversary of the opening of the trail.

Cross US 85 and continue on NM 120 through the town of Wagon Mound. After a couple of blocks, turn right on Catron Street and go a short distance to the junction of Long Street. Here on the porch of the municipal building to the right is the displaced DAR marker for Wagon Mound. Return to NM 120 and turn right (east) toward Roy.

Continue driving past the Wagon Mound school complex on the right at the edge of town. Soon there is a dirt road to the right that leads to two cemeteries at the base of the Wagon Mound, easily seen from the highway. Follow the dirt road to the entrances. The Protestant Hillside Cemetery is on the left, while the Catholic Santa Clara Cemetery is on the right. In it is an extraordinary white marble tombstone of the SFT freighter Charles Fraker. Of mixed German and Cherokee ancestry, Fraker was closely involved with the Santa Fe trade during its last days. He married María de Luz (Lucy), a daughter of Manuel LeFevre, a French Canadian trapper who settled in Taos in the 1820s. (Another of LeFevre's daughters, Dolores, married Uncle Dick Wootton of Raton Pass fame.) The tombstone, somewhat damaged by time or vandals, shows a magnificent ox team and covered wagon in bold relief.

At this location the Wagon Mound towers overhead behind the cemetery. From the high ground here, look north and a bit east to observe the route (though not the ruts) of the Cimarron Cutoff coming from the Rock Crossing of the Canadian toward the Wagon Mound. In May 1850, a war party of Utes and Jicarilla Apaches used this same vantage point to watch the approach of the Santa Fe-bound stage carrying ten men and the U.S. Mail. They concealed themselves behind the low rounded hill just to the southwest of the cemetery, then suddenly attacked. After a furious battle, all the whites were killed and the stage destroyed. Days later a military patrol from Las Vegas found the human remains, scattered by wolves, and buried them. The Santa Clara Cemetery, established many years later, may be on the site of that earlier burial.

Return to NM 120 and turn left back toward the town. At a high point in the road before reaching the school complex, look in the distance to the west (straight ahead) for a good view of Santa Clara Canyon, the site of its spring surrounded by trees. At the interchange you have a choice. An interesting side trip can be made from here to the Ocaté Crossing on the Mountain Route, or you can head directly for Fort Union.

SIDE TRIP TO OCATÉ CROSSING

To get to Ocaté Crossing, drive west on NM 120. When you reach the top of the hill, you can see ruts on both sides of the highway. Many traders heading for Fort Union went west from Wagon Mound to connect with the Mountain Route rather than continuing south on the Cimarron Cutoff to La Junta (present-day Watrous).

At about 14 miles look for the signed Mora Ranch Road on your right. Turn here and continue 1.5 miles to Ocaté Creek, parking on this side of the creek. The crossing, or ford, is to your right. Ruts can be seen leading down to the creek and up the south side. This route is a continuation of the one leading south from Rayado. From this point it was a straight trip south to Fort Union.

By 1860, there was a ranch at the crossing, established by A. J. Calhoun. By 1877, he had built a gristmill and a stage station at the site. He and other family members are buried in the small cemetery behind the corral. The corral and cemetery are a short (100-yard) walk west from the road. Today, the corral is just several lines of stones, the cemetery fenced a few yards west.

From here you can continue on Mora Ranch Road over the creek another 6 miles, although the road is not always good. At 4 miles is Apache Mesa on your left. Trail ruts are evident on the left between the road and the mesa. Just past Apache Mesa it is advisable to turn and retrace your route to Wagon Mound.

At the interchange, rejoin Interstate 25 headed toward Fort Union and Watrous. Just beyond Wagon Mound, to the left between the highway and the railroad tracks, are SFT ruts, which are clearly visible. From the air they stand out boldly, but at ground level from the highway they are more difficult to see. About 1 mile from Wagon Mound is a Highway Department storage yard to the left. There a dip in the fence on the south side indicates the route of the trail.

At about 6 miles from the interchange, the trail crosses from left to right. A rancher has placed a sign at the crossing on the right side of the highway.

Apache
Mesa

Calhoun
Stage
Station

Ocaté
Crossing

Ocaté

Mora Ranch Rd.

Creek

OCATÉ
CROSSING

ıııııı Santa Fe Trail

120

To Wagon
Mound

Approximately 13 miles from Wagon Mound, exit at the Fort Union Rest Stop on high ground to the right. In this roadside park are an official New Mexico Highway Marker, "The Santa Fe Trail," and a DAR marker, the latter moved here a few years ago from the vicinity of Colmor. In the lobby of the visitors' building is a small SFT exhibit containing a map and historical photographs.

About 1 mile beyond this rest stop is another one in the eastbound lane of the interstate, not accessible to westbound travelers. At that stop is another DAR marker (moved here from its original location west of Watrous) and an official New Mexico Highway Marker, "Capulin Volcano."

For the next 8 miles, paralleling the highway on the right, is one of the longest stretches of ruts to be seen anywhere. They are unsurpassed. At a high point about 2 miles beyond the last rest stop, the country falls away in a vast sweep, providing a spectacular vista rimmed by mountains in the distance. In this area it is possible to pick out a secondary trail (at 7 miles from the rest area) that diverges and heads right toward Tiptonville. For the past few miles the wooded Turkey Mountains have been visible to the right of the highway. Beyond them the Mountain Route of the SFT follows their western flank to Fort Union and its original junction with the Cimarron Cutoff at Watrous.

FORT UNION

Approaching the interchange on the north side of Watrous, SFT ruts can be seen on both sides of Interstate 25. Exit here and, at the end of the off-ramp, turn right onto NM 161 for the 8-mile drive to Fort Union.

At about .5 mile after entering this road, a grassy lane intersecting from the left leads down to the small Tiptonville Cemetery. Stay on the highway, and at .7 mile a narrow gravel road intersects from the left. Follow it .5 mile, and where the road bends sharply to the right the ghost town of Tiptonville begins.

To the left front of the intersection, is a large well-preserved adobe and rock quadrangle, once the Tiptonville store and reputedly a stage stop. Although it is private property, you can get a good view of two sides of the complex from the road. The SFT passed directly along the road in front of the store. Today, there is a line of trees marking its route to the south. When the trail reached the Mora River about 1 mile below, it crossed to Barclay's Fort (described below).

From the road bend at the Tiptonville store, you can see the ruined walls of a house close by on the left. This was the residence of William Tipton (1825–1888), who came over the SFT and was prominent in the territory during the Civil War and after. The son-in-law and business partner of trail figure Samuel Watrous, Tipton settled 2 miles north of his in-laws, founding Tiptonville on the trail leading down from Fort Union. His large two-story house burned in 1957.

Continue a short distance past the bend and a large cottonwood on the right. Immediately inside the fence is a dirt bank and behind it the ruins of the old Tiptonville Masonic Lodge, whose membership included soldiers from Fort Union. Just past the lodge on the left side are the remains of the Rev. Thomas Harwood's Methodist mission school, built in 1869. After his arrival via the SFT, Harwood became a circuit preacher using Tiptonville as his headquarters.

Continue straight ahead .5 mile past other deserted buildings until the road ends in a T. Turn right and go .25 mile to rejoin NM 161. There turn left toward Fort Union once again. Very soon notice a deep notch in a low ridge to the right of the highway representing some of the many SFT ruts in this area. A network of alternate trails led from Fort Union to Tiptonville and Watrous, and from here on traces can be observed on both sides of the road.

NM 161 ends in the parking lot of Fort Union National Monument. The approach to the fort and the site itself offer superlative views of a landscape that has experienced only minor changes since the days of the wagon caravans. Herds of antelope can often be seen grazing on the surrounding plains, and rangers warn visitors, at least in the summer, to watch for rattlesnakes. The monument is one of the most exciting places along today's trail, and there is so much to be seen that several hours should be allotted for a tour.

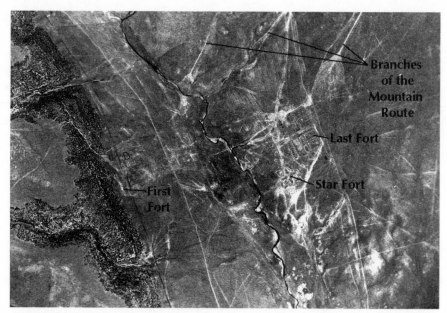

Fort Union with multiple ruts of the Mountain Route on a soil conservation aerial photo.

A small but excellent visitors' center and museum, with very helpful National Park Service personnel, provide an introduction to the fort and its history. In addition, publications relating to the site and to the SFT are also for sale.

The long self-guided tour around the parade ground and through the ruins is furnished with interpretive signs and audio speakers. At the rear of the fort, a marker calls attention to the ruts of the Mountain Route of the SFT coming down from the northwest side of the Turkey Mountains.

Fort Union was established in 1851 to replace Santa Fe as Military Department headquarters because the New Mexico territorial capital was regarded as "a sink of vice and extravagance." Soldiers from the new post patrolled the western end of the SFT to protect it from the kind of Indian raids that had led to the stagecoach massacre at Wagon Mound in 1850. The army also maintained a large quartermaster depot from which military supplies, freighted over the SFT, were dispersed to forts all across the southwestern frontier.

Over the years three separate forts were constructed. The first was located about 1 mile west of the visitors' center. Looking across the open plain, its few scattered ruins can be seen near the foot of a long wooded ridge. A ranch road leads to the location, but it is closed to the public except for one day a year. Check at the monument headquarters for the date if you are interested in visiting this site. That first fort was described by Marian Russell in her trail memoirs as in part having palisade walls. Individuals traveling with her book may wish to read her vivid account of life at Fort Union.

In August 1861, a second installation, the Star Fort, was begun on the plain east of the original post. An earthwork in the form of an eight-pointed star, it was built to repel an anticipated Confederate attack, which never materialized. Its location is west of the visitors' center, well-marked on the walking tour.

The last site of Fort Union, begun in 1863, adjoined the Star Fort on the north. The ruins of its large adobe and stone buildings are the central feature of today's monument. Arrival of the railroad in Watrous in 1879 lessened the fort's importance, but it was not closed until 1891. This is one trail stop worth visiting again, particularly to catch some of the fort's summer events when reenactment groups in period uniforms put on exhibitions.

Return via NM 161 to the interchange at Interstate 25.

WATROUS (LA JUNTA)

Cross Interstate 25 on the overpass, following the sign to Watrous, and enter old US 85. Note that the highway is lined with huge black willow trees. Homer Hastings, former superintendent at Fort Union, claimed that the original cuttings were brought in wagons over the SFT by Samuel B. Watrous, who arrived in this area in 1849 and built a large adobe store and residence. This structure is now incorporated into the beautiful white building with a pitched roof that serves as the Doolittle Ranch headquarters (private property). It faces US 85 on the left about .75 mile from the Interstate 25 interchange. Watrous traded with soldiers from Fort Union and travelers on the SFT. One of his daughters was married to William Tipton, founder of nearby Tiptonville, and another wed George Gregg, manager of the Sapelló Stage Station (described below). Watrous and his son died mysteriously in 1886, probably murder victims.

Just beyond the Watrous/Doolittle house, NM 161 crosses bridges, first over the Mora River and then over the Sapelló River. To the left of the highway, the two small streams come together at what the Spaniards called La Junta, meaning the junction. That name became doubly applicable later when the Mountain Route and the Cimarron Cutoff of the SFT united nearby to again form a single trail on the final stretch to Santa Fe.

About 1 mile north and west up the Mora River, British-born Alexander Barclay, a former employee of the Bents, built an adobe fort in 1849 that served as a major stopping place on the SFT and a relay station for the Independence to Santa Fe mail. The ruins were washed away in a flood in 1904, and the site, now on a private ranch, is not open to the public.

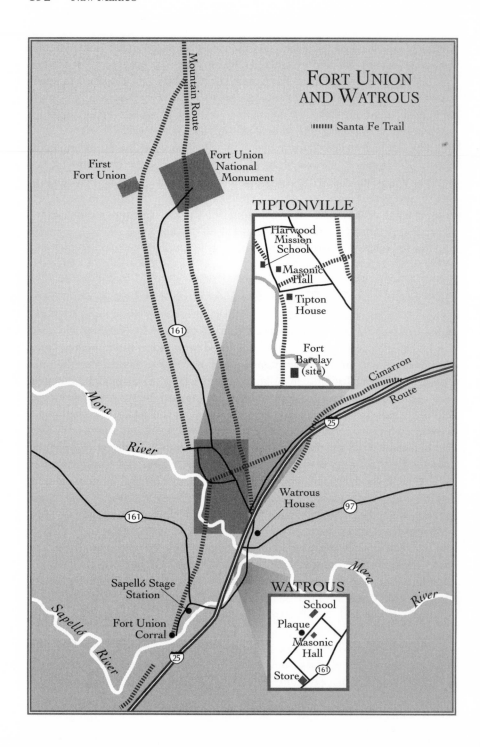

FORT UNION
AND WATROUS

IIIIIII Santa Fe Trail

Mountain Route

First
Fort Union

Fort Union
National
Monument

TIPTONVILLE

Harwood
Mission
School

Masonic
Hall

Tipton
House

Fort
Barclay
(site)

161

Cimarron

Route

Mora

River

25

Watrous
House

97

161

Mora

River

Sapelló Stage
Station

WATROUS

School

Plaque

Masonic
Hall

Fort Union
Corral

Sapelló

River

Store

161

25

The Watrous House at Watrous, New Mexico. Parts of the building may date from the 1850s.

By the late 1840s, individuals eastbound for Missouri had begun using the La Junta area as a rendezvous site where travelers camped until a caravan large enough to ensure safety could be formed. Here officers were elected and regulations adopted that would govern the wagon train on its trip to Independence. In this respect La Junta was the counterpart of Council Grove, the main rendezvous point on the eastern end of the trail. When the Santa Fe Railroad tracks reached this vicinity in 1879, the railroad changed the name of the small community from La Junta to Watrous, mainly to honor Samuel B. Watrous, who reportedly donated land for the right-of-way, but also because there was another place called La Junta on the main line in southeastern Colorado.

Continue on US 85 a short distance to the tiny, post-trail community of Watrous. Turn onto the second dirt lane that intersects the highway from the right. Go one block toward the park, passing on the right a tiny church built by Reverend Harwood from Tiptonville, said to be the oldest Protestant church still standing in New Mexico.

The lane ends in a T at a ball field. Turn left on the gravel street. To the right in the park is the Registered National Historic Landmark plaque for La Junta. Across the street from the plaque is the abandoned Masonic Lodge with a beautiful stone front containing an arched doorway and windows. Like the lodge in Tiptonville, it included among its original members soldiers from Fort Union.

Continue straight ahead on the street in front of the park for another two blocks. Then turn left and go one block to rejoin US 85. At that intersection

The portal, or porch, at the Sapelló Stage Station, on the outskirts of Watrous, New Mexico.

on the right is the old Schmidt and Reinkens General Store, which postdates the SFT but is a nice stone structure.

Turn right (south) on US 85 and go a mile or so out of town to the second (south) Watrous interchange on Interstate 25. An official New Mexico Highway Marker, "Watrous," is on the right. There go under the overpass and enter NM 161 toward Las Golondrinas. Go .5 mile to the first gravel road intersecting the paved road from the left and turn onto it.

Ahead and to the left you will see a newly stuccoed house with a pitched roof and stone chimney. This is the Sapelló Stage Station once operated by Barlow, Sanderson and Company as a "home station" where coaches made half-hour meal stops. The manager, George Gregg, must have sold alcohol as well because the place was known locally as Gregg's Tavern. In 1868, a stage-coach driver got into a fight with the station employees and was stabbed to death. A private residence now, the station is well preserved.

Across the road on the right beyond the fence good trail ruts lead close to the station. The actual union of the Mountain Route and Cimarron Cutoff is believed to have been at the Sapelló Crossing in the valley behind the station.

Drive straight ahead on the gravel road .3 mile past the stage station to the Fort Union Corral on the right. The corral, a large enclosure of native stone now on private property, was reportedly built after the arrival of the railroad in

Watrous. Army horses were off-loaded from stock cars and held here briefly before being driven the approximately 8 miles to the fort.

Return to the interchange and continue on Interstate 25 south toward Las Vegas. For the first several miles after rejoining the interstate watch for SFT ruts along the high ground to the right. At the first rise, the trail crosses from the right side to the left and remains south of the highway to Las Vegas.

LAS VEGAS

At the Onave exit about 8 miles from Watrous, is an important water divide. To this point traders were in the drainage of the Mississippi and Arkansas Rivers and their tributaries, but after this point they were in the drainage of the Pecos and Rio Grande Rivers.

About halfway between Watrous and Las Vegas, Hermit's Peak can be noted in the range of mountains that fill the horizon on the west. It is the tallest peak in the chain, hump-shaped with a sheer face of pink granite. However, the color is only evident in the early morning hours when the slanting sun strikes it. The peak is named in honor of Giovanni Maria Augustini (or Agostini), the hermit whose cave at Council Grove has already been described. He arrived in Las

The Baca House and stone wall near the Upper Plaza in Las Vegas, New Mexico.

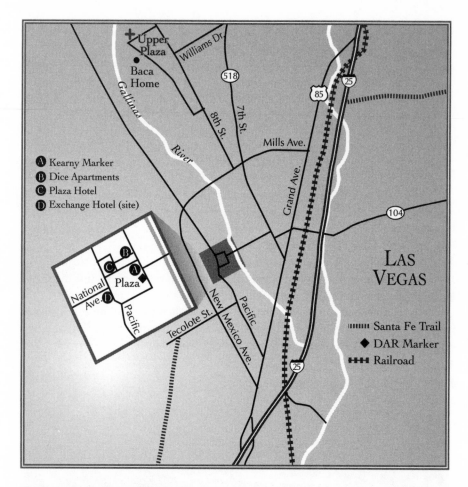

Vegas in 1863 with a freight caravan of the Romeros, who with the Bacas were one of the two leading merchant families of the town. Augustini reputedly performed a number of cures and miracles, but the crowds he attracted caused him to flee to the flat-topped mountain 14 miles east of Las Vegas and resume his life as a hermit. He remained there three years and then headed for southern New Mexico, where he was murdered in the Organ Mountains near Las Cruces in 1867. A few pilgrims from the Las Vegas area still climb Hermit's Peak to visit a shrine honoring Augustini.

About 4 miles from Las Vegas, Interstate 25 curves to the left heading almost due south. Along here the wide valley of the little Gallinas River begins to parallel your route on the right (west), forming a trough between the highway and the foothills of the mountains beyond. In the valley were the well-watered meadows (*las vegas* in Spanish) that gave the area its name. Here SFT

Multiple SFT ruts inside Kearny Gap near Las Vegas, New Mexico.

caravans camped to give their stock a good feed and rest before braving the pass through the mountains on the last leg of the trip to Santa Fe.

Until 1835 there were no permanent settlers in the area, the first New Mexican town encountered by the wagoners being San Miguel on the Pecos River, 20 miles farther. But about 1835 a group of San Miguel residents moved to the grassy valley, establishing Las Vegas.

The town actually had two small communities, or plazas. The first, Upper Plaza, was on an east side bench above the Gallinas River, while Lower Plaza was 2 or 3 miles downstream on the west bank, which is now near the center of present-day Las Vegas. Sometimes wagon trains that had no business in either plaza skirted the valley on the east (to the left of Interstate 25) and swung west through Kearny Gap south of the modern city.

To see traces of the trail as it entered town, continue past the first interstate exit to the second (Exit 345). Get off here and turn left, cross over the freeway, and take the entrance back towards the north. At about 2 miles on the right, you will see dramatic ruts—one deeply-cut swale and another less pronounced to its right. At the bottom of the hill, to your left, the trail forded the small creek and headed for Lower Plaza. Mike Olsen, historian at Highlands University, believes that caravans either stayed low and followed the route of today's Grand Avenue or went up the hill to connect with a trail from Mora.

Continue north on the interstate to the next exit (Exit 347) and get off headed south. Drive toward the city on old US 85, which parallels the interstate. At the first major intersection, Mills Avenue joins US 85 from the right (west).

Turn right (west) on Mills, go .8 mile to the intersection of 7th Street (also NM 518 here), and turn right (north). After about 1 mile turn left on Williams Drive, and go about .7 mile to 8th Street. Turn right here and drive .5 mile (just past a Mennonite Mission on the right) to a dirt road coming in from the left. Take this road, and in one block you will be at old Upper Plaza. The plaza is in good shape, with several old adobe houses and the trail-era church still intact. The plazas were planned as rectangles, and you can see that shape.

At the stop sign in front of the church, turn left and proceed a few hundred yards to a house on the right (number 505 on the mailbox). This is the home of José Albino Baca, now a private residence closed to the public. Baca, a prominent SFT trader, built a large three-story adobe mansion in the 1850s for his family and the headquarters of his freighting and mercantile business. However, only about half of the second story remains, as the house has been much remodeled in recent years. Along the road and around the rear of the house, is a beautiful stone wall, inside of which SFT wagons once parked.

Return to NM 518 (7th Street), where you may elect to turn left (north) and make a 60-mile round-trip to SFT sites at La Cueva and Mora. If not, turn right (south) on 7th Street toward the center of Las Vegas. After describing the trip to Mora, our narrative will pick up again in Las Vegas.

SIDE TRIP TO LA CUEVA AND MORA

Several miles north of Las Vegas, NM 518 crosses the small dam that impounds Storrie Lake. At about 5 miles after the dam, is a pullout on the east (right) side of the highway with an official New Mexico Highway Marker, "Hermit's Peak." From this location there is a good view of the peak directly to the west.

Behind the pullout immediately to the east are superb ruts of the old Mora to Las Vegas wagon road, which may be regarded as a branch of the SFT. Some caravans coming from the States left the main SFT in the vicinity of Fort Union and struck almost due west 15 miles to the town of Mora, located in the valley of the Mora River at the eastern foot of the Sangre de Cristo Mountains. Mora was then an important place, a distribution center for communities lying in the high country beyond and a producer of surplus farm products, particularly wheat. From Mora the caravans would turn south to Las Vegas, their route completing two sides of a triangle, with the main SFT from Fort Union to Las Vegas forming the third side.

Just beyond the Hermit's Peak pullout, NM 518 tops a ridge and goes down into a small valley. A wide swath of fine trail ruts, some deeply eroded, stretch

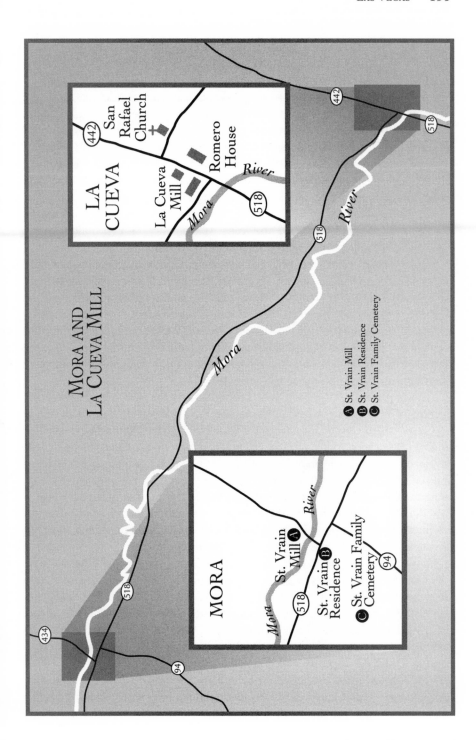

along the east side of the road from this point on. At about 10 miles from the Hermit's Peak pullout, the ruts are exceptional, first on the right side of the highway and then crossing to the left.

After another 2 miles, NM 161 to Watrous intersects NM 518 from the right (east). The eye can follow the route of NM 161 as it leads through a gap in a ridge of hills about 1 mile away, also the course of the Mora River. Fort Union is approximately 12 miles due east. The trail from there traversed the gap, following the north bank of the river on its way to La Cueva and Mora. From NM 518, you can see the deserted adobe buildings of the ghost town of Buena Vista strung along the riverbank for quite a distance, all private property.

At 3 miles beyond, NM 518 forks to the left as it enters the Mora Canyon. The right-hand fork is NM 442 to Ocaté. At this junction, in a pullout to the left, is an informational sign "La Cueva National Historic District."

To the right, along NM 442, are the magnificent ruins of La Cueva Mill. An extensive stone and adobe complex includes the well-preserved mill with its wheel and race, store building, storage structures, and large stone-walled corral. The site is part of the William Salman Ranch. Although it is private property, there is a small store at the north end of the complex, and you can wander through the gardens in the old stone corral. A great deal can be seen from the road, and the complex is a photographer's dream. Today, this is one of the most interesting and scenic places on the entire SFT.

A sign facing NM 442 gives a brief history of the mill. Shortly after the opening of Fort Union in 1851, Vicente Romero established a ranch with mill at La Cueva to grow grain and forage for the new post. At one time he controlled some 33,000 acres, much of it in the bottomlands along the Mora River. He developed an intricate irrigation system to water his vast fields of wheat and corn, and reportedly engineers came from Europe to study his techniques. His mill, using machinery freighted over the SFT, supplied a huge quantity of flour to Fort Union, from which it was distributed to other military posts in the Southwest. Although the sign says the mill was established in the 1870s, it probably was in operation by the 1850s or at the latest the 1860s.

Directly across the road from the mill, on the east side of NM 442, the rear of Vicente Romero's large two-story adobe house is visible through the trees. Now authentically restored, it is a private residence and the headquarters of the Salman Ranch. A long double veranda with white trim runs across the front of the building. By continuing up NM 442 a short distance past the mill and taking the road intersecting from the right that leads to San Rafael Church (an adobe structure with pitched roof and arched windows), it is possible to catch a glimpse of the front of the Romero House just past the church. Soldiers from Fort Union were frequent guests at the many parties given by the Romeros when the house was a center of social activity.

From La Cueva, continue west on NM 518 about 5 miles to Mora. Early in 1847, a revolt against the newly established American rule that began in Taos and resulted in the death of Charles Bent there spread across the mountains to Mora. Eight members of a SFT caravan were killed here, including L. L. Waldo, a younger brother of traders William and David Waldo. In retribution, the American army leveled much of the town with artillery.

In 1855, Ceran St. Vrain, noted SFT figure and longtime associate of the Bents, moved to Mora from Taos and established a store and mill. The following three points of interest in town associated with the SFT relate to him:

A. St. Vrain Mill

Drive to the center of Mora on NM 518. Take NM 434, which intersects from the right (north) and go one block to cross the Mora River. Just beyond the bridge the highway curves, and on the left is the large three-story stone St. Vrain Mill. It is boarded up but still roofed and from the front looks to be in fair condition, although major cracks at the rear indicate that the beautiful building is in a precarious state. The mill is thought to have been built in 1855. At least one account suggests that the original mill was a frame structure that afterward burned and the current stone building, which replaced it, was constructed in 1864. In any case, the St. Vrain Mill as it now stands is an impressive sight. Like the present La Cueva Mill downriver, it furnished flour to the quartermaster at Fort Union.

B. St. Vrain Residence

Return one block to the intersection of NM 434 and NM 518. Turn right, and stop immediately. On the left (south) side of NM 518 is the St. Vrain residence, a long adobe building with brown stucco, unmarked. The room at the extreme east end is a tavern and liquor store. A wing extends back along the west side so that the building now appears to be L-shaped. Probably when St. Vrain lived there (until his death in 1870), the other two sides were enclosed, in good New Mexican style, to form an open courtyard, or *placita*, in the center.

C. St. Vrain Family Cemetery

Return on NM 518 east one block, then turn right on NM 94. After approximately 1 mile, NM 94 ascends a hill, and there is a pullout on the right, adjacent to a small cemetery. Walk to the cemetery and look east to a small hill with a monument, which is in the St. Vrain Cemetery, on private land. Ceran's grave is in the center of the little cemetery, surrounded by those of his family. Just outside the fence on the north side is a marker for Col. George W. Cole, 2nd U.S. Cavalry.

Return to Las Vegas via NM 518.

LAS VEGAS TOUR CONTINUED

Follow 7th Street into the center of Las Vegas. At the intersection with National Avenue, turn left and go east on National several blocks to the intersection of Grand (US 85). On the southwest corner (to the right) in the stone municipal building, is the Rough Riders Memorial and City Museum. The Chamber of Commerce and some municipal courts are also in this building.

Although not primarily focused on the SFT, the museum is worth a visit. Teddy Roosevelt recruited members of his famous Rough Riders unit from this area to fight in the Spanish-American War. For many years Las Vegas held an annual Rough Riders Reunion. The collection contains mementos of the unit as well as other historical artifacts. Moreover, there are plans to make one room of the museum into a SFT exhibit.

Go west on National Avenue to the intersection of 8th Street and the beginning of New Mexico Highlands University campus. Traders camped here at what became the university grounds. On the north edge of the campus, are apartments for students, one called Gregg House. There are interesting plaques in an open hallway in front of this building commemorating the SFT and Josiah Gregg. Return to National Avenue.

Continue straight ahead through the campus three blocks to the bridge over the small Gallinas River. Here National Avenue is on the exact route of the SFT as it heads for the river crossing and the old Lower Plaza just beyond. On the northeast bridge abutment at about knee level, is an inscription commemorating stagecoaching on the SFT, while the northwest abutment is dedicated to the Coronado Expedition, which crossed the Gallinas River in this vicinity in 1541. The southeast abutment has an inscription honoring Gen. Stephen Watts Kearny and his march over the SFT. Kearny entered Las Vegas a colonel and left a general since his promotion papers arrived while he was here.

Cross the bridge and continue one block west to the historic Las Vegas Plaza, where there is a DAR marker in the park near the gazebo. In the northeast corner of the plaza, is a tall petrified log to which is attached a wooden marker with historical text about Kearny's proclamation to the citizens of Las Vegas.

The most historic building on the plaza is the cream-colored, flat-roofed adobe with white trim located in the row of units along the north side at numbers 210 to 218. Now known as the Dice Apartments, it is actually a series of stores, reportedly the location used by General Kearny on August 15, 1846, as a platform from which he read a proclamation annexing New Mexico. After his march over the SFT from Bent's Fort, Kearny camped on the ridge to the east where the Highlands University campus is now and from there went to the plaza for the ceremony. He and the *alcalde* (town mayor) used a ladder to climb to the flat roof, from which Kearny spoke to the townspeople assembled in the plaza below.

Adjacent to the Dice Apartments on the west, almost in the middle of the block, is the renowned Los Artesanos Book Shop. Specializing in fine western Americana, it always carries a good stock of books about the SFT. Past the bookshop on the northwest corner of the plaza is the Plaza Hotel. Established in 1880 soon after the arrival of the railroad and closing of the SFT, it played host to numerous dignitaries in the past.

On the west side of the plaza, National Avenue exits in the middle of the block. Entering National, on the left is a one-story professional building, the site of the Exchange Hotel, built in 1850 by Dr. Henry Connelly and a partner named Mitchell. Connelly was heavily involved in the Santa Fe trade. In the first year of the Civil War, he was appointed territorial governor, and with the advance of the Confederates in early March 1862, Connelly and other officials fled Santa Fe for Las Vegas, where they set up a temporary capital in the Exchange Hotel. After the Battle of Glorieta later in the month, Santa Fe again became the seat of government.

Behind the hotel on the west a large corral served SFT travelers. Stagecoaches also stopped here and used the livery facilities. A narrow wing of the hotel ran along the north side of the corral, its rooms facing on present-day National Avenue. The Exchange Hotel survived until 1959, when a fire destroyed the main building facing the plaza. However, part of the wing behind, a small building with pink stucco and brown trim bordering the street, escaped damage and is now used for storage.

Take Pacific, which leaves the southwest corner of the plaza, and drive south. Pacific is on top of the SFT for several blocks leaving the plaza. Continue on Pacific over a bridge to Tecolote Street, turn right, and drive past New Mexico Avenue to where Tecolote turns to gravel. From here, trail ruts can be seen climbing the hill to the front left. Return to New Mexico Avenue, turn right, and continue to US 85. Turn right here and follow US 85 to its junction with Interstate 25. An on-ramp straight ahead leads to the interstate, however veer left under the overpass and beyond it turn right (south) on to NM 283 at the sign pointing to Mineral Hill.

Continue on NM 283, which for the next mile parallels the interstate on the right. Then NM 283 makes a turn and passes over the interstate pointing west toward Kearny Gap, a natural pass in the high ridge ahead. Before reaching the pass, you will see a pullout on the right with a marker, "Puertocito de la Lumbre." This is the approximate location of the meeting between Capt. William Becknell and about four hundred soldiers under the command of Capt. Pedro Gallego. It was here that Becknell learned that he was to be welcomed in New Mexico and not imprisoned as others before him had been. If

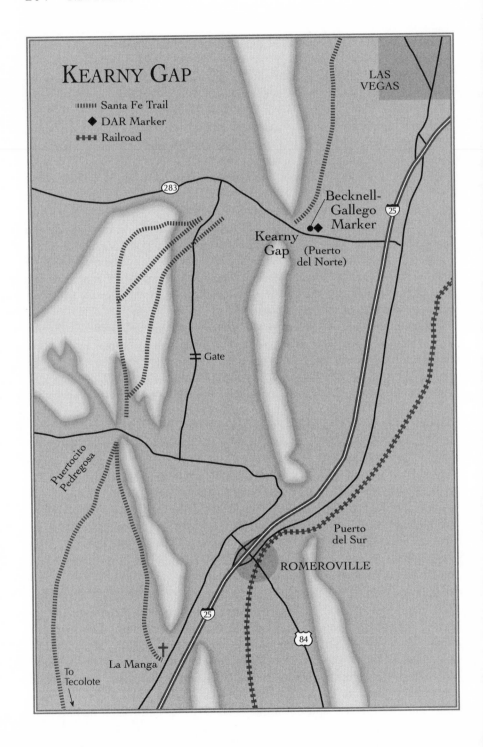

KEARNY GAP

⑉⑉⑉⑉ Santa Fe Trail
◆ DAR Marker
╫╫╫ Railroad

283

LAS VEGAS

Becknell-
Gallego
Marker

25

Kearny
Gap   (Puerto del Norte)

═ Gate

Puertocito
Pedregosa

Puerto
del Sur

ROMEROVILLE

25

84

† La Manga

To
Tecolote

Washout near Kearny Gap, New Mexico.

there is a moment that can be called the opening of the SFT, this time and place is it. The story of the meeting is related in an article by Michael Olsen and Harry Myers in a recent issue of *Wagon Tracks* (Olsen 1992). There is also a new DAR marker at the site.

Approaching the gap, ruts of the SFT curve toward it from the right, the route leading from Tecolote Street in Las Vegas. If you look carefully up the valley to the right, you will see the deeply cut washouts on the side of the hill. The main route of the SFT, used by General Kearny and his troops in August 1846, went through the pass. Before Kearny's time, the gap was called Puerto del Norte (North Pass) to distinguish it from Puerto del Sur (South Pass), which is about 2 miles farther south and is now threaded by Interstate 25.

Once through the gap, note an abandoned iron bridge to the left (south) of the highway. Just over the bridge the old road climbs a low ridge. At its top Spanish or Mexican settlers once had a round defensive tower (*torreón*), to defend access through the pass.

Just inside Kearny Gap, the SFT split into several branches, which are clearly shown on Lt. George Wheeler's geographical survey map of the mid-1870s.

A northern branch followed the present road to the little village of San Gerónimo, from where it struck off over the mountains almost due west. After passing through the community of Las Colonias, it emerged on the Pecos River at present-day Pecos, where it rejoined the main trail. Even though it was much shorter, this must have been a very difficult route for wagons, and we suspect it was a trail favored mainly by pack trains. Traces can still be seen from the highway as far as San Gerónimo.

The middle branches, the principal routes, led from Kearny Gap in a southwesterly direction up a long valley but very quickly veered to the right, crossing through a small pass in the long wooded ridge on the west.

The south branch at first paralleled the middle branch, but where that trail turned west through the pass, the south branch continued up the valley another mile or so to Puertocita Pedregosa (Little Rocky Gate).

To view the ruts of the middle and south branches, continue on NM 283 .4 mile past the abandoned iron bridge. Take an unmarked gravel road on the left (south), impassable when wet, and just after climbing the gentle hill (at about .2 mile) you will see a series of five swales in the valley to the right front, two deepened by erosion. One is to the left of the gravel road, while another four are to the right of the road. They all climb the ridge to the right and head for a pass leading to Tecolote.

You must turn around here as there is a locked gate farther along this road. Return to the frontage road paralleling the interstate, turn right on the frontage road, and drive to Romeroville.

PUERTOCITA PEDREGOSA

South of Las Vegas, Interstate 25 makes a sweeping curve to the west and passes through Puerto del Sur along with the Santa Fe Railroad tracks. The frontage road lies between the interstate and the tracks and goes through Puerto del Sur just before Romeroville (South Pass). This was a secondary route for still another branch of the SFT, used by a portion of Kearny's army in 1846, although the main force went through the gap 2 miles north that now bears his name. Once inside Puerto del Sur, this branch of the SFT moved off in a northwesterly direction to join the main trail at Puertocita Pedregosa.

To reach Puertocita Pedregosa, continue past Romeroville to US 84. If you turn left here, you would go to Santa Rosa, but instead turn right and cross over the interstate to the stop sign. Turn right on a paved road that starts back toward the east, parallel to the interstate. Shortly it turns to the left (north), and after about 1 mile becomes a gravel road, making a couple of curves before pointing west toward Puertocita Pedregosa.

Approaching the mouth of the gap, a road intersects from the right (north) at a junction about 2 miles from Interstate 25, where there is a sign reading

"Ojitos Frios Ranches." This is a new subdivision road in good condition, and some signs of the trail can be seen along it. A locked gate prevents you from driving all the way through to NM 283.

Back at the junction continue west into Puertocita Pedregosa, which is a winding canyon for about .5 mile. Just before exiting the pass you can see two valleys converging to your right, where the several routes of the SFT passed. As you exit the pass on the west side, well-defined ruts are on the left, leading off in a southwesterly direction. Just out of sight the trail split: the left branch went toward the interstate and on to Tecolote, while the right branch went just to the left (east) of Tecolote Peak and then threaded its way to Tecolote. From this point return to the frontage road paralleling the interstate and turn right toward Tecolote.

TECOLOTE

The frontage road immediately climbs a hill, and when it descends you see a small church on the right in the distance, the site of La Manga. If you look just to the left of the church, you can see ruts of the trail descending the hill toward the frontage road. This is a continuation of the left fork of the trail that branched at Puertocita Pedregosa.

Continuing on the frontage road, Tecolote Peak looms to your right. The other branch of the trail passes by its base. At a high point in the road, a break in the trees and an open valley on the right provide a panoramic view of the distant mountains to the north, with Hermit's Peak being the most prominent. From this perspective it presents the outline of two huge tilted and connected blocks, quite unlike the shape observed from the plains approaching Las Vegas.

Turn right into Tecolote on a dirt road that leads two blocks to the plaza. Facing the plaza is an interesting adobe church, while opposite it is an old, unpaved highway going toward Tecolote Creek. Since Romeroville you have been following old Route 66 that came from Santa Rosa. If you walk to Tecolote Creek here, you can see the broken bridge that formed part of the old highway. On the corner of the plaza and this road, is a DAR marker, behind a wire fence and inside the yard of a deserted adobe house.

Tecolote (which means "owl" in Spanish) retains the historical flavor of an earlier day. Readers of Marian Russell's journal will recall her account of the trading post she and her husband operated here after he left service at Fort Union. In his book *The Road to Santa Fe*, Hobart Stocking says he saw their building being demolished in the late 1960s (Stocking 1971). In later trail days, Tecolote was maintained as a U.S. Army forage station, and reportedly large stables and a headquarters building were in evidence as late as the 1930s.

BERNAL

Return to the frontage road and turn right toward Bernal. After 1.5 miles you will be in a small valley, where the SFT crossed from right to left. In another mile the trail passes back to the right of the road. As you continue, you will see Tecolote Hill, a major hurdle for traders looming in front that was anticipated with apprehension. Ascending the hill required traders to double the teams to 12 yoke of oxen, and even then it was a full day's work. We discovered the route they used by finding the old paved highway, which used the same route to climb the hill. About 3.2 miles from Tecolote the valley is to the right, and approximately .5 mile up that valley is the narrow pass they used.

Stay on the frontage road to where you can turn left, cross the interstate, and enter Bernal. The road is not marked but is the very next left turn. The road ends in a T, turn left (east) and go about 50 yards to a clump of junipers on the right (south) side of the road. Here is a DAR marker, easily missed.

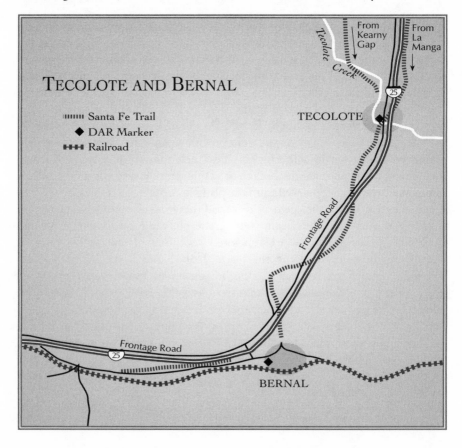

To the right rear in the distance is Starvation Peak, a flat-topped butte properly called Bernal Hill. According to legend, though unverified, a band of travelers, either colonial Spaniards or Santa Fe traders depending on the version, was attacked by Indians and fled to the summit, where they starved to death after a long siege.

A SFT stage station was once located in the vicinity of nearby Ojo de Bernal (Bernal Spring), but the exact location is open to debate. By continuing east past the DAR marker, the village's interesting church can be visited.

SAN MIGUEL DEL VADO

Instead of returning to the frontage road, continue west on the road on which the DAR marker is located, which was old Route 66, at least until the late 1930s. As you drive for the next 3 miles, look for trail ruts only a few yards from the road, mostly on the right. At 3.2 miles from Bernal, about where the railroad tracks cross on the left, the trail split. The left branch went to San Miguel, while the right branch stayed up high and headed for San José.

Continue on the gravel road under the interstate, where it rejoins the frontage road. Drive to NM 3 a few miles ahead. Turn left (south) on paved NM 3 to San Miguel, about 3 miles south of the interstate.

In the initial years of the Santa Fe trade, San Miguel del Vado was the first New Mexican community encountered by caravans arriving from the States. William Becknell received a warm welcome here in 1821 on his inaugural journey. Entering the village, established in the mid-1790s, a large adobe church with its twin towers is on the right (west). The church was built in 1805, and although it has been remodeled many times, the outline of the facade remains basically the same as it was in 1846 when SFT traveler Lt. J. W. Abert captured it in a watercolor. Near the church door is a bell whose casting indicates that it was made in Ohio in 1861. It was freighted over the SFT to San Miguel del Vado and according to popular belief was one of the last bells cast in the East before foundries were converted to making cannons at the outbreak of the Civil War. (A bell with a similar inscription, now in the Catholic church at Belén, south of Albuquerque, apparently was brought over the SFT at the same time.) Also on the bell note the name of the priest, Don Juan Guerin, and the names of the two *padrinos*, literally godparents, who were sponsors of the bell.

During the Mexican period, San Miguel del Vado was a port of entry, where the Missouri merchants had their first dealings with Mexican customs officials. Close to the river is a sprawling building that some claim is the old customs house. However, it was more a place where soldiers stayed while waiting to escort wagon trains. Escorts roamed far out on the trail to keep traders from caching goods to avoid customs duties, which actually were probably paid in Santa Fe.

The old village with its several hundred inhabitants had a defensive plaza—contiguous adobe houses forming a large rectangle with an open area in the center and a single gate that could be closed during Indian attack. Just past the church the road cuts through the center of the old plaza. Although many of the houses on the plaza have disappeared, enough remain to outline the original rectangle. Behind the church are the ruins of a number of stone and adobe houses outside the plaza area, which date from trail days. The SFT forded the Pecos River just east of the main plaza (*vado* means ford in Spanish). Standing at the entrance of the church, look straight ahead (due east) across NM 3 to a small lane that leads down to the Pecos River a block away. Take a walk there to see traces of the ford.

Return on NM 3, cross under the interstate, and continue to the frontage road, which is now about .5 mile straight ahead. Turn left onto the frontage road, and in .5 mile on the right you can spot ruts of the trail headed for San José. Continue on the frontage road across the Pecos River and turn left at the first road past the river, which will take you into San José.

SAN JOSÉ DEL VADO

Several miles up the Pecos River at San José del Vado was an alternate ford for the SFT on a shorter cutoff with a rougher approach. San José del Vado began to assume more importance as San Miguel declined after the 1835 founding of Las Vegas farther east. San Miguel then was no longer the first community encountered by wagon trains.

San José was built around a fortified plaza like San Miguel, but more of the houses survive here making the arrangement clearer. A large church, post-dating the SFT, is in the center of the plaza.

Follow a road that leaves the southeast corner of the plaza. About a block later, there is a DAR marker on the right side of the road. Continue several more blocks to an abandoned steel girder bridge over the Pecos. This may have been the site of the original ford, but we have not been able to verify that.

Return to Interstate 25.

PECOS

At San José begins Glorieta Mesa (or Rowe Mesa), whose towering escarpment remains on the left for the next 20 or 25 miles. Maps of the 1870s show

The ruined church at Pecos National Historical Park, New Mexico.

that the SFT (by that date often labeled the Fort Leavenworth Road) roughly followed the route of present-day Interstate 25 and the Santa Fe Railroad tracks, which are to the left. The earlier SFT probably took this same path since the country to the right is very rough, broken by arroyos leading down to the deep canyon of the Pecos River.

At just over 11 miles from the San Juan/San José interchange, leave Interstate 25 at the Rowe/Pecos exit (Exit 307). Take NM 63 leading toward Pecos National Historical Park. Within a mile or two, SFT ruts can be seen to the left of the highway, where the clearing of piñon timber has left a grassy pasture. After 1.4 miles, you will enter Pecos National Historical Park.

At about 3.4 miles from the exit ramp of Interstate 25, NM 63 passes the old headquarters of Greer Garson's Forked Lightning Ranch. It is on the right (east) side of the road, a salmon-colored adobe building with bright blue trim, now part of the park. An ox yoke hangs from the top of the porch, while near the corner of the porch, next to a blue wagon wheel, is a DAR marker. In addition, there is a marker attached to the front claiming that this building is an "Historic Stagecoach Stop and Trading Post Built in 1810," although the source of this date is unknown to us.

The headquarters is on the site of Kozlowski's Ranch and Stage Station. It incorporates some of the original walls of the station. Martin Kozlowski, a Polish immigrant, entered New Mexico after 1846. Later he acquired this site on the SFT and constructed ranch buildings using materials scavenged from the ruined Pecos mission and Indian pueblo 1 mile away. Meals provided to stage passengers by his wife, including fresh trout from the Pecos River, were said to be the best on the western end of the trail.

Just past the ranch house, NM 63 crosses a bridge. Kozlowski's Spring, the reason he located here, can be seen on the right, down in the creek bed. This was also the site of the Union headquarters in late March 1862, when the Blue and the Gray fought the Battle of Glorieta several miles to the west.

At .6 mile ahead is the entrance to Pecos National Historical Park on the left (west) side of NM 63. Here are extensive Indian ruins and the remains of a huge Spanish colonial mission church. The land immediately around the ruins was donated to the park many years ago by Buddy Fogelson and his wife Greer Garson. After they died the park acquired additional land, including Kozlowski's Ranch and the Greer Garson summer house.

Pecos, located on the east side of Glorieta Pass at the gateway to the plains, has a long and fascinating history, beginning with a visit by members of the Coronado Expedition in 1541. It was a major landmark on the SFT, mentioned in practically all trail journals, including those of Josiah Gregg and Susan Magoffin. Excellent publications on Pecos are available at the visitors' center, and a film shown there focuses, in part, on the SFT. You can also drive to a picnic ground near the park headquarters, where ruts can be seen behind the headquarters building. In addition, although the Greer Garson summer house has nothing to do with the SFT, if you are interested in viewing it check at the visitors' center.

Continue north on NM 63 to the center of the modern community of Pecos. At a Shell station on the right, NM 50 intersects from the west. Turn left onto it, and immediately on the right is an official New Mexico Highway Marker, "Pecos." Follow winding NM 50 toward Pigeon's Ranch and stage station.

PIGEON'S RANCH

At 4.3 miles from the junction of NM 63 and NM 50, is a roadside pullout on the right. To the right rear of the pullout are two markers, both commemorating the Battle of Glorieta, between Union and Confederate forces, that occurred on March 28, 1862—often described as the Gettysburg of the West. One marker, placed by the Texas Division of the United Daughters of the Confederacy, remembers the Confederate dead. The second, placed later, is for the Colorado Volunteers who made up a significant portion of the Union forces. Union troops advancing from Fort Union on the east and Confederates coming from Santa Fe on the west both followed the SFT. This area is now part of the Pecos National Historical Park, which eventually hopes to move

Pigeon's Ranch, Glorieta, New Mexico, June 1880. Photo by Ben Wittick. Neg. No. 15782, School of American Research Collections in the Museum of New Mexico.

the present highway to a ridge on the left, making it possible to show where the various actions took place during the battle.

At .5 mile beyond the pullout, on the right side of NM 50, are the remains of Pigeon's Ranch. In the 1850s, Alexander Valle, of French background from St. Louis, established a ranch and SFT hostelry on the site. According to a common story, he was nicknamed Pigeon because of his fondness for "cutting the pigeon wing" at fandangos. Although that explanation has been questioned, the place was

Pigeon's Ranch and stage station on the SFT and site of the Civil War Battle of Glorieta.

universally referred to as Pigeon's Ranch. Only three adobe rooms adjacent to the highway survive of what was once a twenty-three-room complex. Mounded ruins are behind the building, and the stone footings of a corral are attached on the west end. A porch on the front, now gone, bordered the SFT. Across the road to the left are a few fruit trees from the earlier orchard.

During the Battle of Glorieta, the ranch alternately changed hands between Union and Confederate forces. Briefly it served as a makeshift hospital, where bodies of dead soldiers were stacked to the ceiling in one room. Most of the fighting occurred in the open area to the west, beyond the present highway bridge and on both sides of the road. There is an official Scenic Historic Marker "Glorieta Battlefield" on the left .3 mile beyond Pigeon's Ranch.

In June 1864, Kit Carson spent a night at Pigeon's Ranch telling stories of his exploits to members of the Doolittle Commission, a U.S. Senate investigative body sent west to study the condition of the Indians. However, for reasons not readily apparent few latter-day SFT travelers mentioned stopping at Pigeon's Ranch.

TO JOHNSON'S RANCH SITE

One mile beyond Pigeon's Ranch, NM 50 reaches an interchange that leads back onto Interstate 25 to Santa Fe. The high point on the interstate directly ahead is the unmarked summit of Glorieta Pass, where the highway curves to the left. Traces of the SFT are hidden in the trees on the left.

Between mile markers 296 and 295 on the left, is an informal pullout, accessible only from eastbound lanes. Behind the pullout, on private property, you can see a memorial that commemorates the Battle of Glorieta, as well as a skirmish here two days before the major battle at Pigeon's Ranch.

At 5 miles from entry onto the interstate is Cañoncito at Apache Canyon. Here blasting for the railroad and Interstate 25 has widened what was once a narrow wagon gap on the SFT. In August 1846, Governor Manuel Armijo fortified the gap with the intention of opposing Kearny's advance on Santa Fe, but he abandoned the position before any hostilities occurred.

As Interstate 25 passes out of the gap, take the off-ramp at Exit 294. Turn right at the stop sign, and immediately to your left will be Scenic Historic Marker "Cañoncito at Apache Pass." Adjacent to the marker is a DAR marker, which disappeared in the 1950s and was found and restored in 1988. From the marker drive east past the small, quaint Cañoncito church with its bright red roof. You are now heading back toward the mouth of the gap, parallel to the interstate.

Continue past a yellow stucco house down to the bottom of the hill, where a dirt road intersects from the left. At this intersection on the left is an old corral adjacent to the site of Johnson's ranch house and stage station. Large gray logs inside the corral are the vigas, or roof beams, from the old station, which was leveled in the 1950s by the owner.

Anthony P. Johnson of St. Louis came to New Mexico in the late 1840s. Afterward he worked as a teamster out of Fort Union. From an officer there he borrowed $400 to purchase this ranch in 1858. His adobe and rock residence with a porch across the front became a stop for stagecoaches on the last stretch of trail before Santa Fe. Johnson was absent in March 1862 when Confederate troops occupied his ranch, using it as a headquarters and supply depot for several days prior to the Battle of Glorieta. He sold the ranch in 1869 and was murdered by outlaws in 1879.

At this point you can either return to Interstate 25 and continue to the end of the SFT in Santa Fe or stay on the road passing the church and take it to Santa Fe. The latter way more closely follows the SFT, and is the route described below.

SANTA FE

At 9 miles from the Cañoncito church, turn right on Gancho Way. (If you took Interstate 25, take Exit 284, turn right at the stoplight, and continue to this same point.) Soon you will see the New Mexico Academy on the left and come to Old Santa Fe Trail. Turn left on Old Santa Fe Trail, and look immediately to the right to view a DAR marker, about 15 yards behind a barbed wire fence and difficult to see.

Continue on Old Santa Fe Trail 3 miles, passing the Southwest Head-quarters for the National Park Service on the left just after a turn in the road. The road entering from the right here is Monte Sol. Turn right onto it, and immediately you will see one of the new SFT "XING" markers on your right. The trail crossed here and then went on toward the Santa Fe Plaza, paralleling Old Santa Fe Trail.

Go back and follow Old Santa Fe Trail to where it joins Old Pecos Trail at a stop sign. After you turn right here, you are on the SFT the remaining ten blocks to the plaza. One block after the stop sign East Buena Vista joins from the left, and on the southwest corner is a marker, with the barely discernible words "Santa Fe Trail." The sponsor of this marker and its placement date remain a mystery. Continue on Old Santa Fe Trail to the center of Santa Fe.

Santa Fe's maze of streets requires that you obtain a city map. Many hotels, shops, galleries, and restaurants have free maps and historical brochures. In summer there is usually a tourist information booth maintained on the porch, or portal, of the First National Bank of Santa Fe on the west side of the plaza. Moreover, Santa Fe has a visitors' center located in the Lamy Building, adjacent to the San Miguel Chapel on Old Santa Fe Trail.

The End of the Trail Chapter of the SFTA has developed a fine guide to Santa Fe entitled *Santa Fe: A Walking Tour (Self-Guided)*, which can be found at the information booth on the plaza or the Santa Fe Visitors' Center in the Lamy Building.

In addition, the many local bookstores sell a variety of city guides that provide directions to numerous points of historical interest not associated with the SFT. Especially recommended is the magazine shop in the lobby of La Fonda Hotel on the plaza, or the Museum Shop of the Palace of the Governors, which has a good selection of books about the SFT.

Individuals visiting Santa Fe for the first time should be aware that it is crowded during the height of the tourist season, from mid-June to Labor Day weekend. The Santa Fe Opera draws thousands at this time, and on many week-ends there are special events, including fiestas, craft shows, the Santa Fe Rodeo, the Spanish Market, and, in August, the famed Indian Market. Thus during the high season accommodations may not be available without reservations, and parking may be scarce. Downtown hotels and the finer restaurants charge big-city prices. In fact, they are exorbitant! However, more modestly priced motels and restaurants can be found along Cerrillos Road, which begins four blocks south of the plaza and eventually joins Interstate 25 going to Albuquerque. The best times to visit are in April and May, and September through mid-October.

A tour of SFT sites should begin at the plaza. Points of interest A through P, described below, are within a three- to four-block radius of the plaza and are best reached by walking. The remaining sites are a little farther out, and all but experienced walkers will probably prefer to reach them by car. Consult our map or inquire locally for directions.

THE PLAZA AREA

A. The Santa Fe Plaza

The Santa Fe Plaza marks the official end of the 1,000-mile SFT. As one of the oldest historic sites in America, dating back to the founding of the city by the Spaniards in 1610, it has been designated a Registered National Historic Landmark marked by a bronze plaque mounted just inside the entrance to the Palace of the Governors.

In the earliest days of the Santa Fe trade, Missouri merchants unloaded and sold their wares here in the open air. But soon they began to rent space for stores in the rambling adobe buildings surrounding the plaza. Before 1846, one end of the historic Palace of the Governors was occupied by traders.

B. End of the Trail Monument

Located on the southeast corner of the plaza, this historic granite stone is the last of the approximately 170 DAR markers that travelers have been finding along the trail since Franklin. It signals the completion of a journey that commenced at the Beginning of the Trail Monument, in New Franklin near the Missouri River. The Santa Fe marker was dedicated in special ceremonies on August 21, 1911. A map of the trail incised on its face has an error. Can you find it?

C. Palace of the Governors

This building, dating from the early Spanish colonial period, was closely associated with the SFT. For many years prior to 1846, it was the residence of Governor Manuel Armijo, who was deeply involved in overland trade. Gen. Stephen Watts Kearny, after crossing the Mountain Route of the SFT and occupying New Mexico for the United States, raised the American flag over the palace and took up temporary quarters inside.

Today, the Palace of the Governors is a part of the Museum of New Mexico. Although the exhibits change, there are usually some relating to the SFT. On display is a stagecoach that was used on the trail for many years, labeled "Mud Wagon." And New Mexico's bicentennial covered wagon, which traveled part of the SFT in 1976, can be seen in the patio.

D. The Kearny Monument

A small stone monument on the plaza facing the entrance to the Palace of the Governors honors Gen. Stephen Watts Kearny and his famous 1846 march over the trail.

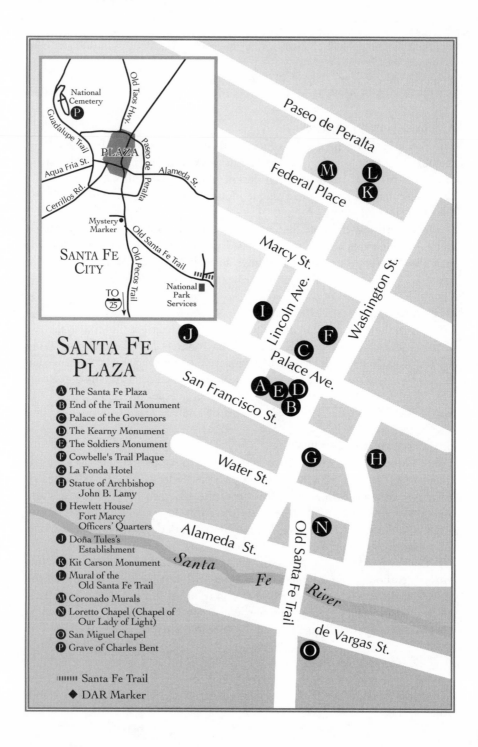

National Cemetery ⓟ

Old Taos Hwy.

Guadalupe Trail

PLAZA

Aqua Fria St.

Cerrillos Rd.

Paseo de Peralta

Alameda St.

Mystery Marker •

SANTA FE CITY

Old Santa Fe Trail

Old Pecos Trail

TO 25

National Park Services

Paseo de Peralta

Federal Place

Ⓜ Ⓛ Ⓚ

Marcy St.

Lincoln Ave.

Washington St.

Ⓘ

Ⓙ

Ⓕ

Ⓒ

Palace Ave.

San Francisco St.

ⒶⒺⒹ
Ⓑ

Water St.

Ⓖ

Ⓗ

Alameda St.

Ⓝ

Santa

Fe

River

Old Santa Fe Trail

de Vargas St.

Ⓞ

SANTA FE PLAZA

Ⓐ The Santa Fe Plaza
Ⓑ End of the Trail Monument
Ⓒ Palace of the Governors
Ⓓ The Kearny Monument
Ⓔ The Soldiers Monument
Ⓕ Cowbelle's Trail Plaque
Ⓖ La Fonda Hotel
Ⓗ Statue of Archbishop
     John B. Lamy
Ⓘ Hewlett House/
     Fort Marcy
     Officers' Quarters
Ⓙ Doña Tules's
     Establishment
Ⓚ Kit Carson Monument
Ⓛ Mural of the
     Old Santa Fe Trail
Ⓜ Coronado Murals
Ⓝ Loretto Chapel (Chapel of
     Our Lady of Light)
Ⓞ San Miguel Chapel
Ⓟ Grave of Charles Bent

⁍⁍⁍⁍ Santa Fe Trail
◆ DAR Marker

E. THE SOLDIERS MONUMENT

Dedicated in 1867, this 33-foot column, surrounded by an iron fence in the center of the plaza, honors Union soldiers who died at the Battle of Glorieta (March 28, 1862) on the SFT near Pigeon's Ranch. Another inscription honors pioneers (among them many trail travelers) who died in battles with hostile Indians. The marker originally called these Indians "savages," but that word was later "edited off" by a vandal. The monument can be seen in early photographs showing ox caravans arriving in the plaza.

F. COWBELLE'S TRAIL PLAQUE

Located on Washington Avenue at the east end of the Palace of the Governors, under an iron hitch rail, this bronze plaque honors early trail drivers.

G. LA FONDA HOTEL

On the outer corner of the plaza, opposite the End of the Trail Monument, this historic hostelry, entirely rebuilt in the 1920s, was known as the Inn at the End of the Trail. The hotel, whose fame extended to Missouri and beyond, was host to some of the best-known individuals who came over the trail.

Facing the La Fonda Hotel, across Old Santa Fe Trail and about 12 yards east of that street's junction with San Francisco Street, is one of the DAR's special bronze trail plaques set into the wall of a commercial building.

H. STATUE OF ARCHBISHOP JOHN B. LAMY

This fine statue, which inspired Willa Cather's famous novel *Death Comes for the Archbishop*, is located at the entrance to St. Francis Cathedral, built by Lamy at the east end of San Francisco Street just past La Fonda Hotel. Lamy made numerous trips over the SFT by wagon train and stagecoach. In a famous crossing of 1867, his caravan was attacked by Comanches, and though it was first erroneously reported that he and the priests and nuns accompanying him had been massacred, all eventually reached Santa Fe safely.

NORTH OF THE PLAZA

Leave the plaza by the Fine Arts Museum (on the site where Marian Russell's mother ran a boardinghouse in the 1850s) and walk north on Lincoln Avenue.

I. HEWETT HOUSE/FORT MARCY OFFICERS' QUARTERS

Located behind the Museum of Fine Arts Museum at 116 Lincoln, this extensively remodeled building is one of two surviving officers' quarters of old Fort Marcy. (The other one is a block northwest at 135 Grant Avenue.) General Kearny ordered construction to begin on Fort Marcy in August 1846. A blockhouse was built on a prominent hill about 600 yards northeast of the plaza, but it was never garrisoned. (Inquire locally if you want to visit that site.) Instead, decaying Spanish military installations behind the Palace of the Governors were used for barracks and warehouses. In the 1870s, during the last decade of the SFT, seven two-story gabled officers quarters were built along Lincoln and Grant Avenues. When Fort Marcy was abandoned in 1894, these quarters passed into private hands, and five were demolished. The one now on Lincoln was purchased in 1916 by Frank Springer (publisher of the *Cimarron News* and attorney for the Maxwell Land Grant Company, both closely identified with the trail), who remodeled the structure in the Spanish-Pueblo architectural style. Springer gave the building as a residence for Museum of New Mexico Director Edgar L. Hewett, who occupied it until his death in 1946. Today, the building houses offices of the Museum of New Mexico Foundation.

J. Doña Tules's Establishment
Doña Tules maintained a gambling establishment at 142 West Palace in what is now the Palace Restaurant. Many trail diaries and journals mention this noteworthy place of diversion for the traders.

K. Kit Carson Monument
This tall stone column is located at the end of Lincoln Avenue in front of the main entrance to the U.S. Courthouse. Carson (1809–1868), a mountain man, scout, and soldier, was perhaps the most famous person associated with the SFT. He traveled it many times and, although his home was in Taos, he was a frequent visitor to Santa Fe and a member of this city's Masonic Lodge, which still preserves his rifle.

L. Mural of the Old Santa Fe Trail
Located immediately on the left just inside the main door of the U.S. Courthouse behind the Kit Carson Monument, the mural was painted by Santa Fe artist William Penhallow Henderson as part of the New Deal federal art projects in the early 1930s. It shows a wagon train from Missouri approaching Santa Fe through the eastern hills. Other historical and scenic murals of interest are also in the building.

M. Coronado Murals
Located in the lobby of the U.S. Post Office just west of the Carson Monument and the U.S. Courthouse, the two murals show explorer Francisco Vásquez de Coronado and the Pueblo Indians in 1540. They were painted by local artist Gerald Cassidy in 1921.

SOUTH OF THE PLAZA

Return to the plaza and follow the street signs for Old Santa Fe Trail, beginning on the west side of La Fonda Hotel, the route by which you came to the plaza.

N. LORETTO CHAPEL (CHAPEL OF OUR LADY OF LIGHT)

The building faces Old Santa Fe Trail behind La Fonda Hotel. In the early 1850s, Archbishop Lamy brought six nuns of the Order of Loretto over the SFT to establish a girls' academy surrounding this site. The Gothic chapel was begun in 1874 and completed in 1878, while freight wagons still rumbled past.

O. SAN MIGUEL CHAPEL

Located on Old Santa Fe Trail, one block beyond the Santa Fe River Bridge, this chapel, destroyed in the Pueblo Revolt of 1680, was rebuilt in 1710 and is sometimes referred to as "the oldest church in the U.S.A." In 1859, Lamy brought the Christian Brothers over the trail to manage the chapel and found a school for boys on adjacent lands. Both this structure and the so-called "Oldest House" next door were familiar sights to travelers on the SFT. Next to the chapel is the Lamy Building, which contains the Information Center for New Mexico and the City of Santa Fe.

NORTHWEST OF THE PLAZA

P. GRAVE OF CHARLES BENT

Celebrated SFT trader Charles Bent was appointed first civil governor of New Mexico after the conquest by General Kearny in 1846. The following January he was killed in an uprising while at his home in Taos, and subsequently his body was brought to Santa Fe for burial. His grave can be found in the National Cemetery ten blocks northwest of the plaza (see map for directions from the plaza).

Entering the main gate of the National Cemetery, drive straight ahead to the office. Turn right here, then right again, continuing past an adobe service building. The grave is about 50 yards beyond the adobe building, with an oversized white marble stone on the left toward the back of the cemetery. Next to it is a tall brown sandstone marker for Maj. Lawrence Murphy, one of the figures in the notorious Lincoln County War in which Billy the Kid was a participant. Behind Bent's grave is the grave of William F. Amy, who came over the SFT by stagecoach in 1861 to become Indian agent for the Utes and Jicarilla Apaches at Cimarron. He succeeded Kit Carson as the agent for those tribes and while at Cimarron became closely associated with Lucien Maxwell. Amy also served a term as secretary for the New Mexico Territory.

SIDE TRIP TO TAOS

In 1825, Commissioner George C. Sibley and his trail survey party reached Taos, which he had intended should serve as the official end of the SFT. Even though Taos had the disadvantage of being locked in by mountains and virtually inaccessible by wagon from either the east or south, it also had advantages. It was becoming a resort for American trappers operating in the Southern Rockies and a center of the fur trade. The Mexican government maintained a port of entry there. And because of its location in the northeast part of the province Taos was the closest settlement to both Raton Pass on the Mountain Route and the Rock Crossing of the Canadian on the Cimarron Cutoff. Notwithstanding, Taos failed to become a major trail terminus.

From Santa Fe drive north on US 84/US 285 to Española, about 20 miles. From there take NM 68 north to Taos, approximately 75 miles from Santa Fe. At Velarde the highway enters the scenic canyon of the Rio Grande and some 10 miles south of Taos emerges onto a high plateau that extends to the foot of the

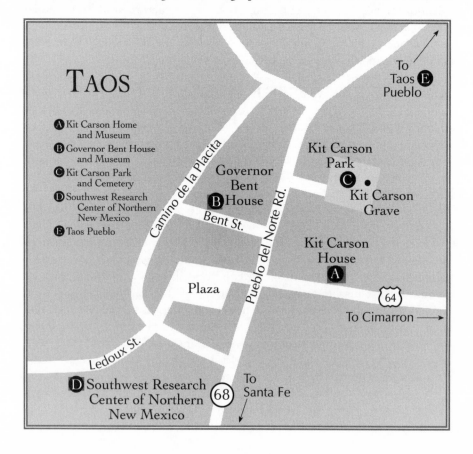

TAOS

Ⓐ Kit Carson Home and Museum
Ⓑ Governor Bent House and Museum
Ⓒ Kit Carson Park and Cemetery
Ⓓ Southwest Research Center of Northern New Mexico
Ⓔ Taos Pueblo

To Taos Ⓔ Pueblo

Kit Carson Park

Ⓒ •
Kit Carson Grave

Camino de la Placita

Governor Bent Ⓑ House

Bent St.

Pueblo del Norte Rd.

Kit Carson House
Ⓐ

64
To Cimarron →

Plaza

Ledoux St.

Ⓓ Southwest Research Center of Northern New Mexico

68 To Santa Fe

Sangre de Cristo Mountains. If you look carefully to your left after you crest the hill, you can see the deeply-eroded canyon cut by the Rio Grande.

Boasting eighty art galleries, Taos is a smaller and more charming version of Santa Fe, with a helpful Chamber of Commerce. (Address: Drawer 1, Taos, NM 87571.) Historic Taos Plaza in the center of town is the site where formerly all mountain trails converged. Nearby are at least four points of interest associated with the SFT:

A. KIT CARSON HOME AND MUSEUM
Located on US 64 East, one block east of the plaza on Kit Carson Road, this structure was built about 1825 and was owned by Carson from 1843 to 1868, serving as both residence and office during the years he was agent for the Utes and Jicarilla Apaches. In addition to fine exhibits, there are several furnished period rooms that impart the flavor of trail days. The only portion of the building that is original is the front section facing the road. There is an admission fee. Across the street from the Kit Carson home is the renowned Taos Book Shop, specializing in volumes on the Southwest.

B. GOVERNOR BENT HOUSE AND MUSEUM
Located one block north of the plaza on Bent Street this house is where SFT trader Charles Bent spent more of his time during his last years than at Bent's Fort on the Arkansas River. He was assassinated here in January 1847 while serving as the first appointed civil governor under American rule. It is difficult to ascertain which part of the house is original. There is a hole punched through an interior wall, said to resemble the one through which Bent's family and friends escaped. Admission fee.

C. KIT CARSON PARK AND CEMETERY
On Pueblo del Norte Road, NM 68, at one block north of the plaza on the east is Kit Carson Park. The graves of Kit Carson, his wife Josefa, and other notables are enclosed within a fenced cemetery at the rear of the park. Padre Antonio José Martínez, who married Kit and Josefa and who was a foe of the Bents, has a fine carved headstone (recently vandalized) that was made in the East and freighted over the SFT. A number of excellent historical markers have recently been added to the cemetery.

Kit Carson grave in Taos, New Mexico.

D. SOUTHWEST RESEARCH CENTER OF NORTHERN NEW MEXICO
After following Ledoux Street from the southwest corner of the plaza one long block, the center is on the left next to the Harwood Foundation. It houses the combined libraries of the Harwood Museum, the Millicent Rogers Museum, and the Kit Carson Museum. The latter, of interest to trail buffs, has some resources pertaining to trail research. Nearby is the Blumenschein House, the entrance fee for which is included with the entrance fee for the Kit Carson House. Blumenschein was a prominent Taos artist.

E. TAOS PUEBLO
From the entrance of Kit Carson Park, continue north several blocks to a Y. In the center of the Y, is an official New Mexico Historical Marker, "Taos Pueblo." Take the right-hand fork 2 miles to the pueblo. There is an entrance fee.

This spectacular adobe pueblo played a prominent role in the history of the Southwest, but its association with the SFT is only marginal. In 1843, Governor Manuel Armijo took a large force from Santa Fe over the Cimarron Cutoff to escort the annual SFT caravan westward. At Cold Spring in the present-day Oklahoma Panhandle, he sent ahead a party of one hundred Taos militiamen under Capt. Ventura Lobato, including many Taos Pueblo Indians. In southwestern Kansas, Lobato was attacked by raiders from the Texas Republic, who killed or captured almost all his command. The severe losses sustained in the incident embittered Taos Indians against Americans as well as Texans. This enmity is believed to have led them to participate in the murder of Charles Bent and others four years later. At the edge of the pueblo, you can still see ruins of the church that became a refuge for the rebels and was battered down by Col. Sterling Price's artillery during the U.S. Army's assault in February 1847.

SIDE TRIP TO ALBUQUERQUE

While Albuquerque, on the Rio Grande 60 miles southwest of Santa Fe, was not situated on the SFT, many Missouri traders passed through it on their way south to El Paso and Chihuahua City. This route, beginning at Santa Fe, became known to SFT merchants as the Chihuahua Trail but was really the old Camino Real of colonial days. Several individuals prominent in the Santa Fe trade settled in Albuquerque and opened stores on or near the plaza. Most important among them was German-born Franz Huning, whose wagons were attacked at the Plum Buttes and whose trail journal has been published.

From Santa Fe take Interstate 25 south to Albuquerque. About halfway there is a large stone monument with a plaque dedicated to the Mormon battalion. Leave the interstate at Exit 257 and take the frontage road on the west side of the freeway. The marker is about 1 mile south on this road. After arriving in Santa Fe, the Battalion followed this route south to pick up what was to become the Gila Trail leading to California.

The small city of Bernalillo is just off the interstate at Exit 242. One of New Mexico's wealthiest merchants, José Leandro Perea, lived here. He was the most prominent Hispanic merchant in 1860 and 1870 according to Susan Boyle in *Los Capitalistas: Hispano Merchants and the Santa Fe Trade*. From Bernalillo, Perea's caravans went east to the village of Placitas and continued northeast to connect with the SFT at Johnson's Ranch. A substantial portion of the trade on the SFT was carried out by Hispanic merchants such as Peréa. Many of the wealthy Hispanic families sent their sons to schools in Missouri as well.

Continue to the main interchange in Albuquerque, where Interstate 25 intersects with Interstate 40. Exit to Interstate 40 heading west to Grants. After about a mile take the Rio Grande Boulevard exit and turn left (south) on Rio Grande to Old Town Plaza, the former center of Albuquerque. There are numerous historical markers in the center of the plaza, some of which relate to the period of the SFT. On the northeast edge of Old Town, at 2000 Mountain Road N.W., is the Albuquerque Museum, whose splendid historical exhibits include sections on Coronado and the Chihuahua and Santa Fe Trails. Admission is free.

The fourth and last Madonna of the Trail statue (or Pioneer Mother) on the SFT is located near the courthouse between 3rd and 4th Streets at Lomas, a major street that enters Old Town from the east joining Central Avenue one block south of the plaza. Follow Lomas to 3rd Street, turn left (north), and go to the next corner. Located to your right, the Madonna of the Trail statue was supposed to have been placed in Santa Fe in 1927, but artists and writers there rejected it as being ugly and not representative of the region's Spanish pioneer women, so the DAR moved the statue to Albuquerque.

SELECTED BIBLIOGRAPHY

Boyle, Susan Calafate. *Los Capitalistas: Hispano Merchants and the Santa Fe Trade*. Albuquerque: University of New Mexico Press, 1997.

Brown, Joseph C. *Survey of the Western Boundary of the State of Missouri, 1823*. Originals located in Missouri State Department of Natural Resources, Rolla, Missouri.

Brown, William E. *The Santa Fe Trail*. St. Louis, Mo.: Patrice Press, 1988.

Clapsaddle, David K. "The Dry Route Revisited." *Overland Journal* (Summer 1999): 2–8. Reprinted in *Wagon Tracks* (November 1999): 8–11.

Coues, Elliott, ed. *The Journal of Jacob Fowler*. Minneapolis, Minn.: Ross and Haines, 1965.

Crease, Craig. "Lone Elm and Elm Grove: A Case of Mistaken Identity?" *Wagon Tracks* (August 1991): 10–13.

Davis, H. Denny. "Franklin: Cradle of the Trade." *Wagon Tracks* (May 1993): 11–17.

Duffus, Robert L. *The Santa Fe Trail*. Albuquerque: University of New Mexico Press, 1999.

Field, Matt. *Matt Field on the Santa Fe Trail*, edited by John E. Sunder. Norman: University of Oklahoma Press, 1995.

Franzwa, Gregory M. *The Oregon Trail Revisited, Silver Anniversary Edition*. Tucson, Ariz.: Patrice Press, 1997.

_____. *The Santa Fe Trail Revisited*. St. Louis, Mo.: Patrice Press, 1989.

Gardner, Mark L. *Wagons for the Santa Fe Trade: Wheeled Vehicles and Their Makers*. Albuquerque: University of New Mexico Press, 2000.

Gregg, Josiah. *Commerce of the Prairies*, edited by Max L. Moorhead. Norman: University of Oklahoma Press, 1990.

Gregg, Kate L., ed. *The Road to Santa Fe: The Journal and Diaries of George Champlin Sibley*. Albuquerque: University of New Mexico Press, 1995.

Hamilton, Jean Tyree. *Arrow Rock: Where Wheels Started West*. Arrow Rock, Mo.: Friends of Arrow Rock, 1972.

Hafen, LeRoy R. *The Mountain Men and the Fur Trade of the Far West*. 10 volumes. Glendale, Calif.: Arthur H. Clark Co., 1965–1972.

Horgan, Paul. *Lamy of Santa Fe*. New York: Farrar, Straus, and Giroux, 1975.

Hughes, John Taylor. *Doniphan's Expedition*. College Station: Texas A and M University Press, 1997.

Kirwan, John S. "Patrolling the Santa Fe Trail: Reminiscences of John S. Kirwan."*The Kansas Historical Quarterly* (Winter 1955): 569–87.

Lavender, David. *Bent's Fort*. Lincoln: University of Nebraska Press, 1972.

Long, Margaret. *The Santa Fe Trail*. Denver, Colo.: Kistler Company, 1954.

Louden, Richard. "The Military Freight Route." *Wagon Tracks* (May 1993): 7–10.

Lowe, Percival G. *Five Years Dragoon*. Norman: University of Oklahoma Press, 1965.

Magoffin, Susan Shelby. *Down the Santa Fe Trail and into Mexico, 1846–1847: The Diary of Susan Shelby Magoffin*, edited by Stella M. Drumm. Lincoln: University of Nebraska Press, 1982.

Marmaduke, Meredith Miles. "Santa Fe Trail: M. M. Marmaduke Journal." *Missouri Historical Review* (October 1911): 1–10.

Olsen, Michael L., and Harry C Myers. "The Diary of Pedro Ignacio Gallego Wherein 400 Soldiers Following the Trail of Comanches Met William Becknell on His First Trip to Santa Fe." *Wagon Tracks* (November 1992): 1, 15–20.

Quaise, Milo, ed. *Narrative of the Adventures of Zenas Leonard*. Chicago: Lakeside Press, 1934.

Raytown Historical Society. *Raytown Remembers*. Clinton, Mo.: The Printery, 1975.

Russell, Mrs. Hal, ed. *Land of Enchantment: Memoirs of Marian Russell Along the Santa Fe Trail*. Albuquerque: University of New Mexico Press, 1993.

Sappington, John. *The Theory and Treatment of Fevers*. Arrow Rock, Mo.: Friends of Arrow Rock, 1993.

Slusher, Roger. "Lexington and the Santa Fe Trail." *Wagon Tracks* (August 1991): 6–9.

Stocking, Hobart E. *The Road to Santa Fe*. New York: Hastings House, 1971.

Strate, David K., ed. *West by Southwest: Letters of Joseph Pratt Allyn, a Traveler Along the Santa Fe Trail in 1863*. Dodge City: Kansas Heritage Center, 1984.

Twitchell, Ralph E. *The Military Occupation of New Mexico, 1846–1851*. Denver, Colo.: Smith-Brooks Company, 1909.

Vestal, Stanley. *The Old Santa Fe Trail*. Lincoln: University of Nebraska Press, 1996.

Wetmore, Alphonso. "Major Alphonso Wetmore's Diary of a Journey to Santa Fe, 1828." *Missouri Historical Review* 8 (July 1914): 177–97.

_____. *Gazetteer of the State of Missouri*. St. Louis, Mo.: C. Keemle, 1837.

Wright, Robert M. *Dodge City: The Cowboy Capital*. Wichita, Kans.: Wichita Eagle Press, 1913.

INDEX

Note: Page numbers with maps are indicated in **bold.**